REFLECTIONS ON WRIGHT

REFLECTIONS ON WRIGHT

Essays on the Career of Speaker Jim Wright

Edited by

JAMES W. RIDDLESPERGER JR.
ANTHONY CHAMPAGNE

FORT WORTH, TEXAS

Library of Congress Cataloging-in-Publication Data

Names: Riddlesperger, James W., Jr., 1953- editor. | Champagne, Anthony, editor.
Title: Reflections on Wright : essays on the career of Speaker Jim Wright / edited by James W.
    Riddlesperger Jr., Anthony Champagne.
Description: Fort Worth, Texas : TCU Press, [2024] | Includes bibliographical references and
    index. | Summary: "Reflections on Wright is a collection of essays on Jim Wright from his
    early years through his retirement from the House of Representatives. Wright was one of the
    most influential members of Congress in the latter part of the twentieth century and had a
    major role in policies such as the interstate highway system and American policy in Central
    America. Foreclosed from moving to the Senate, Wright eventually sought to become Majori-
    ty Leader and won in a hotly contested race against California's Phil Burton. Both as Majority
    Leader and as Speaker, Wright proved himself an exceptionally strong leader. Indeed, Wright
    pushed his agenda so strongly that it led to grumbling among members of his caucus. With
    attacks on his ethics by Georgia Republican Newt Gingrich, attacks that heralded a new level
    of viciousness between the two parties in the House, Wright resigned and returned to Fort
    Worth. For most of the remainder of his life, he taught at Texas Christian University"-- Pro-
    vided by publisher.
Identifiers: LCCN 2024005200 (print) | LCCN 2024005201 (ebook) | ISBN 9780875658179
    (trade paperback) | ISBN 9780875658780 (ebook)
Subjects: LCSH: Wright, Jim, 1922-2015. | United States. Congress. House--Speakers--Biog-
    raphy. | Legislators--Texas--Fort Worth--Biography. | United States--Politics and govern-
    ment--1981-1989. | LCGFT: Essays. | Biographies.
Classification: LCC E840.8.W75 R44 2024 (print) | LCC E840.8.W75 (ebook) | DDC
    328.73/092 [B]--dc23/eng/20240215
LC record available at https://lccn.loc.gov/2024005200
LC ebook record available at https://lccn.loc.gov/2024005201

TCU Box 298300
Fort Worth, Texas 76129
www.tcupress.com

Design by Preston Thomas, Cadence Design Studio

CONTENTS

ACKNOWLEDGEMENTS

The editors were enriched by having an ongoing relation-ship with Speaker Jim Wright for more than twenty years, including numerous conversations in his office or over a lunch table. Speaker Wright was generous with his time and re-markably circumspect about his career, at times completely un-guarded in his observations about politics during his time in office and both the highs and lows of his career.

We were able to conduct interviews with many people who worked with Jim Wright in his congressional offices—in Washing-ton and in Fort Worth. We were able to talk with Dorothy Beard, Steve Charnovitz, Paul Driskell, Lanny Hall, John Mack, Kathy Mitchell, and Norma Ritchson, all of whom served on Wright's staff at important junctures of his career. They knew Wright well and were invariably loyal to him in their reflections of his service in office. We interviewed several of his congressional colleagues, in-cluding Bill Alexander (D-AR), Jim Chapman (D-TX), Pete Geren (D-TX), David O'Brien Martin (R-NY), and Charles Stenholm (D-TX), all of whom provided important context to evaluating

1

Wright's career. We thank former Secretary of State James Baker for agreeing to an interview as well. Former Fort Worth Mayor Bob Bolen made himself available for an interview, as did Wright's daughter, Ginger McGuire. The book was enriched by their gifts of time and their wisdom.

Former students of Wright at TCU generously provided memories of the class they took with Speaker Wright, including John Athon, Louisiana State Senator Thomas Pressley (R-Shreveport), and Melanie Harris. They were among a large number of students who offered positive reviews for the experience of taking Wright's class.

Thanks to the assistance of LeAnna Schooley with the Center for Texas Studies at TCU. We are grateful for the assistance of Mary Saffell and Samantha Brown, librarians in Special Collections at Mary Couts Burnett Library at TCU. We are indebted to the professional staff at the TCU Press, including press director Dan Williams (who co-edited *The Wright Stuff* with the editors), Kat Thomas, and Abigail Jennings.

We were lucky to get high quality contributions from top scholars whose essays make up the contents of the book.

Finally, as always, we thank our families for their ongoing support and tolerance of our quirks and our escapes for "working lunches" as the book project was underway. We especially thank our wives Beatriz Champagne and Kris Riddlesperger.

CHAPTER 1

Eulogy

MARTIN FROST

Member, US House of Representatives, 1979–2006

In the words President John F. Kennedy said about Jim Wright, "No city in America was better represented in Congress than Fort Worth."

I'm here today to speak on behalf of the scores of people—many of whom were Texans—that Jim Wright helped along the way with their careers. He was our mentor, our colleague, and our friend. We were better public servants because of Jim Wright, and many of those members, past and present, Democrat and Republican, are here with us today to honor Jim.

In a minute, I'm going to speak about what Jim did for my career, but it really speaks volumes for what he did for a lot of others, too.

Jim Wright was an extraordinary leader, both for the people of Fort Worth and for our nation. He always remembered the people who sent him to Washington and worked tirelessly to make our country even better every day he was in office. Few congressmen in recent times have had a greater impact than our friend Jim Wright.

I met Jim Wright in 1958, when he was a young congressman beginning his second term and I was a sixteen-year-old. Jim was the guest speaker at the Temple Beth-El youth group in the basement of the old synagogue building on West Broadway, near downtown.

I had never met a national politician before, and he made a deep impression on me that day. I remember to this day some of what he said, and more of that a little bit later.

Seven years later, in 1965, I showed up in Washington as a young reporter covering Congress for a magazine, and the first thing I did was to go see my hometown congressman, Jim Wright. Jim and his chief of staff, Marshall Lynam, were very helpful to this young reporter, suggesting whom I should get to know on congressional committee staffs. Three years later, in summer 1968, Jim helped me get a job on Hubert Humphrey's national presidential campaign staff while I was a student at Georgetown Law School.

The last two people I saw before I headed back to Texas following graduation in 1970 were Jim and Marshall. I told them that I hoped to come back to DC someday as a congressman in a neighboring district. I had no intention of ever running against Jim Wright.

Fast forward to 1976 when I was North Texas coordinator for the Carter-Mondale general election, when carrying Texas was still in doubt. They wanted to stop only in Dallas. As a Fort Worth boy, I told them they also had to come to Cowtown and that I knew that local Congressman Jim Wright would put on one hell of a show for them, and that's exactly what Jim did. He filled the downtown convention center with more than ten thousand people early in the afternoon that Sunday. It made great television, and Carter became the last Democratic presidential candidate to carry Texas.

Shortly after that election, Jim Wright became House majority leader by one vote in a hotly contested secret ballot election. He certainly knew how to count.

Two years later, I was elected to Congress from the Twenty-Fourth District, which, in fact, adjoined the Twelfth District that Jim represented. Jim went to Speaker Tip O'Neill and made sure I was named to the powerful House Rules Committee, an appointment that almost never went to a freshman member.

From that day on, Jim Wright and I became both colleagues and friends. He was my mentor during the eleven years we served together, and I learned an enormous amount just watching him in action. When I inherited the Black community in southeast Fort Worth following the 1991 redistricting, I only used one picture in my mailing: a photo of Jim Wright and me. There wasn't anything else the voters in that part of my district needed to know. They continued to be my base for the remainder of my twenty-six years in Congress, and just to make sure people in Fort Worth knew that I had strong ties to Fort Worth, even though I now lived in Dallas, he used to tell anyone who would listen that I went to high school in his district at Fort Worth's Paschal, and he went to high school in my district at Dallas's Adamson.

When Jim taught a course at TCU on Congress for twenty years after leaving Congress, I was proud to be a guest lecturer for him every single year. The last time I saw Jim was in spring 2014, when I was working on a book about Congress. We visited for about an hour in his office at TCU. His body was frail, but his mind was as sharp as ever.

I learned how to be an effective congressman by observing Jim as a colleague and as a junior partner on a variety of matters that helped Fort Worth. He never forgot the people who sent him to Washington. He was a stalwart in his work on behalf of defense workers at what is now Lockheed Martin, formerly General Dynamics, and Bell Helicopter in Fort Worth.

He played a significant role in the decision by American Airlines to move its corporate headquarters from New York to the Metroplex, and he was a strong supporter of DFW Airport, the jobs magnet for this part of the state.

We worked together—and by the way, he did the heavy lifting—to convince the railroad to make its right-of-way available for the Trinity Railway Express connecting Fort Worth and Dallas. No request from anyone in Tarrant County was too small to win Jim's help.

Also, Jim's role in promoting the careers of promising African Americans from Fort Worth was of great significance. He brought Lorraine Miller, a young woman from the southeast side of Fort Worth, to Washington to work on his staff. Years later, she became the first African American to serve as clerk of the US House and recently served as interim national president of the NAACP. Just a few years ago, Jim played a key role in the election of Marc Veasey, who became the first Black congressman from Fort Worth.

One of Jim's greatest strengths was molding a disparate group of Democrats into an effective majority when he became Speaker. During his first year as Speaker in 1987—and Tony [Coelho] and Steny [Hoyer], you will remember this—Congress passed all thirteen appropriation bills before the start of the new fiscal year on October 1, something that is almost never done today.

I remember his response to a question from the audience at that speech at Temple Beth-El in 1958. He was asked what a congressman does when he feels one way about an issue and his district feels the other way. He responded that the job of a congressman was to reflect the views of his district as often as he could. He then added that he reserved a small percentage of votes, perhaps 10 percent, to vote against the majority of his district if he felt something was vital in the national interest. He then added that it was his responsibility to go back to his constituents to explain his vote and hopefully convince them that he was right and they were wrong. He added that if a congressman couldn't successfully do that, he wouldn't be reelected, and that was as it should be.

He did a very good job following his own advice. I did the same and found that he was exactly correct.

Fort Worth is a great city today because of Jim Wright. We all owe him an enormous debt of gratitude. We will never see his like again.

CHAPTER 2
Eulogy

BILL ALEXANDER

Member, US House of Representatives, 1969–1993

J immy and Ginger, Kay, Lisa, and all the Wright family, I feel
that we are kin. To all of his friends who are here today, I join
you in tribute to one of my dearest friends. I kept up with Jim
through the years, even after he left Washington and returned to Texas, and following his recovery from surgery, I gave him a call one day,
and he invited me to come to Fort Worth. So my son and I—Alex,
who is here with his sister Ashley, who came to TCU at a later time—
boarded our plane and came to DFW. In those days Jim was driving,
and so he met us at the airport. I'd never been outside of DFW before,
so I didn't know what to expect. As we left the terminal, I noticed all
of the concrete infrastructure that supports the airport: the entrance
ramps, the exit ramps, the overhead bridges, the long ride to the interstate. I never saw so much concrete in all my life. I turned to Jim,
who at one time, as most of you know, was a senior member of the
Public Works Committee, and I said to him, "Jim, how much money
did the Public Works Committee spend on this airport?" He looked
at me and rolled his brow and lifted his big bushy eyebrows and he
said to me, "Not a penny more than the law allowed."

Jim was probably one of the most successful members in Congress, and with that success, people encouraged him, and he ran for

majority leader. As all of you probably followed in the news, it was a very contentious race, and on the day of the vote, I was appointed to be a judge. So after the votes were cast, I adjourned with the other members of the election group and counted the votes. We counted them twice, and Jim won by one vote.

I got up from the chair in the Speaker's lounge—the Speaker's lobby, we call it—rushed through the door to the House chamber, and Jim was sitting on the second row on the Democratic side in the hall of the House. I rushed up to him and I said, "Jim, you won." He was surprised because no one knew the outcome of that election. He looked at me, and he said, "Are you sure?" I said, "Jim, I counted the votes, and if you hadn't won, Phil Burton said he would send me to Alaska."

Following in the footsteps of Sam Rayburn and Lyndon Johnson, Jim asserted leadership in Congress at a time of confusion in the Senate and the White House, demonstrating a unique ability to command our nation's political resources to get things done. This went across the aisle to the Republicans and even down Pennsylvania Avenue to the White House, which is sometimes a million miles away if you serve in Congress.

Jim Wright had fought in World War II to defend the values of the Greatest Generation, as Tom Brokaw describes this generation, a generation of men and women united in common purposes of family, country, duty, honor, courage, and service. During World War II, he flew many combat missions. I haven't really been able to discern exactly how many yet because there's such a debate over it. Maybe somebody will tell me before I go back to Washington. He served as a bombardier and was awarded the Distinguished Flying Cross for his bravery.

Jim believed that government should serve the people as well as the economic interests, which also must be represented, and provide federal assistance to communities and states like Arkansas, where I'm from. It's in need of capital development in order to provide infrastructure to try to attract industry and jobs for our people. That was, in his view, providing building blocks for the foundation of the economic development that benefits all of us. All you've got to do is look around in Texas a little bit to find out if it works.

The criticism of Speaker Wright, which is in the news, instead of all of the accomplishments that we know he achieved, was his strong leadership during a changing Congress. Some of my former colleagues from Congress are here today, and they know what I'm talking about.

Beginning with the 1968 election, which was my first election to Congress, the ideals and values of the Greatest Generation began to evolve. A Congress run by Southern Democrats, who chaired mostly the important committees in the Congress, was gradually replaced by a younger generation of congressmen and senators, many of them in the other party. When he left Congress, even his political enemies often remarked that, had he stayed in Congress, he would have been the greatest Speaker since Henry Clay.

His time as Speaker laid down historic markers. He was the last great figure in Congress to keep alive the idea of infrastructure development—that came from the New Deal—that would help our economy.

After him came what we call Reaganomics and the tidal wave of polarization of our two political parties and the continuing mindless cannibalism, which we can still see evident today between the parties and even within the parties in Congress.

Criticism of Speaker Wright's forceful leadership came from Republicans and Democrats alike; although, at the time he stepped down, the principal antagonists came from within our own party. I was there, and I know who they are.

What followed was a profound change in the power structure in Congress, shifting away from the power and authority lodged in a handful of key Southern committee chairmen to a dispersion of power among proliferating committees and subcommittees, encouraging intensifying rivalries and even political fratricides throughout the House. His departure marked the end of an era when Southern

Democrats dominated in both the House and the Senate, along with a gradual evolution of the Congress toward social issues.

It marked the transition from Southern leadership of Congress to a growing concentration of power of the Democratic Party in our nation's biggest cities, many of them in the North, opening a widening rift between our nation's small towns and rural areas and the political interests of the inner cities. The way was opened for lobbyists to shift attention away from schools and roads and bridges and water systems that helped our people to special interests of Wall Street banks and a commercial agenda.

A fluent speaker of Spanish, he took the initiative to intervene in the political crisis in Nicaragua and crafted peace talks that laid the foundation for elections. When I assisted him in this so-called junket, in his endeavor, I found that what we tried to do generated much consternation among President Reagan's White House staff. Later, another great Texan, James Baker, observed that what Jim Wright did with his intervention in Nicaragua turned the corner for that nation and helped the United States and Nicaragua to come to better terms with one another.

Jim Wright was not only a master of the political structure and the rules in Congress, he also was an author, a professor. He lectured at Texas Christian University with eagerness to inspire and guide our nation's youth.

In the tradition of Sam Houston and Sam Rayburn, Jim Wright was a giant. I was his chief deputy whip in the Congress, the worst job in the House of Representatives, but it was worth all the knocks and the cuts and the bruises and the criticism that I endured to fight for the values established by the Greatest Generation. Unfortunately, those ideals were changed by a new breed of voter who believes that Washington is not a solution; rather, Washington is the problem. He was my dear friend, and I stood with him in every fight for the values that won World War II and provided the building blocks and foundation for the greatest economy on Earth.

God bless Jim Wright.

CHAPTER 3
Eulogy

PAUL DRISKELL
Special Assistant, Majority Leader Jim Wright

Martin, Bill, Betsy, Mike, Kenneth, Mr. Leader, Steny Hoyer—the one man in this sanctuary today who knows the full weight and measure and the responsibilities of the job this prince of peace executed so beautifully for so many years. Dear Steny, thank you for your presence today. How very special, how honored he would be, how much he would love this congregation today. This is a delegation of community builders.

Mr. Wright loved Sam Rayburn dearly, and he often quoted him. Many people wondered why Mr. Rayburn went back to Bonham, Texas, after announcing he was going to leave the House, and Rayburn's answer was simple: "Bonham is a place where people know it when you're sick, and where they care when you die."

You have validated Jim Wright's recitation of that quote, all of you today, by honoring him in coming here. You knew he was ill, and you cared that he died. How he would celebrate you. How he must be enjoying this. He loved people of accomplishment. He loved people who contributed and built. Mr. Rayburn used to always say, "A jackass can kick a barn down; it takes a carpenter to build one." It's no accident that our Lord was a carpenter—and parented by a carpenter in his early years.

I'd like to give you a sense of Speaker Wright, Jim Wright, my friend. It may be unique. As I have thought about him so much and as I visited him in those final days, things came to me that I would have never imagined. He was, in fact, the first gifted multi-tasker. Now, if you know anything about Jim, he despised anything to do with technology, but he was a multitasker. Let me explain what I mean.

Some of the people in this room—Tony, John—had been working diligently because Mr. O'Neill had told us privately he was going to retire. So we were trying to collect the requisite number of votes for Jim to become Speaker of the House two years out. February 7, 1985, eleven o'clock in the morning, a national press conference was held in the office that Steny Hoyer's offices are in today. He met the national press. He was surrounded by his colleagues. These were people who loved him and wished well for him, and he made the announcement that he had achieved the requisite number of votes to capture his dream, to be Speaker of the House. He put at peace, if you will, a body that's not given to peace easily about the next years and how things would follow.

Fifteen minutes later, he grabbed me by the arm and escorted me and my now-wife, Donna, up the back stairs with thirty-one other people to the House chaplain's office, where Chaplain Ford married us at Henry Clay's desk. Then he walked back downstairs with us and we had a reception in the office. He pulled Donna and me aside and he said, "I only have two things to tell you two: Paul, always hold her hand, and never go to bed mad."

Mr. Speaker, sometimes you set the bar too high. I have removed pillows from my bed so as not to elevate the temptation for Donna to smother me.

There are so many things privately that I loved about him and that we shared. He had a passionate love for boxing. He knew boxing like Nat Fleischer, the famous author who recorded almost everything of significance about American heavyweight boxing. We went to the Golden Gloves. We went to the Olympic trials. We went to tons of professional fights. It was like going to fights with Nat Fleischer, and he would he sitting there and he would be reciting to you the ring scores of the Firpo-Dempsey fight. With every hobby and interest he had, he wanted to know everything there was to know about it. If you ever saw the roses that he cultivated, you'd understand that in spades. He was a gifted horticulturist. He was a great teacher.

Kay, you and I sat two and a half years ago just about where Steny is sitting, and you told me how he taught you and Ginger, Jenny, and Lisa about God. In fact, he used a wagon wheel and said that was the universe and God was the hub. The spokes represented the people, and the rim, where all the damage and impact takes place, was the furthest from God. He admonished you that it was your job, it was your responsibility, it was a testament of your faith to move closer down those spokes because you would be closer to more people, and as you were closer to more people, you'd be closer to God. What a gift!

I've often wondered, and I think everyone in this sanctuary today wonders, why God lets us see certain things at certain times. It seems rather odd. Last week, just the day before his passing and only a few days after my last visit with him, there was a documentary about George Foreman. I happened to turn it on. George Foreman, the famous heavyweight, struck fear and terror in everyone's heart—undefeated, knocked poor Joe Frazier down eight times. The interviewer asked him a question. He said, "Who was the greatest champion of all time in your estimation?" George Foreman didn't hesitate. He said, "Muhammad Ali." That stunned the interviewer.

Muhammad Ali had defeated George Foreman in Zaire, Africa, and usually when a boxer loses to another one, it was a lucky punch or you're just a little better that night, not the greatest champion that ever lived. He didn't hesitate. He said, "Muhammad Ali."

The interviewer said, "Why? Why do you choose him?" He said, "Well, if you saw the fight in the eighth round, he hit me twice in the face." If any of you remember or happened to have seen it, George Foreman began to cartwheel. He began to turn and fall to the floor. As he was falling, Muhammad Ali, as all boxers are trained all their life to do, cocked his arm to hit him with what is known as the "killing punch."

George Foreman said, "I looked up out of my left eye, just partially conscious, knowing I was going to the floor, and he never threw that punch. So for me, he's not the greatest champion that ever lived for the punches he threw; it's for what he didn't do. It's the punch he didn't throw."

The very people who besmirched and impugned this prince of peace at the end of his public career, when they fell on hard times and they fell by the sword they had so recklessly wielded, not once in private—and certainly never in public—did Jim Wright throw that punch. He could not retaliate. He didn't just talk Christian forgiveness, he lived it. His higher calling at that time was to find a way to inspire students at TCU to engage in public service and to think about the possibilities of what they could build, like the beautiful people in this room today. He didn't throw that punch.

I was fifteen years old, standing in front of a black-and-white television, and I watched Robert Kennedy say, "When he shall die, take him and cut him out into stars, and he shall make the face of Heaven so fine that all the world will be in love with night and pay no worship to the garish Sun." I didn't know at fifteen just what that meant. At sixty-five, I marvel how Bobby Kennedy could have mustered the strength and the insight to say that about the brother he loved, in some ways his best friend, and, oh, by the way, the president of the United States.

I understood because of this church [the First United Methodist Church of Fort Worth] and because of my association with Jim that all of us have a spark of divinity. We are all made in God's image, and that spark is there, but what I didn't understand was that there are a special few who possess a flame, a torch. It's bigger. It's more committed. It's something we can appreciate. It's not necessarily something we readily understand.

It's not by accident that there's an eternal flame that burns at John Kennedy's grave. It's partly for all the accomplishments: the Peace Corps, the space program, all of those things. That's why millions go there to pay respects. The other part of it is that during the most sensitive time in our nation's history, when we were the closest to engaging in a nuclear holocaust, when every adviser that president had was admonishing him to take advantage of the tactical and strategic position we occupied for those precious few days and strike Cuba with nuclear weapons, he didn't throw that punch. We're all breathing good air and loving our friends and conducting our lives because of that divine torch.

The thing I think I will miss most is a private passion that Jim had and I shared. He loved movies. The singular thing that we really appreciated together was we happened to think that Robert Duvall was the greatest American actor that's ever lived. Jim's favorite movie was *Tender Mercies*, and my favorite film was *The Natural*. In *The Natural*, Robert Redford played Roy Hobbs, the gifted baseball player. Robert Duvall was the cynical sportswriter. Wilford Brimley was the crusty old coach.

There's that beautiful soliloquy where Robert Duvall walks in and says to the coach, "Coach, who is this Roy Hobbs?" The coach turns on his heels and says, "I don't know who Roy Hobbs is. I just know he's the best there is and the best there ever will be."

Jim Wright, you are "The Natural."

There probably has never been a man in American history whom I can recall that so eloquently used the English language. He helped those of us who only have sparks appreciate the flame with his application of our language.

It seems a shame that I can't find words in my language to encompass all that he was, and yet he will always be. Only in Spanish: *Vaya con Dios*—Go with God. Light of our land. Vaya con Dios, friend of my life.

Weatherford Mayor Jim Wright astride a horse in a 1952 parade. *Photo property of Jim Wright Collection, TCU Special Collections, TCU Library. Used by permission. Note: unless otherwise marked, all photos are from this source.*

Historical family home of Jim Wright in downtown Weatherford. *Photo by Jim Riddlesperger.*

Wright stands on a boat with one foot on the roof of a flooded Fossil Creek home, 1957. Wright would make a name for himself in Fort Worth by gaining federal funding to build levees for flood control.

When Lyndon Johnson resigned from the US Senate to become vice president, Jim Wright ran, along with sixty-nine other candidates, in a special election for Johnson's seat. Here is a picture of Wright during that campaign in 1961. Wright placed 4th in the field of candidates and never sought office outside the House seat after that campaign.

Jim Wright rides in a ticker-tape parade in downtown Fort Worth, 1970.

Congressman Jim Wright walks with President John F. Kennedy to their cars after Kennedy's Fort Worth speech, November 22, 1963. They would fly together from Fort Worth to Dallas on Air Force 1 prior to the motorcade in which Kennedy would be assassinated, just hours later.

This cartoon celebrates Jim Wright as a congressman who brought public works spending to Fort Worth, including the Bureau of Engraving and Printing's Western Currency Facility in North Fort Worth.

Wright poses on horseback in the Fort Worth Stockyards. Wright was instrumental in securing federal funds to help develop the Stockyards, which had become dilapidated after the Armour and Swift meat packing plants closed, into the thriving tourist area that it is today.

Congressman Jim Wright poses with former Fort Worth and 12th district Congressman Frederick Garland "Fritz" Lanham who served in Congress from 1919 until 1947. Eight years later, Wright was elected to the seat, serving from 1954–1989.

Jim Wright poses with his two successors in House District 12, Pete Geren (1989–1997) and Kay Granger (1997–present), on February 22, 2013. *Photo property of Jim Wright Symposium at TCU. Used by permission.*

CHAPTER 4

Jim Wright's
Early Congressional Career

★

MARK BEASLEY
Emeritus Professor, Hardin-Simmons University

On January 6, 1987, Representative Jim Wright was sworn in as the forty-eighth Speaker of the House of Representatives, after serving in Congress for thirty-two years, the last decade as majority leader. He enjoyed continued political success in large part because of the many skills he had mastered and the lessons he had learned early in his political career, having served a single term in the Texas House of Representatives (during the Fiftieth Legislature, 1947) and as mayor of Weatherford for four years (1950–54). Those skills continued to increase as he conducted his first congressional campaign in 1954 and throughout his early tenure in the House of Representatives. During that first congressional race, Wright adopted campaign principles that he utilized in future elections and revealed a combative instinct for political survival—when confronted with adversity—that he retained for the length of his public career. From the beginning, Wright relished his role as a legislator, developing an abiding respect, if not a deep affection, for the institution of Congress. He also possessed deep ambitions, but not only for himself; he continually strived to make a difference for his district and his political party. Early on, Wright established

himself as an effective communicator, as a writer as well as an orator. And during the early years he acquired a lifelong fondness for
and commitment to Latin America.[1]

First Congressional Campaign

Early in 1954, Wright, opting for political service over business,
decided to run for Congress for a number of reasons. Many people
in the district viewed four-term incumbent congressman Wingate
Lucas with contempt, as "essentially just an errand boy for . . . the
[Fort Worth] 'Seventh Street' crowd," a small group of wealthy local men headed by newspaper publisher Amon G. Carter. Others
were anxious for a more responsive, less conservative representative;
Lucas, for example, had antagonized many working people with
his opposition to any increases in the minimum wage and with
his general antilabor attitude. Although Lucas would be tough to
beat because of such powerful backing, Wright was not deterred.
According to one contemporary, Wright was an "attractive candidate" who had the support of his hometown, had been making
numerous speeches to service clubs and church groups throughout the five-county area, and was relatively well known. Friends in
Weatherford as well as in Fort Worth encouraged him. Persistent
prodding paid off. On March 29, 1954, during a twenty-minute
televised speech, he revealed to the North Central Texas viewing
audience his desire to be their next congressman—"the noblest and
most honorable enterprise to which a young man could aspire."[2]

Wright, at age thirty-one, thus began his first contest for Congress, a Democratic primary campaign that proved both challenging
and educational. During the next four months, Wright tested political skills acquired as a state legislator and as a local mayor. He also
adopted campaign principles that he utilized throughout his congressional tenure as well as effectively applied television techniques
in elections. And in the process he gained self-confidence and the
respect of District Twelve voters, who reelected him seventeen times.

This hard-fought campaign proved to be, Wright said, "A watershed in my life."[3]

Throughout the spring and early summer of 1954, Wright, with the help of many volunteers, worked assiduously to reach voters. Weatherford supporters wrote personal endorsements to their friends in Fort Worth (Tarrant County) and in the surrounding counties of the district (Parker, Somervell, Johnson, and Hood), thus expanding Wright's circle of acquaintances. A local banker conducted a letter-writing effort, recommending Wright to other businessmen throughout the area. Other proponents sent out copies of a *Weatherford Democrat* editorial lauding Wright, held house meetings for him, and organized Saturday motorcades to outlying towns. Wright spent many mornings shaking hands with workers at local manufacturing plants as well as numerous afternoons knocking on doors or greeting potential voters in various cities. And beginning on June 28, 1954, during the last four weeks of the Democratic Party primary, Wright, together with other office seekers, participated in the customary speaking itinerary almost every night.[4]

Even though such efforts proved valuable, Wright soon discovered that television was his most effective campaign tool—a development underscored by the apparent reluctance of Amon G. Carter's *Fort Worth Star-Telegram* to publicize his campaign. On May 14, for example, Wright officially opened his election effort with a $1-per-plate barbecue at the Will Rogers complex in Fort Worth, attracting more than 1,200 people. Although the dinner was a rousing success and the program—broadcast over local radio—was well received, the *Star-Telegram* (the most widely circulated newspaper in West Texas) simply ignored, Wright asserted, "the largest political event in the town's recollection." He thus realized that television would be the major means for the electorate to hear his message. As a result, he pioneered this new method of communication by talking directly to people in their living rooms in prime time. He soon purchased many relatively inexpensive time segments, ranging from five to thirty minutes. Wright still used radio and newspaper advertising, but he quickly discerned his effectiveness over television, saying it "was my medium." And people responded; after each broadcast they recognized him on the street as well as sent letters of support. He later recalled: "I owe the success in that first campaign, at least in part, to the availability of television."[5]

Wright developed several standards that guided the general tone of his political campaigning for the remainder of his congressional career. He arbitrarily limited contributions to $100 (adjusted in later years to accommodate the rate of inflation). In his first television speech, Wright candidly discussed the expenses of financing political contests, contending that voters should know the costs—at least $25,000 for a congressional seat—and where the money is coming from. He also wanted all contributions to come from individuals, not pressure groups and lobbying organizations with an ax to grind. To accept such money, he asserted, was not "right or moral," especially if "men finding their way into the halls of government [had been] bought and paid for in advance." Consequently, on several occasions Wright declined to accept funds from labor unions who had specific legislative objectives. And he refused to fall "into the gutter" of negative campaigning, hoping to compete in a positive vein and not indulge in dubious attacks on his opponent.[6]

In 1954, however, Wingate Lucas opted for the gutter. In his opening television speech on June 28, he targeted Wright as the "anointed" candidate of labor "racketeers" who had "passed the word that Wingate Lucas must go." He suggested that Wright might "speak and vote for the Communists and others who are disloyal," implying that they were the source of a $5,000 contribution supposedly turned down by Wright. Lucas also insisted that his opponent was running a campaign "masterminded by a left-wing conspiracy." On yet on another occasion he claimed that Wright favored "a world government, one to which our own government would be subservient." Later, Lucas went so far as to accuse Wright, who was a young Democrat in 1945, of protesting the failed adoption of a seventh-grade textbook praising Soviet Russia. And he asserted that in 1948, Parker County voters failed to return Wright to a second term in the state legislature because his neighbors were "outraged by his left-wing stand" on labor issues and "found [him] . . . to be faithless in his one effort at legislative service." During the last week of the campaign, Lucas even claimed that Wright used his position as a lay minister for the Presbyterian Church "with the sole selfish desire of furthering his campaign." Of course, his political advertisements reiterated these themes, continually questioning Wright's character and business dealings while warning the public not to be taken in by "meaningless, flowery oratory that offers no realistic proposal of effective representation."[7]

Wright, although wanting to conduct a positive campaign, was compelled to respond vigorously. On June 29, he answered Lucas on television, introducing his speech with a story about meeting the incumbent's young daughter at a recent political rally. He had assured her that "I'm not going to say anything ugly about your daddy." Looking directly into the television camera, he declared: "Tonight I'm going to keep that promise to that little girl." But, Wright asserted, his opponent should not "mistake gentility for weakness." He then replied to the slurs point by point. His campaign was not masterminded by any left-wing conspiracy but was run by himself. He made the decisions; he wrote the speeches. He denounced the "frantic name-calling," then asked: Could he have been elected mayor of Weatherford three times, served as commander of the local VFW post, or been selected as one of five outstanding young men in Texas the previous year if he was radical or left-wing? The answer, he concluded, was obviously not. Next, Wright deemed preposterous that labor racketeers supposedly were out to get Lucas—or that he was responsible. But he did note that many of the honest working people of the district were "anxious to have any kind of a change." And Wright insisted that he was not the candidate of labor or of business or of any other one segment of the economy but "wanted to be free to be a congressman for all the people or no congressman at all."[8]

As the campaign continued, Wright countered his opponent's attacks as well as answered insidious rumors. He branded every slander as "fantastic"—or the like—charging that Lucas often showed a "complete lack of concern for the truth." He denied reports of his 1945 support for any school textbook praising Soviet Russia. He defended his one term in the state legislature, stressing that his votes on labor issues were evenly split between management and organized labor. And he contended that his 1948 reelection defeat did not mean that his neighbors had lost confidence in his ability. After all, Weatherford citizens had elected him mayor three times, thereby affirming their trust in his ability and character. He also repudiated potentially damaging rumors of being funded by the CIO (Congress of Industrial Organizations), of favoring socialized medicine, and of opposing pay raises for city employees. And he viewed as ridiculous the assertion that politics motivated his church work. Again, on television Wright, effectively rebuking Lucas, stated that he had spoken at many churches outside the district and that his church work in Granbury predated his run for Congress by several years. "In the churches I visit," Wright explained, "we go there to pray not politic."[9]

As the campaign progressed, additional allegations of wrongdoing threatened to derail the Wright election effort. At a mid-June political rally at Euless, a Lucas backer charged that the National Trades Day Association, the sales promotion business in Weatherford co-owned by Wright and his father, conducted lotteries that were "just as much gambling as . . . slot machines." Wright quickly discounted such accusations as acts of "men who are becoming desperate." But two weeks later, US Postal Service inspectors (to the delight of Lucas supporters) filed civil charges against Wright and his firm, citing violations of postal regulations. The complaint maintained that the association conducted "a scheme for obtaining money through the mails." Federal authorities scheduled a hearing in Washington for

July 22, just two days before the primary election, forcing Wright to spend precious time defending his business rather than campaigning against Lucas, who denied any role in the postal complaints. Rumors quickly circulated that Wright might withdraw from the race.[10]

Wright aggressively defended himself. Despite the incumbent's protestations to the contrary, he steadily maintained that the charges were "obviously a political move to discredit . . . [him] by someone who had a personal interest in his election or [his] defeat." Wright cited comments by a Lucas supporter who made a "similar slur" two weeks earlier and the congressman's passing reference to it during a recent television speech. Pointedly, he questioned the timing of the inquiry, asserting that his opponents sought to "keep him so busy answering this complaint that [he wouldn't] have time to campaign." But they were wrong, Wright announced; their tactics would not work because "the people [would] see through it." He also countered all rumors of his pending withdrawal by urgently summoning supporters, by means of telegrams, to meetings in Fort Worth and Weatherford, whereupon he declared his innocence in the postal matter and promised to fight to the end. On July 6, Wright once again used television, his most effective campaign tool, to defend himself, eloquently asking his supporters not to be bitter over the politically inspired charges recently made against him. He reaffirmed his desire to run a clean campaign and to keep fighting until the "last vote is counted." As a further measure, Wright hired Horace J. Donnelly Jr., of Washington, DC, one of the most prominent attorneys on postal law, who persuaded the Postal Service to postpone any hearing on July 21—just three days before the election.[11]

Wright remained optimistic about his election chances despite all the rumors and accusations. Lucas, by such tactics and charges, was obviously worried. Otherwise, Wright questioned, why would a four-term congressman, unless vulnerable and scared, needlessly assail a lesser-known opponent from a small town? Wright, in turn, because of his rebuttals to the growing litany of allegations, attracted a lot more attention, a fact that was certainly important. Wright supporters were increasingly indignant and his responses to the charges were often calculated to make other people incensed by them—and they were. As a result, he began to gain confidence with every day that passed.[12]

Wright's opponents kept the postal controversy at the forefront of the campaign, but their tactics seemingly misfired. Lucas's backers continually questioned Wright's business practices and character on radio and television. Political advertisements echoed similar criticism. At one stop during the local stump-speaking tour, Lucas himself, speaking last, insisted that he was not accusing Wright of any wrongdoing in the postal affair but contended that a "congressman, like Caesar's wife, must be above suspicion." The implication irritated Wright and he readied a response. On July 15, before a large crowd at an Arlington Heights Park, Lucas, speaking first, once again repeated his admonition. Wright countered that "a congressman, like Caesar's wife, must be above casting suspicion." The crowd erupted in applause, confirming to Wright that the Lucas comments had backfired.[13]

During the last two weeks of this increasingly contentious campaign, two more incidents indicated that Wright was gaining strength. On July 14, Democratic Party office seekers appeared at a Fort Worth political rally scheduled before a minor league baseball game at LaGrave Field; candidates purchased tickets and distributed them freely to their supporters in an attempt to pack the park. Local factory workers, predominant among the 9,500 in attendance, roundly heckled the antilabor Lucas while warmly receiving Wright. And on July 22, just two days before the election, a Weatherford event provided another boost. A large hometown crowd at the football stadium booed Lucas, whose negative campaign had angered many in Parker County. Wright, outwardly embarrassed but silently appreciative of his neighbors, announced to the crowd: "Please show courtesy to our guest," and a disheartened Lucas quickly finished his comments. Wright later recalled that those two episodes indicated, "I was winning."[14]

But to ensure victory, Wright needed a fitting climax to this campaign. That could mean only one thing: he must neutralize, indeed overcome, the influence of Fort Worth power broker and publisher Amon G. Carter. On July 22, only two days before the Saturday election, the *Star-Telegram* ran a front-page endorsement of Lucas in its widely circulated afternoon edition, announcing that the voters would not be fooled by vague promises or substitute inexperience for experience. An angry Wright responded quickly, composing an election eve magnum opus on a borrowed typewriter. He bought an almost full-page advertisement (costing $974.40) in the next morning's edition, addressing an open letter to Mr. Amon G. Carter. Wright told the publisher that he had finally "met a man . . . who is not afraid of you, who will not bow his knee to you, and come running like a simpering pup at your beck and call." He castigated Carter and his newspaper for virtually ignoring his campaign and for misrepresenting his stands on issues. "Is this how you have controlled Fort Worth so long," Wright inquired, "by printing only that which you WANTED the people to read?" Wright also protested that "it is unhealthy for ANYONE to become TOO powerful, TOO influential, TOO dominating. The people are tired of 'One-Man Rule.'" Then he predicted: "The PEOPLE are going to vote for me. . . . And if I am your Congressman, as I think I am going to be . . . I will be YOUR Congressman, just as I will be EVERYONE'S Congressman, not your personal, private Congressman, but a Congressman for ALL the people!"[15]

On election day, July 24, 1954, the voters of the Twelfth Congressional District affirmed the Wright manifesto. He handily won the Democratic nomination with a 60 percent majority, outpolling Lucas in all five counties. And in a state then dominated by a single party, he easily defeated his Republican opposition in the November general election. In the process of the bitterly fought contest, he had furthered his political education, discovered the value of television in campaigning, adopted lifelong principles, and emerged stronger and more self-confident. A boyhood dream fulfilled, Jim Wright was on his way to Washington.[16]

On Congress: "Wouldn't Swap Jobs with Anyone in the World"

Wright found his first year in Washington both challenging and exhausting. Although he considered himself an energetic person, having juggled a business while serving as mayor of Weatherford, he was unprepared for the strenuous demands of congressional service. Committee conferences, floor debates and votes, talks with colleagues, meetings with visitors and lobbyists, and staff discussions filled his weekly calendar. Dozens of invitations for events in Washington as well as in Texas piled up. By July, he wrote to a friend that the city was "a hectic rat race." As adjournment neared late in July 1955, he lamented that the "House was running at break-neck speed," in "too big a hurry"; many bills, according to Wright, had escaped rigorous examination. And yet, he relished his position, heartily agreeing with his Texas colleague Jack Brooks of Beaumont that he had "no intention of making a career out of this job. Twenty-five or thirty years . . . [would] be entirely long enough."[17]

During these early years, life as a congressman remained hectic for Wright. On a typical day he arrived at his office by 8:00 a.m. and "read the daily mail" (an average of 160 pieces per day reached his office) and rapidly dictating replies; he also scanned the *Congressional Record*. Constituents visiting Washington often stopped by; almost one hundred passed through his suite each week. By 10:00 a.m., he usually was attending meetings of the Public Works Committee or one of its subcommittees, whereupon bills would be considered, testimony heard, and witnesses questioned. At noon the House convened. He either ate a quick lunch with a group of visitors from home or with several colleagues at the House dining room, attentive to the bell system that notified members of imminent votes. On the House floor, debate and voting often extended from 4:00 p.m. to 7:00 p.m. If unconcerned about House floor activities, Wright returned to his office early enough to greet more visitors, return phone calls, dictate replies to letters, meet with staff, and consult with colleagues on bills or projects of mutual interest. Often during the evening he dined with constituents, attended to his increasing correspondence, or tried to get home in time to spend a few minutes with his children. Finally, in the quiet of the late evening, Wright concentrated uninterrupted for an hour or two on the preparation of a speech, the agenda of the next day's committee, or a project within his district. Despite the constraints of time, Wright wrote to one constituent, that he "wouldn't swap jobs with anyone in the world," because it was the "most challenging and fascinating work in the world . . . and the most rewarding in terms of human values."

Wright, although relishing political life, worried about the public perception of Congress. In 1962 when allegations surfaced that certain lawmakers were blatantly misusing public funds, he shared the same disgust and disillusionment with his constituents. He stressed, however, that those who engaged in such practices were a tiny minority. In his view, the typical congressman was a "sincere, hardworking" individual possessing "more than the ordinary sense of dedication."[18]

Wright continued to defend the reputation of the Congress. In August 1963, he refuted allegations written in *Life* magazine that the Public Works Committee considered projects on the basis of "political advantage first and the public welfare second." Earlier in the year, after *Parade* magazine published an article entitled "Congressmen Who Cheat," he had labeled the piece "irresponsible," chiding the journalist Jack Anderson for his "blanket indictment," which cast doubt on the Congress. He challenged Anderson and his unnamed informant to produce any evidence to support such charges. In turn, Wright wrote the editors of *Parade* asking for the opportunity for rebuttal. When his request was rejected, he published his response in the Washington weekly *Roll Call*, declaring that Congress and a "responsible press" needed to commence "a vigorous and concerted program to restore and protect the integrity of the law-making branch of . . . [the] government."[19]

For the remainder of his congressional career, Wright retained this same affection, respect, and concern for the institution he served for over three decades. In his May 1989 speech that signaled his intent to resign as Speaker of the House, Wright confessed that "for 34 years I have had the great privilege to be a Member of this institution, the people's House, and I shall forever be grateful for that wondrous privilege. I never cease to be thankful to the people of the 12th District of Texas for their friendship and their under-standing and their partiality toward me. Eighteen times they have voted to permit me the grand privilege of representing them here in this repository of the democratic principle."[20]

Labor for Party

Throughout his early career in Congress, Jim Wright worked dili-gently on behalf of his political party on a state and national level, especially during the biennial election cycle. In 1956, Wright, with his own reelection secured, labored unavailingly on behalf of Lyn-don Johnson. For more than a year he had promoted the Texas sen-ator as a "favorite son" candidate for president, endorsing him as the only one who could "effectively unite the party and restore the South firmly to the [Democratic] fold." Wright, at Johnson's request, attended the state Democratic Convention at Dallas in May to help ensure a smooth-running event. The Johnson forces expected prob-lems, having recently defeated the conservative element of the party (led by Governor Allan Shivers), at the precinct and county level. Wright, however, failed in this endeavor, unable even to prevent his own Tarrant County delegates from bitterly dividing along conserva-tive/liberal lines. For example, they battled viciously over hometown delegates to the Democratic National Convention. Because three people were vying for two available spots, Wright removed himself from the delegate list to allow room for all three contenders and hopefully avoid a negative story in the press. But the local newspaper used the situation, as Wright lamented, "to do a neat knife job on that poor, strife-ridden bunch of fools who . . . [did not] even know how to win graciously." Through a misunderstanding, Wright failed to make the at-large delegate list. He traveled to Chicago anyway, at Johnson's insistence ("I want you and am going to need you at Chicago"), where he worked behind the scenes to secure the nomination for Texas's "favorite son"; Adlai Stevenson, however, prevailed once again—as he had in 1952.[21]

In the fall of 1956, Wright continued to work for the national Democratic ticket. He had gone all out for Stevenson four years earlier in a state and a district in which this was not the popular course for political aspirants to follow. He now offered advice to Stevenson about campaigning in Texas, including an appeal not to "let them photograph you again in Bermuda shorts." Along with other state Democratic leaders, he recorded radio spots endorsing their presidential nominee. In October he temporarily joined a chartered campaign bus tour of the state upon its arrival in his district; specifically, he introduced party spokespersons to his constituents and helped to raise funds. Then he embarked on a speaking itinerary throughout North Texas to laud Stevenson. Wright, booked solidly right up until Election Day, hoped somehow to undercut the popularity of the Republican president in an increasingly conservative state—but to no avail; a majority of Texans voted for Eisenhower, as they had just four years earlier.[22]

Two years later, in the fall of 1958, Wright worked diligently to enhance his own party and thereby enhance his own reputation. Before leaving Washington early in September, he had accepted thirty speaking engagements in Texas, the most important one being before the state Chambers of Commerce Association in Houston. Repeatedly he outlined several dangerous trends affecting the nation's future, such as the erosion of states' rights, the executive usurpation of legislative powers, and a waning respect for the Supreme Court. He had sought to "stake out a reasonable ground of moderation" as well as to demonstrate that he was a "different kind of liberal."[23]

Reactions were gratifying. Audiences found his speeches compelling. A Houston editorial approved of his "penetrating look at the country." A Dallas columnist claimed that Wright was "giving some conservative-minded Texans a few afterthoughts" and that he was "winning a lot of friends in the process." As a result, within two weeks, Wright became co-chairman of the Democratic National Committee's Speakers Bureau for the 1958 congressional campaign. He campaigned on behalf of Democratic candidates in West Virginia, Delaware, Maryland, Utah, South Dakota, Indiana, and Tennessee. While in Washington he also helped coordinate speakers for nearly five hundred Democratic dinners and rallies across the nation. And although a relative newcomer (having served only two terms in Congress), he became recognized, one North Texas reporter noted, as one of "four Texas Congress members" (the others being Senators Johnson and Yarborough and Speaker Rayburn) who deserved "credit for bringing victory to Democratic candidates in areas which were almost certain to go Republican."[24]

Throughout the spring and early in the summer of 1960, Wright strongly promoted Lyndon Johnson for president. Despite a heavy schedule in Washington, Wright represented the majority leader at the Kansas state convention, helped organize campaigns in several states, and delivered speeches on Johnson's behalf throughout Texas. At each stop Wright characterized Johnson as "the ablest, best qualified, and most responsible leader" in America, a man with a "broader vision" who as president would "serve all of America." In mid-June Wright performed dual roles at the Texas state convention in Austin. On the eve of the meeting, the Johnson forces, hoping to avoid any political embarrassment, enlisted Wright as a behind-the-scenes peacemaker. Conscious of the bitterness that had divided the loyalist and conservative factions since 1952, he repeatedly conferred with liberals to gain their acceptance of a loyalty resolution supporting the party nominees on the national, state, and local levels. And as the keynote speaker, Wright championed Johnson as "the most effective majority leader in the past 50 years." He was pleased by his efforts; Johnson won unanimous backing at the convention.[25]

In July 1960, Wright traveled with the Texas delegation to the Democratic National Convention in Los Angeles to work for Johnson. He spoke before several state delegations on his fellow Texan's behalf. In public statements he boldly predicted that Johnson's forces would block Senator John F. Kennedy of Massachusetts from gaining "the nomination on the first two ballots" and "then his 'bandwagon' . . . [was] going to fall apart."

When Kennedy soundly defeated Johnson on the first ballot, the Texas delegates, although disappointed, were not surprised. Speculation now centered on the vice-presidential choice, and Wright labored for Johnson. He talked to people within the Kennedy camp, including brother Ted Kennedy. He advised them that if Kennedy solicited the help of the majority leader on the basis that his party and nation needed him, then LBJ would accept the vice-presidential nomination; any other approach, Wright feared, would cause his proud friend to reject the offer. Once the pairing was announced, Wright claimed that Johnson would "add strength, maturity and acknowledged skill to the ticket," indeed the "very ingredients which the ticket otherwise lacked."

Wright enthusiastically backed the Democratic ticket. Before the July convention he had emphasized to constituents that he was pro-Johnson and not anti-Kennedy, believing that both men were at least as well-qualified to be the next president as was the Republican nominee, Vice President Richard M. Nixon. Wright further viewed his party as much better qualified to provide the leadership necessary to restore the nation's "once strong position in a world severely threatened by the Communist menace." As a result, after Congress adjourned in September, he spoke at numerous party rallies in

East Texas and along the Gulf Coast as well as joined both Kennedy and Johnson during a mid-month swing through his district. Until election day in November, Wright continued to campaign throughout Texas, explaining to state Democratic officials that he did not "want to have any idle time" when he could be "getting some votes for the nominees."[26]

Labor for District

From the beginning of his congressional career, Wright was ever cognizant of issues important to his district and region, striving to become a congressman who "could make things happen." Wright certainly recognized the significance of environmental matters to North Texas. Based on his experience as mayor of Weatherford and as president of the League of Texas Municipalities (now the Texas Municipal League), Wright believed that "clear, usable water" was perhaps the "single most important item for the future of America." In 1956 he endorsed legislation focused on water pollution, insisting that the issue was "a national problem and a national responsibility and one that we cannot avoid." On a related issue, Wright wrote that soil conservation was "nearest to . . . his heart," dating from his 1947 term as a Texas state legislator. In March 1955, in his first speech before Congress, he denounced efforts to eliminate the field activities of the US Soil Conservation Service, saying that only the federal government was equal to the task. For the next three years he appeared annually before the House Appropriations Subcommittee, pleading forcefully against cuts in soil conservation programs. He steadily maintained that "money spent for conservation [was] really an investment." Wright also consistently promoted water resource development. As a representative of North Texas, where both drought and flooding menaced his constituents, and as a member of the Public Works Committee, he became an active and successful voice for flood control appropriation. Responding to critics of federal investment in such projects, Wright pointed out how such funding saved citizens millions of dollars annually and insisted that the federal flood control program would pay for itself many times over.[27]

Wrestling with civic rivalry and partisanship certainly motivated Wright into action. Over a three-year period (beginning in 1956), postal officials sought to transfer a small contingent of transport workers from Fort Worth to Dallas "for the good of the service," but Wright regarded such a move as a foot in the door to shift more than two hundred employees eastward. He further surmised that the real purpose behind the relocation was to reward the only Texas district represented by a Republican, Congressman Bruce Alger. As a result, Wright campaigned fiercely, characterizing his fight as "one lone Texas congressman against the whole [Eisenhower] administration." Five different times the move was announced and Wright, with the aid of Speaker Rayburn, stoutly resisted, stating on one occasion that "they'll have to steam-roller me to get it through." They never did. The regional post transportation office remained in Fort Worth, even adding twenty new personnel. "Persistence," Wright concluded to one hometown associate, "does pay off sometimes, I suppose."[28]

In 1956 the prospect of a new federal building in Dallas spurred Wright once again to defend Fort Worth. After the Eisenhower administration announced plans to construct a $24.5 million structure in Dallas to house federal agencies, Wright sought a delay to ascertain the impact of such a building on his district. Publicly he did not begrudge the rival city this project, but he feared that such a project "might provide future temptation to move agencies and government services from Fort Worth to Dallas." To allay such concerns, Wright used his influence on the House Public Works Committee to receive written assurances from the administrator of the General Services Administration (GSA) confirming that the project would not relocate any federal offices eastward from Fort Worth. Because of financing problems in 1957, however, the Dallas building was not constructed for several years. And before it was formally authorized by the Public Works Committee, Wright gained an agreement to erect a hometown federal complex, to be completed before its Dallas counterpart. Only then, Wright later recalled, would the GSA have "no excuse for their moving things from Fort Worth to Dallas."[29]

In 1961, Wright waged a battle over an issue important to his hometown, and lost. Since 1958 he had become an active proponent of the Fort Worth–built B-58 supersonic bomber. For the next three years, like a proud parent, he followed the progress of the local Convair plant (a division of General Dynamics), especially since eighteen thousand families depended on it. An abrupt cancellation of the B-58 would devastate the area economy. Then in 1960, the Eisenhower administration changed their priorities, offering no new funding for manned bombers, including the older B-52 as well as the new B-58.

Early in 1961, the new Kennedy administration sent a revised defense budget to Congress without provisions for further purchases of strategic combat aircraft, signaling that missiles were the newest weapon of choice. As a result, Wright became a self-appointed one-man sales force to reinstate bomber money in the military budget. His campaign proved instrumental in rallying several relevant House and Senate committees to act. And his efforts seemingly paid off. In August 1961, Congress approved $515 million for long-range bombers. But Wright could not overcome opposition, particularly General Curtis LeMay, the incoming Air Force chief of staff, who was dead set against the B-58, in part because he favored Boeing, the Seattle manufacturer of the B-52s, over General Dynamics. Attempts to sway Secretary of Defense Robert McNamara failed. For several months Wright even had sought an audience with President Kennedy, but he had been unable, he complained, "to penetrate the armor of the president." Consequently, on October 27, Secretary McNamara announced that the appropriated funds for more bombers would not be spent, and production of the B-58 would end in 1962. Wright, by his own admission, "had fanned out."[30]

Another General Dynamics (GD) aircraft presented an opportunity for recovery. Late in 1961, GD officials conferred with Wright about a project that could compensate for the pending phaseout of B-58 production. For several months company engineers had labored over a design for a new type of fighter plane— the TFX (or Tactical Fighter Experimental). Both the Navy and the Air Force had traditionally utilized separate aircraft production programs, but Secretary McNamara, despite the skepticism of senior military officers, had pushed for a single airplane for both services, a craft capable of operating from naval carriers as well as from short runways on land. In December 1961, initial military evaluations determined that the Boeing and General Dynamics design proposals, among the six submitted, had most clearly met the military specifications.

Wanting to prevent another arbitrary decision like the one that had led to the B-58's death knell, Wright searched for a strategy to ensure that GD received a fair chance. Since General LeMay favored Boeing and Secretary McNamara presumably listened to his military leaders, Wright discussed his quandary with Vice President Johnson, who suggested talking personally with President Kennedy. When Wright hesitated, Johnson assured him that the president liked him and appreciated his support of such administration programs as the Alliance for Progress, the space program, and the Peace Corps. Consequently, the vice president arranged an audience.

In January 1962, Wright joined Kennedy and Johnson in the Oval Office, and was greatly encouraged. The president listened intently and did not interrupt. Wright, instead of focusing on the obvious economic impact the company had on his district, stressed the importance of maintaining the Fort Worth plant from a national viewpoint. He cited several factors, including the sizeable investment taxpayers already had in the massive facility. The recent cancellation of the B-58 program, he noted, threatened this national asset; a modern and efficient manufacturing factory would soon become idle. And the dispersion of a highly experienced management team would not serve the country's interest. Furthermore, Boeing had a backlog of business, but the Fort Worth facility needed the TFX contract to survive. In response, President Kennedy complimented his presentation and then implicitly indicated that "if the price . . . [was] in the ballpark, the Fort Worth plant . . . [would] get the job."[31]

In November 1962, Wright anxiously awaited word about the TFX contract. For nearly a year he had used the influence of his office in campaigning for the General Dynamics bid. After winning his reelection race handily, Wright returned to Washington, having heard disturbing reports that the Defense Department had twice recommended Boeing for the TFX contract, but Ken O'Donnell, the president's right-hand man, assured Wright that "the plane will be built in Fort Worth." Then on November 24, Wright received official confirmation that General Dynamics was to build the TFX, a contract, according to a local editorial, that would have "a stabilizing effect upon the plant, its personnel and the general economy of Fort Worth."

Most importantly during his early career, Wright battled for improved airline service for his constituents. In 1958 and 1960, he had appealed to the Civil Aeronautics Board (CAB) for better flights to Carter Field (located in eastern Tarrant County) because commercial airlines had favored Dallas's Love Field and had diminished service to Fort Worth, despite excellent facilities there. In 1962, Wright changed tactics and helped convince the CAB to investigate the need for a Dallas-Fort Worth regional airport; hearings began in July 1963. Eleven years later, Wright helped dedicate such a facility, situated midway between Fort Worth and Dallas. His constituents, he later proudly affirmed, no longer had to drive to Dallas to fly commercially.[32]

Ambition

Wright's ambition continued to grow during his early congressional career, fueled by his upbringing and personality and his earlier service in the Texas House and as the mayor of Weatherford.

He carried with him an impatience to get things accomplished, to make a difference. Wright, although enjoying his tenure on the Public Works Committee, had the opportunity to switch to the Foreign Affairs Committee. He thought that the Foreign Affairs Committee seemed "to carry a little more stature" and would probably grant him "expanded opportunities to render a contribution to the national welfare." Yet, he considered that such a change might reduce his effectiveness to his own District. Unable to reach a definite conclusion, he consulted with Speaker Rayburn, who told him that he could have either committee assignment, but that he should "take . . . [his] time and think it over." In the end, Wright stayed with Public Works, realizing that he would have greater seniority in that committee and that his other choice, although a prized assignment, had limited jurisdiction in the House. He also realized "the advantages of being a team player who could make things happen in Congress for folks back home."[33]

By the end of 1957, Wright, despite several achievements for his district, refused to become complacent. Imbued by his parents with an intense drive to excel, he was supremely confident of his capabilities. He labored intensively to demonstrate his effectiveness as a legislator, to both his colleagues and his constituents. True, he was pleased with his accomplishments to date, but he had higher aspirations. From the beginning of his tenure, consciously or unconsciously, Jim Wright sought to be "more of a player," to have have a more prominent role, to be a bigger part of the machinery of Congress, never content "to just sit there . . . and cast a vote."[34]

In August 1958, *Esquire* magazine named Wright as one of five members of Congress among the fifteen Bright Young Men in American politics—and justifiably so. His performance in the 1958 congressional campaign, speaking for Democratic candidates, earned high marks from party officials. As a result, late in 1959, Wright received in the mail an editorial endorsing his debt-reduction bill from a conservative Dallas newspaper; a friend had wryly scrawled in the margin that Wright was "really gaining ground when the *Dallas News* climbs aboard." Capitol watchers tracked his political rise. In 1957, Wright had been identified as a "comer." By the end of 1958, one Fort Worth correspondent claimed that Wright had "arrived." In 1959, a Houston writer speculated that he "might be the man to watch" if a Texas senatorial seat opened up. And another from Dallas in 1960 tabbed him as a "young man going places."[35]

With the election of Kennedy in 1960, Wright decided to undertake a challenging opportunity. For months the press had speculated about his running for the US Senate, if Lyndon Johnson won higher office. In turn, friends throughout Texas had sent letters of support. Publicly, Wright demurred on the subject, but privately he encouraged such talk. And as he had toured the state campaigning for the national ticket, he had quietly acquired backing for a possible senatorial bid. Wright, eager to play a more vital role in the incoming administration, declared his candidacy for Vice President Johnson's unexpired Senate term on November 18, 1960. He was the first to announce his intentions, hoping that his stature as a candidate "would scare others out of the race."

Wright remained confident of his chances and optimistic about his future. As a veteran campaigner, he was widely recognized as an excellent speaker, both on the stump and on television. He was well known and "apparently well-liked" (according to a Fort Worth newspaper) in Central and West Texas but was less familiar to voters in the eastern and Gulf Coast areas of the state. To compensate, he vowed to emerge victorious by "getting up earlier, going to bed later, working harder, traveling more miles and shaking more hands." Tarrant County provided him with a solid base. At a Fort Worth luncheon in December 1960, more than four hundred local business, professional, and civic leaders—both Republican and Democrat, conservative and liberal—met to promote his candidacy. Twelve area mayors, together with most regional newspapers, lauded him. His campaign tour of the state for the Kennedy-Johnson ticket had paid dividends; at least half of the sixty-two members of the State Democratic Executive Committee favored him, with twenty-two of them serving as county or district campaign chairmen. Wright also expected partial labor backing, despite some discontent over his record. In addition, no other member of the Texas congressional delegation entered the race, so his experience in national politics remained an asset. And he hoped to run with the full support of Lyndon Johnson, believing that his association with the vice president would enhance his standing. Wright had, according to one political observer, "much to gain and little to lose by running for the Senate." Even if defeated, he "would become," the *Fort Worth Press* predicted, "well-known to voters across Texas and would be in a good position for another statewide race."[36]

The notion that his early decision to run would deter opposition proved to be, Wright later admitted, foolishly misguided. He considered the candidacy of conservative Dallas businessman William A. Blakley (whom Governor Price Daniel had selected as the interim senator) without alarm, because the public would choose him, a moderate, over an ultraconservative. Such a selection, however, soon became complicated. Former college professor John Tower, a Republican, joined the contest, hoping to capitalize on his strong showing against Lyndon Johnson in the November 1960 senatorial election. Many liberal Democrats, who viewed Wright as too conservative, backed Maury Maverick Jr., of San Antonio—a fervent Kennedy supporter who was not ashamed of being called a liberal—or state senator Henry B. González of San Antonio. And the political middle became crowded once state attorney general Will Wilson decided to run. In the end, seventy-one individuals—a record number for the same office in the state—registered to appear on the ballot for US senator.[37]

Additional obstacles confronted Wright. His devotion to Johnson alienated a number of liberal Democrats, among them Senator Ralph Yarborough, who was reportedly cool toward Wright's candidacy. Wright had also angered a segment of organized labor by voting for the Landrum-Griffin bill; thus, the Texas AFL-CIO

Committee on Political Education endorsed Maverick. Although refusing to give unions a "blank check" or to serve as their "rubber stamp," Wright had been more sympathetic to their cause, he believed, than anybody who had the "remotest chance to win." Several Fort Worth labor groups recognized this fact and broke ranks to back Wright. His Washington connections, however, proved disappointing; Wright received no help from either Lyndon Johnson or Sam Rayburn in his bid for the Senate. Campaign funds were always in short supply, even though at one point late in the contest Wright reportedly was the high spender and the top recipient of donations among the candidates. In addition, pressing congressional matters occasionally forced him to spend valuable campaign time away from Texas. Such absences only highlighted the difficulty in covering the vast state in just four months, a task he later likened to siphoning "all the water out of the Gulf of Mexico with an eyedropper!"[38]

Despite such disadvantages, Wright campaigned vigorously as a unity candidate. He deplored political labels and hoped to overcome the long-standing strife among Texas Democrats by appealing to both conservatives and liberals as an "independent-thinking moderate Democrat." He contended that Texans were "not going to let this Senate seat be controlled by any minority, whether it be of the far right or the far left." In speech after speech he proclaimed the need for a middle-of-the-road senator. But the crowded field only further divided Democrats and threatened to overshadow his distinctive appeal.[39]

As the senate race neared the end, Wright returned from Washington, seeking to break out of the pack. Because he was hopeful that he would win, he traveled ceaselessly—by car, bus, train, even helicopter. He maintained a brutal pace. For example, he averaged eleven speeches daily during his 1,700-mile, six-day helicopter tour, which stretched through forty-eight counties from the Red River to the Gulf Coast. Day after day he greeted voters at untold shopping centers, spoke at countless political rallies, and appeared at innumerable banquets and barbecues. During the last weeks of the campaign, Wright increasingly relied on television to reach more citizens, recognizing his strength in that medium. He also attempted to engage both John Tower and "Cowboy Bill" Blakley in televised debates, but they were the front-runners and were unwilling to take risks. Still, Wright was heartened by the growing response to his candidacy—the newspaper endorsements and enthusiastic crowds; even his Washington Sunday school class sent an unsolicited letter of support to various Texas newspapers.

Wright, however, lost in his bid for higher office, placing a close third in the April election, behind Republican Tower and Democrat Blakley. He remained gracious in public, although he was deeply disappointed. In May 1961, for the sake of party unity, Wright returned from Washington to campaign for Blakley over Tower in the runoff senatorial contest. He vowed to oppose Tower, regarding him as an "opportunistic . . . dangerous" individual who had "such a closed mind that he thinks that he and Barry Goldwater . . . [were] conducting a Holy Crusade." He willingly toured West Texas with an appreciative Blakley, debated on his behalf, and urged Democrats to back their candidate. Wright warned moderate and liberal Democrats that staying away from the polls to protest the conservative party choice would allow the election of the Republican nominee, a move Wright likened to creating a "Frankenstein's monster." Democrats failed to listen to pleas for unity as they stayed away from the polls; a 20 percent voter turnout virtually guaranteed a Tower victory.[40]

Wright spent the remainder of 1961 discreetly exploring whether he could provide the leadership necessary to revitalize the state Democratic Party by running for governor. The possibility tempted him; whoever occupied that office would be in the best position to challenge Tower in 1966. And Wright did want to be a US senator. To that end, within a few days of his defeat, he hinted publicly about seeking the governorship, asserting hundreds of well-wishers had urged him to do so. By the end of May, he privately evaluated his assets and liabilities, identified the next several months as a period "devoted to building upon the assets and eradicating the liabilities," and then set a deadline of December for deciding whether to make "a go-for-broke assault on the Governor's office."[41]

In part, Wright considered running for governor because of his growing frustration with his position in Congress. He was no longer able, at least by his logic, to expand his influence. He was, "in effect, waiting around until someone dies or is defeated" to "move up a notch in seniority toward a chairmanship." He would have to wait ten years before attaining such a post. Until then, he could have only the vicarious satisfaction of making suggestions and ideas that were "later incorporated in legislation under the name of committee chairmen." But Wright was impatient to play a more significant role.[42]

By the fall, Wright was confident of winning the gubernatorial election. But he wrestled with the key question: Did he want the job? He disliked the approach of using the governorship as a stepping-stone to the Senate; he believed such an act both unfair to the state and "not very honorable." Of course, reorganizing and rejuvenating the Democratic Party in Texas was a more compelling reason to run. Still, he vacillated. Unable to resolve the issue in Washington, he returned home late in September to "sample the wind" again by scheduling a number of speeches.[43]

Eventually, on December 16, 1961, Wright decided that he would remain in Congress. And why? He cited that his experience lay in national affairs and that his deepest interests lay in improving US defenses, promoting the economy, and helping Latin America, where he could "do the greatest amount of good." In addition, he wanted to complete work on several projects particularly helpful to Texas. In private Wright confided that he was neither "sufficiently conversant with nor frankly sufficiently interested in the day-to-day problems" of the governorship and that he was unconvinced he could make a "truly important contribution." But equally significant, he could not envision "being tied up and frustrated by a re-calcitrant Legislature." In other words, he lacked the temperament. But most importantly, he wrote to a friend, his "heart just . . . [was] not in this race."[44]

By 1962, Wright became increasingly restless about his role in Congress. Laboring in the shadows of senior congressmen frustrated him, particularly when any real opportunity for lead-ership—a chairmanship—seemed probably a decade away. The Kennedy presidency had inspired, as Wright later wrote, "a veri-table horde of idealistic young political practitioners," all clamor-ing to heed the call for public service. But the deliberate pace of the House caused Wright to believe that the mantle of leadership was passing him by. His administrative assistant, Craig Raupe, had earlier joined the Agency for International Development and after a year in Indonesia had returned to Washington and was enlisting people to represent the Kennedy administration abroad. Wright became acquainted with a number of these dynamic re-cruits and began to wonder if he "couldn't make a bigger impact" by leaving Congress and pursuing a post on the Kennedy inner team.

Wright sought out advice. In 1962 he approached Vice Pres-ident Johnson about joining the administration, perhaps in a cabinet position or as an ambassador to a Latin American na-tion. He also expressed frustration with his present role as well as his worry about not "making a big enough contribution." In response, Johnson pointed out that both he and the president had their share of disappointments as well; in fact, Jack Kennedy, he asserted, was "the most frustrated man in Washington." Still, the vice president assured Wright that such executive appointments could be arranged but confided that the best jobs in this town were in the House and the Senate. With a renewed sense of clar-ity, Wright had to agree.

A driven Jim Wright remained in the House, pursuing leader-ship positions and ultimately becoming Speaker of the House of

Representatives. His ambition certainly continued to grow. But he also retained his impatience, an impatience to get things accomplished, to make a difference.[45]

Effective Communicator

The impact of Wright's communication skills increased over time. As indicated earlier in the chapter, Wright, in the fall of 1958, had emerged as a keynote speaker at numerous events for his party, which also enhanced his own reputation. In the process, even as a relative newcomer (having served only two terms in Congress), Wright became recognized, one North Texas reporter noted, as one of only four Texas members of Congress who deserved "credit for bringing victory to Democratic candidates in areas which were almost certain to go Republican."[46]

Wright realized still further satisfaction for his actions, especially regarding Alaskan and Hawaiian statehood. To him, statehood for both territories was a matter of "common decency and morality." For example, when the bill for Alaskan statehood reached the House floor during the last week in May 1958, Wright delivered an effective and stirring speech for the bill. He warned that the issue "could be the most historically significant decision" confronting the Eighty-Fifth Congress. He challenged his colleagues to affirm the basic principle of self-determination as well as to grant the unfulfilled promise extended to Alaskans "the enjoyment of all the rights, advantages, and immunities" available to all US citizens. And he questioned how Congress could rebuff, and then deny, people who had asked "to be united with us in the whole enjoyment of our freedoms." Wright closed by exclaiming that "whenever we begin to begrudge . . . [freedom] to others and selfishly seek to enjoy it exclusively, . . . then we shall have ceased to deserve it. And, ceasing to deserve it, we may find that we have it no more."[47]

Such advocacy brought recognition and results. George Lehleitner, a New Orleans industrialist and statehood proponent, sent copies of the standout speech to the top five hundred daily newspapers in the country, later noting the "importance of . . . [Wright's] contribution to the success of this effort." Ernest Gruening, former territorial governor, called the oration "the best and most persuasive address" he had ever heard "in support of statehood, at any place or any time." And Bob Bartlett, an Alaskan territorial delegate, claimed that "no one—not even the bitterest foe of the bill—could have failed to be impressed by those ringing declarations." The House, after rejecting a combined statehood bill just three years earlier, now endorsed Alaskan inclusion by a vote of 208 to 166. In June 1958, the Senate followed the House lead, and President Eisenhower formally admitted the forty-ninth state in January 1959.[48]

Even as a junior congressman, Wright steadily gained attention for his skills. His eloquence as a speaker continued to impress colleagues and members of the press. His voice and choice of words reminded old-timers of the silvery oratory of one predecessor, Fritz G. Lanham of Fort Worth. For example, during the floor fight over the National Cultural Center in August 1958, Wright reportedly snapped members to attention by declaring: "All of us like to portray ourselves as real . . . corn-fed, homegrown, log cabin boys. . . . In striking such a pose, it is always kind of easy to ridicule and poke fun at things of a cultural nature. I plead guilty to having done my share of it, but I think . . . that we have reached a state of maturity in this nation when that kind of attitude no longer becomes us. Sooner or later, we have to grow up and stop poking fun at things intellectual and cultural." A Dallas newspaper noted that Wright "was the most effective floor speaker" for the Cultural Center bill.[49]

Wright also wrote well. He had, one Houston columnist claimed, "a touch of Lincoln" about him. Most lawmakers' newsletters were, according to a Washington writer, "as indigestible as their speeches," but Wright's were an exception. His weekly reports were "carefully scanned by hundreds of newspaper correspondents covering Capitol Hill," and his observations were frequently quoted. An Amarillo

editorial proclaimed that "for pure literacy," Wright was "wasted on
the national Congress"; his letters were "usually witty, entertaining,
and informative," resulting in numerous newspapers in his own
district publishing excerpts.[50]

Growing Interest in Inter-American Affairs

Throughout his early congressional career, Wright's personal affection for, as well as his public commitment to, Latin America
deepened, certainly foreshadowing his future role in bringing peace
to a troubled Central America. By the end of the 1950s, Wright,
prompted by his concern with interstate roadways, developed a special interest in the region. As a member of the House Public Works
Committee, he became an active congressional proponent of the
Inter-American Highway, which stretched from the Texas-Mexico
border at Laredo to the Panama Canal, passing more than 1,500
miles through Mexico, Guatemala, El Salvador, Nicaragua, Costa
Rica, and Panama. In the fall of 1958, he attended a highway conference in Mexico, inspected progress of existing roadwork, and in-
vestigated US–Central American relations. He met with the Costa
Rican president and later used his limited knowledge of Spanish
to address the Guatemalan national legislature—"Heady stuff," he
recollected, "for a second-term US congressman." Such experiences helped Wright acquire a lifelong affinity for the region. He returned to Congress, committed to promoting understanding with
Latin America. He applauded US congressional efforts to improve
relations with Mexico by establishing annual meetings of legislators
from both countries to discuss mutual problems. In one newsletter
to constituents he emphasized how important the region was to
the United States, both politically and economically. In another he
discussed why Communism was attractive to many in the region,
outlining how the United States could recapture its lost prestige
and re-create "the friendship so carefully nurtured over the years
through the Good Neighbor policy." And in his own district he

began to cultivate Mexican American understanding. Speaking in Spanish at a 1959 Fort Worth celebration, which marked 149 years of Mexican independence from Spain, Wright expressed his belief that Americans must respect the interests of "our brothers to the South."[51]

In 1960, Wright unexpectedly played a major role in promoting inter-American relations. President Eisenhower had invited members of the Pan American Health Organization, the oldest agency (1902) within the venerable Organization of American States, to build their permanent headquarters in Washington. A bill authorizing the purchase of such land faced unforeseen attacks by opponents from both political parties. A defeat would not only embarrass President Eisenhower but also harm US relations within the hemisphere. After the State Department had learned of the opposition, an official urgently called Wright for help, knowing of his ardent support of Latin America. With debate limited to forty minutes and with a two-thirds vote necessary for passage, the bill faced an uncertain fate. Wright spent the day phoning colleagues; he then appeared on the House floor for the debate. As the last speaker—with a time limit of three minutes—to persuade his fellow congressmen to do the right thing, Wright, groping for the appropriate words, fervently offered: "Although I did not personally vote for this president, I want everyone in this House to know that he is my president. If he is embarrassed in the eyes of the world, then I am embarrassed—because my country is embarrassed." The measure passed, 206 to 40. Later, one Democratic colleague playfully accused him of "pulling the Administration's chestnuts out of the fire." Wright was proud that he had.[52]

Throughout the Kennedy years, Wright's commitment to Latin America continued to deepen. In congressional speeches, published articles, and district newsletters, Wright offered ideas to solve the problems, rooted in poverty and despair, plaguing US–Latin American relations. He supported long-term mortgage credit that would enable individuals to own "family farms, modest homes, and small businesses . . . a sort of Latin American FHA." Wright also suggested requiring all government employees—and encouraging all privately employed US citizens throughout the region—to learn the local language. He continued to promote exchange programs with labor leaders, radio commentators, teachers, and journalists to counter Communist propaganda. And he called on US tourists to use sensitivity when visiting their southern neighbors.[53]

In 1963, Wright continued his involvement with inter-American affairs. Early in the year, Speaker John McCormack of Massachusetts appointed Wright to a vacancy in the House delegation to the forthcoming third annual conference with Mexican lawmakers, beginning an assignment that Wright enjoyed for nearly twenty years; eventually, he became chairman of the US delegation. To sharpen his communication skills, Wright enrolled in early-morning Spanish classes at the State Department's Foreign Service Institute. At the March parliamentary conference in Guanajuato, Mexico, he addressed the assembly in Spanish, a gesture appreciated by his hosts. And in May, Wright delivered a speech in Spanish to delegates attending a Pan-American Highway Congress in Washington, DC. Constituents, colleagues, and Latin Americans noticed his deep interest in regional issues. In recognition for his "efforts on behalf of Pan-American unity and friendship," Wright was elected to the Mexican Academy of International Law as an honorary member, only the third North American up to that time so chosen.[54]

1   On Wright's tenure in the Texas Legislature, see Mark Beasley, "Jim Wright: The Fiftieth Legislature and the Education of a Texas Politician," in *Never without Honor: Studies of Courage in Tribute to Ben H. Procter*, ed. Archie P. McDonald (Nacogdoches: Stephen F. Austin State University Press, 2013), 105–27. On Wright's tenure as mayor of Weatherford, see Mark W. Beasley, "Jim Wright: Mayor of Weatherford Texas, 1950–1954," in *Weatherford Days . . . A Time of Learnin'*, ed. Jim Wright (Fort Worth: Madison, 1996), 113–22.

2   Jim Greer, interview by Jeanne Grisham, October 16, 1992, Jim Wright Collection, Mary Couts Burnett Library, Texas Christian University, Fort Worth, Texas (hereafter cited as JWC); "Jim Wright Address Opening Speech for Congress," audio tape 1, JWC.

3   Jim Wright, interview by Jeanne Grisham, October 1, 1992, JWC.

4   Jim Wright, interview by Ben Procter, March 3, 1992.

5   Jim Wright, *Balance of Power: Presidents and Congress from the Era of McCarthy to the Age of Gingrich* (Atlanta: Turner, 1996), 31; Wright, interview, October 1, 1992, JWC.

6   Jim Wright, interview by Ben Procter, March 16, 1992; "Jim Wright Address Opening Speech for Congress," audio tape 1, JWC; Wright to Ross Matthews, July 7, 1954, in "Campaign, Fort Worth—7/7/54," Special Projects, 84th, 1st, JWC

7   *Weatherford Democrat*, July 7, 1954, 1; *Fort Worth Press*, June 29, 1954, 9; *Fort Worth Star-Telegram*, June 29, 1954, evening edition, 1, 10; *Fort Worth Press*, July 20, 1954, 11; July 21, 1954, 2; *Fort Worth Star-Telegram*, July 22, 1954, morning edition, 28.

8   "Jim Wright Address Opening Speech for Congress," audio tape 1, JWC; *Fort Worth Press*, June 29, 1954, 9.

9   *Fort Worth Press*, June 30, 1954, 5; July 21, 1954, 2.

10 *Fort Worth Press*, June 14, 1954, 4; *Fort Worth Star-Telegram*, June 30, 1954, morning edition, 1.

11 *Fort Worth Star-Telegram*, June 30, 1954, evening edition, 1; July 1, 1954, 18; *Fort Worth Star-Telegram*, July 1, 1954, morning edition, 4; *Fort Worth Press*, July 1, 1954, 1; *Weatherford Democrat*, July 5, 1954, 1.

12 Wright, interview, March 3, 1992; Wright, interview, October 1, 1992.

13 Jim Wright, interview by Mark Beasley, February 8, 1996.

14 Wright, interview, October 1, 1992.

[15] *Fort Worth Star-Telegram*, July 22, 1954, evening edition, 1; July 23, 1954, 8.

[16] Mark William Beasley, "Prelude to Leadership: Jim Wright, 1922–1963" (PhD diss., Texas Christian University, Fort Worth, 1997), 172-83 (primary source for "First Congressional Campaign").

[17] Wright to J. B. Irwin, July 12, 1955, in "Personal [I-L]—7/9/55-7/12/55," General, 84th, 1st, JWC; "The Wright Slant on Washington," July 25, 1955, in "Jim Wright Newsletters: 'The Right Slant'—7/25/55," Special Projects, 84th, 1st, JWC; Jim Wright, interview by Mark Beasley, September 24, 1997.

[18] Wright to Linda Kay Mann, February 15, 1963, in "Wright Personal [2/11/63–2/18/63]—2/11/63–2/25/63," General, 88th, 1st, JWC; Wright to Mr. and Mrs. Tommy B. Felmet, May 5, 1962, in "Colleagues [F-G]—1/31/62-11/12/62," General, 87th, 2nd, JWC.

[19] *Congressional Record*, 88th Congress, 1st session, 1963, Vol. 109, Part 4—House, pp. 4940-4941, https://www.congress.gov/congressional-record; *Roll Call*, April 10, 1963, 1, 8.

[20] *Congressional Record*, 101st Congress, 1st session, 1989, Vol. 135, Part 8—House, p.10431, https://www.congress.gov/congressional-record; Beasley, "Prelude to Leadership," 194–96, 309–10, 312–13 (primary source for "On Congress: 'Wouldn't Swap Jobs with Anyone in the World'").

[21] "The Wright Slant on Washington," February 21, 1955," in "Jim Wright Newsletters: 'The Wright Slant'—2/21/55," Special Projects, 84th, 1st, JWC; Wright to Carlos [Hartnett], May 26, 1956; Lyndon Johnson to Jim [Wright], June 4, 1956, in "Campaign—5/18/56-6/12/56," General, 84th, 2nd, JWC.

[22] Wright to [Adlai] Stevenson, December 13, 1955, in "Campaigns—11/3/55–12/27/55," General, 84th, 1st, JWC; Craig Raupe to Fred H. Schmidt and Jerry R. Holleman, October 30, 1956, in "Federal Communications Commission [Sch-Tank]—10/16/56–1/17/57," Departments, 85th, 1st, JWC.

[23] *Houston Chronicle*, September 20, 1958, Sec. C, 6; Wright, interview, September 24, 1997.

[24] Houston Chronicle, September 20, 1958, Sec. C, 6; Dallas Times Herald, October 3, 1958, article enclose with Albert N. Jacson to Wright, October 28, 1958, in "Invitations [Hut-Hoh]—1/7/58-12/22/58," General, 85th, 2nd, JWC; *Fort Worth Star-Telegram*, November 6, 1958, in "Scrapbook: 1958," 88, RC Box 8/30, JWC.

25 *Fort Worth Star-Telegram*, June 25, 1960, morning edition, 4; *Fort Worth Star-Telegram*, April 26, 1960, 4; *Fort Worth Press*, June 14, 1960, 1.

26 *Fort Worth Press*, July 13, 1960, 4; *Fort Worth Star-Telegram*, July 15, 1960, morning edition, 1; Wright to A. H. Rowan, July 7, 1960, in "Campaign—6/26/60-8/29/60," General, 86th, 2nd, JWC; Wright to Gerald C. Mann, August 20, 1960, in "1960 Election [8/3/60-8/20/60]—8/3/60-8/29/60," General, 86th, 2nd, JWC; Beasley, "Prelude to Leadership," 210-12, 248-49, 268-71 (primary source for "Labor for Party").

27 The League of Texas Municipalities (created in 1913) was renamed the Texas Municipal League in 1958. Wright, *Balance of Power*, 41; *Congressional Record*, 85th Congress, 1st session, 1957, Vol. 103, Part 4—House, p. 4990, https://www.congress.gov/congressional-record; *Congressional Record*, 84th Congress, 2nd session, 1956, Vol. 102, Part 8—House, p. 10267, https://www.congress.gov/congressional-record; Wright to Frank Vollintine, March 19, 1957, in "Agriculture: Vol-Wol—1/10/57–6/28/57," Departments, 85th, 1st, JWC; *Fort Worth Press*, April 11, 1957, in "Scrapbook: 1957," 36, RC Box 8/30, JWC; "The Wright Slant on Washington," February 11, 1957, in "Jim Wright Newsletters: 'The Wright Slant'—2/11/57," Special Projects, 85th, 1st, JWC.

28 Wright to Sam Rayburn, December 4, 1956, in "Fort Worth Postmaster and Post Office—6/11/56–12/4/56," Departments, 84th, 2nd, JWC; Wright telegram to Joe T. Gray, January 5, 1957, in "Post Office: Fort Worth Post Office [Gray]—1/4/57–12/5/58, Departments, 85th, 2nd, JWC; *Fort Worth Press*, December 7, 1956, in "Scrapbook: 1956," 115, RC Box 8/30, JWC; Wright to W. O. Jones, March 11, 1958, in "Post Office: Fort Worth Post Office [Jones]—2/19/58–3/19/58," Departments, 85th, 2nd, JWC.

29 Wright to Franklin C. Floete, July 10, 1956, in "General Services Administration—3/1/56–7/11/56," Departments, 84th, 2nd, JWC; Wright, interview, September 24, 1997.

30 Wright, *Balance of Power*, 78, 80; *Fort Worth Star-Telegram* June 8, 1961, morning edition, 5; *Fort Worth Star-Telegram*, July 26, 1961, 8.

31 Wright, *Balance of Power*, 82-83.

32 Wright, *Balance of Power*, 84; *Fort Worth Star-Telegram*, November 25, 1962, morning edition, Sec. 4, 6; Beasley, "Prelude to Leadership," 202–3, 214–19, 302–6, 308–9 (primary source for "Labor for District").

[33] Jim Wright to Sam Rayburn, December 27, 1956, in "Wright Personal—12/4/56-12/27/56," General, 84th, 2nd, JWC; *Fort Worth Star-Telegram*, January 9, 1957, in "Scrapbook: 1957," 4, JWC; Wright, *Balance of Power*, 41.

[34] Wright, interview, September 24, 1997.

[35] *Dallas Morning News*, September 27, 1959, Sec. 1, 22; *Fort Worth Press*, August 27, 1958, in "Scrapbook: 1958", 65; *Houston Chronicle*, March 24, 1959, np, enclosed with Norman L. McCarver to Wright, March 26, 1959, in "Wright Personal—3/26/59–4/10/59," General, 86th, 1st, JWC; *Dallas Times Herald*, June 28, 1960, 2-C.

[36] Wright, *Balance of Power*, 74; *Fort Worth Press*, August 19, 1960, 5; *Fort Worth Star-Telegram*, January 25, 1961, morning edition, 3; *Fort Worth Press*, November 6, 1960, A-7.

[37] Wright, *Balance of Power*, 74; *Fort Worth Star-Telegram*, December 23, 1960, morning edition, 1.

[38] *Fort Worth Press*, December 9, 1960, 24; *Fort Worth Star-Telegram*, February 5, 1961, morning edition, 2; Wright to Otis Gardner, December 30, 1960, in [loose papers at back of RC Box 150], RC Box 150, Jim Wright Papers, Unprocessed Materials (JWP-UM), JWC; *Fort Worth Star-Telegram*, March 28, 1961, morning edition, 3; Wright, *Balance of Power*, 74.

[39] *Fort Worth Star-Telegram*, January 12, 1961, morning edition, 3; *Star-Telegram*, April 2, 1961, Sec. 4, 1; *Star-Telegram*, March 9, 1961, 1–2. [1] Wright to Mrs. Margaret Carter, May 18, 1961, in "Tarrant #2," RC Box 150, JWP-UM, JWC; *Star-Telegram*, May 14, 1961, morning edition, 16.

[40] Wright to Mrs. Margaret Carter, May 18, 1961, in "Tarrant #2," RC Box 150, JWP-UM, JWC; *Fort Worth Star-Telegram*, May 14, 1961, morning edition, 16.

[41] *Fort Worth Star-Telegram*, April 11, 1961, morning edition, 2; Wright to Dr. Silas Grant, May 32, 1961, in "Letters written from D.C. office, general, 1961, Gov. Race," RC Box 151, JWP-UM, JWC.

[42] *Texas Observer*, July 29, 1961, 1.

[43] *Dallas Morning News*, September 29, 1961, in "JW Press Clippings, 1961 [#1],"RC Box 151, JWP-UM, JWC; *Houston Press*, September 1961, 10.

[44] "Statement of Congressman Jim Wright," December 16, 1961; Wright to Ben N. Ramey, December 18, 1961, in "Harris," RC Box 152, JWP-UM, JWC.

[45] Wright, *Balance of Power*, 86-88; Beasley, "Prelude to Leadership," 213,

222, 290-293, 295-302, 320-21 (primary source for "Ambition").

46 *Fort Worth Star-Telegram*, November 6, 1958, in "Scrapbook: 1958," 88, JWC.

47 Wright to E. L. Sitton, June 10, 1958, in "Labor [Ric-Smi]—1/10/58-8/13/58," Departments, 85th, 2nd, JWC; *Congressional Record*, 85th Congress, 2nd session, 1958, Vol. 104, Part 7—House, pp. 9507-9508, https://www.congress.gov/congressional-record.

48 George H. Lehleitner to Wright, June 22, 1959, in "Wright Personal—4/6/59-7/30/59," General, 86th, 1st, JWC; *Fort Worth Star-Telegram*, August 7, 1958, in "Scrapbook: 1958," 61, JWC; E. L. Bartlett to Wright, June 10, 1958, in "Interior and Insular Affairs, Alaska and Hawaii Statehood [And-Bra]—1/23/58-8/5/58," Legislative, 85th, 2nd, JWC.

49 *Fort Worth Star-Telegram*, August 7, 1958, in "Scrapbook: 1958," 61, JWC; *Congressional Record*, 85th Congress, 2nd session, 1958, Vol. 104, Part 15—House, p. 19182. https://www.congress.gov/congressional-record; *Dallas Morning News*, August 31, 1958, in "Scrapbook: 1958," 66, JWC.

50 *Houston Chronicle*, March 24, 1959, enclosed with Norman L. McCarver to Wright, March 26, 1959, in "Wright Personal—3/26/59-4/10/59," General, 86th, 1st, JWC; *Washington Daily News*, April 3, 1959, 25 in "Scrapbook: 1959," RC Box 8/30, JWC; *Amarillo Daily News*, May 7, 1959, 33, SB 1959, 20, JWC; Beasley, "Prelude to Leadership," 248-52, 258-59 (primary source for "Effective Communicator").

51 Jim Wright, *Worth It All: My War for Peace* (Washington: Brassey's, 1993), 18; "The Wright Slant on Washington," August 29, 1960, in "Jim Wright Newsletter: 'The Wright Slant'—8/29/60," Special Projects, 86th, 2nd, JWC; *Fort Worth Star-Telegram*, September 17, 1959, morning edition, 19.

52 Wright, *Worth It All*, 23; "The Wright Slant on Washington," March 28, 1969, in "Jim Wright Newsletter: 'The Wright Slant'—3/28/60, Special Projects, 86th, 2nd, JWC.

53 Reprint of Jim Wright, "Latin America: Threat and Promise," *Maryknoll Magazine*, May 1962, in *Congressional Record*, 87th Congress, 2nd session, 1962, Vol. 108, Part 6—House, p. 7995, https://www.congress.gov/congressional-record.

54 *Dallas Morning News*, September 29, 1963; *Fort Worth Press*, September 29, 1963, in "Wright Personal [9/27/63-9/30/63]—9/27/63-10/18/63," General, 88th, 1st, JWC; Beasley, "Prelude to Leadership," 263-65, 318-19, 322-23 (primary source for "Growing Interest in Inter-American Affairs")

CHAPTER 5

Jim Wright and Civil Rights: Gradual Support in the Face of Constituent Opposition

★

NEAL ALLEN*

Before rising to party leadership in the 1970s, Representative Jim Wright had to navigate his way through the tumultuous politics of the 1960s. Civil rights was an especially difficult issue, as Wright's reelection depended on support from white Texans who benefited from segregation and saw it as the natural order of society. One constituent, writing a letter in June 1963, set out the danger for Wright:

> I trust and hope that you will vote against every so called "civil rights" measure that is proposed. I feel so strongly about this matter that I will spend the rest of my life working against every member of Congress who lends support to legislation of this kind.[1]

Wright's incoming constituent correspondence on civil rights demonstrates that this vehement opposition to antidiscrimination legislation was wide and deep in the Texas Twelfth District, or at least among the most motivated citizens. The majority of letter

---

* Earlier versions of this chapter were published in the *East Texas Historical Journal* and the *Journal of South Texas*.

writers opposed nondiscrimination legislation and often argued that such legislation amounted to discrimination against white citizens. For example, when discussing with Wright in July 1966 legislation that would eventually pass with Wright's support as the Civil Rights Act of 1968, one constituent argued: "Do everything in your power to defeat the housing bill . . . it is robbing us of our civil rights," and that "if this unfair bill becomes law, we will all be wiped out."[2]

Wright's ability to gain reelection through this period and to maintain his credibility with both the Southerners and Northern liberals necessary to rise to party leadership in the 1970s and 1980s stands as a testament to his political skill and courage. Wright began the 1960s with a mixed record on civil rights and ended it as a supporter of open housing legislation. Review of hundreds of letters sent to his Washington, DC, office reveals that he faced a district hostile to civil rights throughout the period.

This chapter first discusses Wright as a relative liberal or moderate Democrat in Texas politics and his complex relationship with civil rights as a legislative issue. I then discuss the arguments about civil rights made by citizens who wrote to Wright in the 1960s, drawing on archival records from his papers housed at Texas Christian University. I conclude with a discussion of the role of civil rights and property rights in motivating the views of Wright's constituents.

When Jim Wright entered the US House in 1954, he had already served in the Texas House of Representatives and as elected mayor of Weatherford. He was considered a liberal in a chamber controlled by conservative Democrats, in particular because of his willingness to oppose the interests of petroleum producers. He entered the US House from a Fort Worth–based district in 1954, joining a Democratic Texas delegation that included both US senators and twenty-one of twenty-two House seats (all but the Dallas-based Fifth District, which was won by Republican Bruce Alger). Wright's early career was marked by the ambition that would fuel his rise to the speakership, but his focus was statewide. He explored running for Senate in both 1961 and 1966, actually placing a close third in the 1961 election for the remainder of Lyndon Johnson's term.

The civil rights politics of Texas in the 1950s and 1960s were a complex mix of continued Jim Crow segregation along with gradual progress toward integration. Conservative governor Allan Shivers fought against post–*Brown v. Board of Education* school de-segregation with the rhetoric of interposition, echoing the "massive resistance" politics of his counterparts in Virginia and the Deep South. He deployed the Texas Rangers to prevent court-ordered in-tegration in Mansfield and Texarkana. A liberal like Senator Ralph Yarborough, however, could win election to the US Senate in 1957 at the height of the post-*Brown* backlash and fight off a Republican segregationist challenge from future US president George H. W. Bush in the 1964 general election. Speaker Sam Rayburn and Sen-ate majority leader Lyndon Johnson charted a middle path.

Jim Wright as Future Congressional Leader and "Southern Liberal"

Wright was ambitious and upwardly mobile throughout his career, first focusing on winning a Senate seat. When Lyndon Johnson became vice president in 1961, Wright ran for the open Senate seat and finished third, less than two percentage points behind the ap-pointed Democratic senator William Blakley. Wright would have likely beaten Republican John Tower in the runoff, as Blakley lost Texas liberal support because of his conservatism. Wright attempt-ed to gain the nomination to run against Tower in 1966 but ended his campaign after his fundraising fell below expectations.

The complexity of civil rights politics was present in the Metroplex region that sent Wright to Washington. North Texas State College (now the University of North Texas), in nearby Den-ton, denied admission to Black undergraduates until the college peacefully complied with a federal court ruling in 1955, enrolling over 247 Black students by 1958.[3] This pattern of gradual integration stimulated by legal action and peaceful protest activity fits the larger pattern identified by Brian Behnken in his study of the Dallas civil rights experience. He argues that the "Dallas Way" of business-oriented consensus politics provided opportunity for Black protest actions to stimulate gradual integration: "To maintain the positive image of the city and promote business growth, Dallas's leaders proved willing to negotiate with blacks and implement desegregation measures."[4] This movement toward integration occurred while Dallas County sent Bruce Alger, a right-wing, anti-integration Republican, to Congress until 1964.

The Texas Twelfth District that voted overwhelmingly for Jim Wright during the entire civil rights period was demographically similar to the state as a whole, although more metropolitan (100 percent to 74 percent), and with a smaller Latino population (4 percent to 15 percent). Wright benefited from the more Democratic voting habits of his constituents, who in 1968 voted 47 percent Humphrey, 40 percent Nixon, and 13 percent Wallace. This compares with the statewide vote of 41 percent Humphrey, 40 percent Nixon, and 19 percent Wallace. In the 1970 census the district ranked first out of 435 districts for federal government outlays, owing to the large defense industry led by General Dynamics and Bell Helicopter. The Black population of 14 percent was slightly higher than the 13 percent statewide, and even after the Voting Rights Act did not constitute a large part of Wright's nomination or general electorate.[5]

Operating on the left of Texas politics in the 1950s and 1960s, Jim Wright was vulnerable to attack as an integrationist, in particular because of his record as, by Texas standards, a liberal leader of the UT College Democrats while an undergraduate. The student group called for passing antilynching legislation, ending the poll tax, and integrating the university's law school.[6] When running for reelection to the Texas House of Representatives in 1948, Wright's Democratic primary opponent attempted to use the ongoing NAACP litigation

involving the University of Texas Law School against him. Eugene
Miller, a former state legislator, said Wright wanted "every uppity
nigra with a high school diploma" to attend the University of Texas
Law School.[7] Wright responded by running a newspaper ad saying:
"I believe in the Southern tradition of segregation and have strongly resisted any efforts to destroy it." Wright attempted to stay within the mainstream of Texas Democrats, opposing particular facets
of Jim Crow while protecting against right-wing militant attack.

Wright continued his rhetorical support for segregation during
his early service in the US House. When the US Supreme Court
ruled public school segregation unconstitutional in *Brown v. Board
of Education* in 1954 and ruled that schools must be integrated
"with all deliberate speed" the following year, Wright followed the
lead of more-senior Southern leaders in supporting the rejected
"separate but equal" standard that had been precedent since *Plessy
v. Ferguson* in 1896. Then in his first term, Wright said the Supreme Court "erred in judgment. . . . I feel that segregation could
be ideally maintained without discrimination, that it is possible for
facilities to be equal while being separate."[8] This rhetorical support
for segregation, while maintaining his legislative focus on bringing
federal resources to Fort Worth and Texas with his seat on the Public Works Committee, followed the example set by Speaker Sam
Rayburn (D-Bonham) and Rayburn's protégé, then–Senate majority leader Lyndon Johnson. Rayburn and Johnson maintained rhetorical support for segregation, strengthening their ties to Southern
conservatives while also retaining support of the progressive liberal
minority within their respective Democratic caucuses.

The white backlash that swept the South, particularly the Deep
South, in the years following *Brown* eroded this mildly segregationist
middle ground that Wright and other Texas liberal and economically
populist congressmen were attempting to occupy. The congressional
manifestation of the regional backlash was the Southern Manifesto,
a militant segregationist statement of principles produced by Deep
South senators. The manifesto's creators, led by Senator Richard

Russell of Georgia, did not ask Rayburn or Johnson to sign, saving them from a choice that would have inflamed a large portion of the caucus they were attempting to lead. Russell and other senior Southern senators also were attempting to support a future presidential run by Johnson, which would only be possible if he could be acceptable to non-Southern liberals in the party.[9]

Lowly backbenchers like Jim Wright, however, had to make a public choice to sign or refuse to sign. Following the pattern seen in other peripheral Southern states like Florida, North Carolina, and Tennessee, the Texas House delegation split on the issue. Right-wing members from rural areas of the state, like Martin Dies Jr. and John Dowdy of East Texas and O. C. Fisher of West Texas, signed the manifesto and continued to incorporate anti-integrationist arguments into their broader anti-Communist conservatism. Wright Patman of Northeast Texas, whose populist criticism of large financial institutions as chair of the Banking Committee made him a hero to younger Texas liberals like Wright, signed the manifesto. Facing a right-wing primary challenge, representing the part of the state most similar to the Deep South, Patman acted to protect his position of power over other areas of public policy.[10]

Wright, however, joined the majority of the Texas House delegation in rejecting the strident position of the Southern Manifesto. Anthony Badger, attempting to explain why Texas senators and House members rejected the manifesto, attributes the Texas pattern to the influence of Rayburn. The Speaker saw the document as a potential wedge within his fractious caucus. The state's position in the 1950s House was as strong as any in history, with the speakership and several committee chairmanships. This was only possible if the Democratic Party could stay relatively united and in the majority. Rayburn and Johnson were also engaged back home in a struggle for control of the state party against the conservative faction led by Governor Allan Shivers, which wanted to withdraw support from the national Democratic Party's presidential ticket in 1956. Rayburn and Johnson's ultimately successful effort depended on isolating the more militant antifederal government conservatives within the party.

In justifying his more integrationist stance, Wright drew on his Christian (Presbyterian) faith, stating that "hatred is evil in the sight of God. The Negro is a child of God, as am I and as are my kinsmen. He possesses an immortal soul, as do we."[11] Wright would continue this support for limited integration by voting for the 1957 Civil Rights Act, which was limited to the right to vote and had little practical effect on Southern society.[12]

Like many more moderate Southerners in Congress, Wright offered mixed and conflicted positions on the more consequential civil rights legislation of the 1960s. He voted against the 1964 Civil Rights Act, citing support for property rights (discussed in reference to correspondence below). He supported the more popular Voting Rights Act of 1965 and the quite controversial Civil Rights Act of 1968, with its mostly ineffectual focus on open housing. This eventual move to a more integrationist position would serve him well in the most important election of his career, his narrow victory as House majority leader in 1976.

Constituent Letter Data

Like every member of Congress, Jim Wright received letters from constituents and other citizens commenting on issues of the day. Fortunately for students of civil rights, Congress, and Texas history, Wright and his staff preserved incoming correspondence on civil rights legislation from 1963 to 1966, totaling 893 individual letters. This archive opens a window on the opinions of everyday Texans in this period of contestation and transformation of racial norms and rules.

Citizens who write letters to their members of Congress are a clearly self-selected group. A person's decision to write to someone he or she likely knows only from popular media and sometimes from a newsletter marks that person as more interested in public affairs than their fellow citizens who don't write such letters. And letter writers likely hold more definite and considered opinions. Archival data like that under review here is best understood as a measure of motivated public opinion, providing a more narrow but deeper look into the attitudes of citizens on legislative issues than public opinion polling provides.

Letters provide a measure of district opinion, in terms of basic support and opposition and in terms of the substantive content of actual and potential voters. They communicate to legislators and their staff the views of those they represent. Particularly in the 1960s, when polling was infrequent at the national level and virtually nonexistent at the district level, letters provided members a proxy for district opinion.[13] Taeku Lee, in *Mobilizing Public Opinion* (2002), argues that letters to the president have significant advantages as a measure of public opinion over opinion polls in that they do not contain "non-attitudes" and do contain argumentative content.[14]

The Jim Wright Papers at Texas Christian University in Fort Worth contain files with letters sent to his Washington office from 1963 and 1964 addressing the legislation that became the 1964 civil rights bill. The archive also preserves letters from 1966 addressing that year's civil rights proposal, mainly concerning the inclusion of Title IV, an open housing provision that would have applied to sales of owner-occupied homes and rentals of units in structures with at least four units. No letters have been preserved from 1967 and 1968 concerning the modified and weakened open housing bill that became the 1968 Civil Rights Act.

While there is no way to verify that a given folder contains all letters sent to a congressman like Wright on a given issue during a particular time, Wright carefully preserved paper files in his large archival record. All files analyzed here contain both support and opposition to legislation, which supports the assumption that there is not a corresponding "For" or "Against" file that was discarded. It is likely that staff discarded some portion of out-of-district and out-of-state letters, particularly since the practice of congressional offices was often to reply only to in-district letters.[15] The data analyzed below, although limited by multiple kinds of selection bias, corroborates generalizations about support for civil rights legislation and the content of arguments made by constituents.

All letters were coded for "Support" or "Opposition" to civil rights legislation. I included only letters where support or opposition to congressional action is clear from the text. I did not include letters that expressed an opinion but did not express support or opposition, although these were few in number. I did not include letters asking for a copy of legislation, unless the request was part of a larger argument for or against legislation. I counted a letter as commenting on legislation if the writer mentioned a bill number or a proper or informal name for a specific bill or referenced action by Congress. Letters that specifically called for action on school desegregation or limitation of the power of the Supreme Court were not included, although these were also few in number.[16]

Argumentative Content: Letters to Jim Wright

Letters from constituents not only provide data on support or opposition to particular legislation but also reveal the types of arguments that underlie support or opposition. A letter that argues that the 1964 Civil Rights Act should be opposed by their congressman because it is unconstitutional shows a different foundation for opposition than one that comes from a belief that nonwhites are inferior. The kinds of arguments made for and against legislation reveal the reasons for those positions, and also the kinds of arguments writers think will be persuasive.

All letters analyzed in this article were coded for their general stance toward civil rights legislation and for five argumentative types: property rights, constitutional, Communist/Socialist, totalitarian, and white supremacist/racist. Many letters used more than

TABLE 1. **Argument type, Jim Wright letters**

ARGUMENT TYPE	#	%
For civil rights	97	11
Against civil rights	796	89
Property rights	334	37
Constitutional	153	17
Communist/Socialist	71	8
Totalitarian	53	6
White supremacist	26	3

Source: Data from Civil Rights File, Jim Wright Papers, Mary Couts
Burnett Library, Texas Christian University, Fort Worth, Texas.

one type of argument, and the majority of letters used none. Some letters merely called for support or opposition to legislation, and others had argumentative content that did not fit into my typology. I define and discuss each type below with evidence from the Wright collection.

Nearly nine out of ten letters in the civil rights files of Jim Wright express opposition to civil rights legislation. Many letters merely urge Wright to vote against such legislation, as he did in 1964 but did not in 1965 and 1968. Others use creative metaphors to illustrate their opposition. A married couple from Fort Worth wrote on June 4, 1966, that the proposed open housing legislation was "garbage":

> My husband and I are small property owners, and we
> think the bill is so rotten it stinks. When we find any-
> thing around our house that stinks we throw it into the
> garbage. We expect you to do the same with that bill.[17]

Some writers, like this constituent from Fort Worth in 1966, presented fantastical slippery-slope arguments about the push for civil rights legislation:

If Bills of this nature are passed, how far are we from the
legislation that would make it a federal crime for a person
to reject any marriage proposal on the ground the refusal
involves the other party's civil rights? Not too long back,
I would have regarded this question as ludicrous; now it
appears to be no small thing.[18]

Many writers in opposition to legislation presented variations
on the theme of a loss of core American values, often linked with
arguments that civil rights legislation was merely a Trojan horse for
some other nefarious goal. A frequent refrain was that bills were
"10 percent civil rights and 90 percent federal power."[19]

These defenses of the established order in American politics
used several distinct, but often complementary, types of argument.
After reading a subsample of letters, I selected four types that
seemed common or likely in letters: property rights, constitutional,
Communism/Socialism, and white supremacist/racist. After cod-
ing around half of the Wright letters, I added an additional type
for totalitarian.

The most common type of argument, present in 37 percent of
letters, was property rights. A letter received this code if the writer
argued explicitly that legislation was eliminating property rights or
the rights of property owners. I also included letters that argued
that legislation took away the right of owners to make decisions
involving their property. Some letters in this category also made
reference to specific examples, like defending the ability of an owner of a house to rent a room to a person of their choosing.

An illustrative example, from a Fort Worth resident on June 9,
1963, makes reference to Wright's relative liberalism and connects
it to property rights and other values:

I disagree most emphatically with your work in the US
House of Representatives for you have continually spoken
for the trend toward Socialism in this country. I am against
the Administration's proposed Civil Rights Bill. It is an

unconstitutional attempt to deprive American [*sic*] of their
property rights. . . . You have made me a Republican.[20]

This letter, like many others, joins a property rights argument
to other argumentative types discussed later. This letter is typical of
those supporting property rights in that those rights are presented
as universal, not specifically as enjoyed by white Americans only.
A letter from the National Restaurant Association on November
1, 1963, presented a more concrete argument against the public
accommodations section of the bill that became the 1964 Civil
Rights Act:

> By subjecting private business to unnecessary harassment
> and by enabling the Federal Government to exert more
> control over individual rights and over private business,
> the proposals, if enacted, can only result in the diminu-
> tion of free enterprise and of the rights and freedoms of
> all citizens. [21]

The economic focus of Wright's correspondents, and their
sparse use of explicitly racist argument, is similar to other collections of letters from Texas, from other Southern states, and from
the nation generally. A broader analysis of letters to seven other
members of the House, drawn from both parties and all parts of
the country, finds that economic and property rights are the most
common argumentative types in all collections and always significantly more common than racism and white supremacy.[22] The
correspondence of Wright's constituents follows a general pattern
of opposition to nondiscrimination legislation based on economic
and individual rights.

Wright, who would later vote for the 1968 Civil Rights Act
that included restrictions on the choices of residential property
owners, echoed this opposition to legislation on property rights
grounds in his *Wright Slant* newsletter to constituents on June 23,
1963. A property rights critique of then president John Kenne-

dy's civil rights proposals garnered support from letter writers, with one correspondent from Houston writing on June 28, 1963, that Wright's statement was the "highest expression of Americanism."[23] Responding to a constituent letter also from June 1963, Wright drew a clear distinction between public institutions that are legitimately subject to federal government regulation and private institutions that are exempt from it:

> There is in my mind a clear legal difference between publicly owned, tax financed facilities on the one hand, and private business establishments, privately owned and individually supported on a voluntary basis by individual customers on the other.
>
> I believe in the government's duty to protect the constitutional rights of every citizen. But one of these rights is the rights of private property. I do not want to see the government violate this right, any more than I would want it to violate any other constitutional right of our citizens.[24]

This focus on private property that Wright shared with his constituents helps to explain how Wright supported bills focusing on voting rights in 1957 and 1965 but opposed the 1964 Civil Rights Act.

Wright continued this private property focus in the first phases of the open housing debates on the Eighty-Ninth and Ninetieth Congresses. Responding to a Fort Worth letter of June 26, 1966, opposing how "our government has been systematically eroding the rights of one group of citizens to improve those of other citizens," Wright wrote the following on July 1, 1966:

> Thank you for your communication. I think you are correct in your opposition to Title IV of the proposed Civil Rights Bill of 1966. In my judgment, this provision should not and will not be enacted. I have, in fact,

so advised the President. Certainly I could not vote to
remove from the American people a right of choice so
basic and so personal as the selection of those to whom
we might wish to sell or rent our homes. This does not
mean that I favor discrimination against any race. You
and I probably feel about the same way. It will be recalled
that I actively supported the Voting Rights bill last year,
assuring to all Americans these equal and fundamental
rights of citizenship. But just as I opposed certain provisions of the Civil Rights Bill of 1964 as an unwarranted
invasion of the rights of private property, so I do oppose
this new proposal.[25]

Wright also voted with twenty of twenty-two Texas congressmen to remove Title IV (a strong open housing provision) from
the 1966 Civil Rights Act.[26] While Wright's papers do not include
letters from 1967 to 1968, it is unlikely that they would reflect any
change in their opposition grounded in property rights. Letters to
Earle Cabell, representing a similar next-door district, reflected the
same trend of opposition from 1966 through 1968.[27]

Constitutional argument was the second most common type,
at 17 percent of letters. I counted letters in this group if the writer
argued particular legislation was unconstitutional or that constitutional rights were at stake in this issue. While writers occasionally
mentioned specific constitutional provisions, like the Guarantee of
Republican Form of Government clause or the Free Speech clause,
constitutional arguments usually were of the general variety shown
here by a Houston resident on October 14, 1963:

The Civil Rights Bill of 1963 is a further extension of
federal executive power created at the expense of individuals of all races. It is nothing but a law for a controlled
system of life which is in direct opposition to our Constitution. . . . Stand up for Constitutional government
which guarantee States and human rights as God granted

> us these rights by doing everything in your power to
> defeat the so called Civil Rights Bill of 1963.[28]

Related to both property rights and Constitutional arguments is the next most common type, Communism/Socialism, at 8 percent of the letters. I classified letters as belonging to this group if they criticized legislation as Communist or Socialist (which were used interchangeably and negatively in context). Writers would have to explicitly mention either ideology, like a Fort Worth resident did on June 20, 1966:

> High among the objectives of Communism is the
> abolition of the concept of private property. To deprive
> a person by law of the right to absolute ownership of
> property and the ability to choose within certain bounds
> what he may do with it, is to make a mockery of the right
> to life, liberty and the pursuit of happiness as ascribed by
> our forefathers who founded this Nation of ours.[29]

Interference with private property or economic choice of any type is often classified as Communist or Socialist, usually with no reference to the rights of minorities that might have countervailing claims.

The following lengthy quote from a Smithfield, Texas, resident on July 2, 1963, shows how anti-Communism views, support for private property, and a belief in a constitutional theory based on economic rights were reinforcing concepts. This letter to Jim Wright also explicitly casts these concepts as unconnected to racial rights but founded on universalistic concepts:

> We are not against colored people having more freedom;
> however, we Abhor and Detest any ruling that destroys
> free enterprise. We are speaking of the proposal that any
> café owner or owners of various other business establish-
> ments must cater to negroes whether they wish it or not.
> This is merely another step our government is taking

toward becoming a Socialistic State. Businesses should
always have, as in the past, the right to refuse service
to anyone. When the government of the United States
has the power to tell an individual how he must run his
business and to whom he must cater, we no longer have a
government by the people and for the people. Instead, we
have something very similar to what we fought against in
World War II.[30]

This letter also shows another argumentative type, totalitarian-
ism. Letters are classified as using a totalitarian type of argument
if the writer claimed that civil rights legislation (usually the 1964
variant) constituted a government on the same form as the governments of Nazi Germany or Soviet Russia. The following passage
from June 17, 1963, shows this classification of civil rights legislation as creating a totalitarian government:

We, as citizens of the United States, and you, in particular, should be quite concerned with the powers that the
President is trying to assume. We speak of Russia having
a dictator and of Germany having had its Hitler, when
we sit and watch a man that can certainly be classified
as more of a dictatorial individual than either the case of
Russia or Germany.[31]

This letter also claims that President Kennedy is attempting to
become a dictator, a claim also sometimes applied to his brother
Robert as attorney general. Merely making this argument about
increasing presidential power was not classified as totalitarian.

The most interesting finding of this study is the relative absence of explicitly racist or white supremacist arguments. Only 3
percent of letters used a white supremacist or racist argument. I de-
fined this category as including writers who argued that nonwhites
were inferior to whites and who ascribed negative characteristics to
nonwhites or who supported segregation on explicitly separation

grounds. Some writers, like a Fort Worth resident writing on June 6, 1966, make explicitly race-conscious arguments in conjunction with other argument types:

> I do not want to live in the same rooms with Negroes, Mexicans or whatever else wishes to move in with me. I have a bed room and need some one for companionship but I sure don't want a Negro or a Mexican. This makes us as bad as the Communist or Gestapo.[32]

Such arguments, however, only appear in 26 of 893 letters from Jim Wright's Texas constituents.

This relative lack of explicitly racial or racist appeals should not be seen as evidence of the absence of racism or white supremacy by letter writers. It, however, does reveal citizens' assumptions about which arguments will likely persuade their representatives and how underlying racist attitudes were held in conjunction with race-neutral arguments. Letter writers were over twelve times more likely to ground their argument in economics than they were to reference racial characteristics. This focus on universal rights–based arguments, instead of explicitly race-based appeals, is consistent with the insights of recent historians about white backlash to civil rights. In his study of extremist opponents to integration, Clive Webb argues that the far-right, white supremacist backlash, while powerful and emerging from white Southern political and religious culture, did not dominate the "mainstream" of Southern white politics.[33] Letters to Wright reveal the grassroots component of the larger phenomenon of softening white supremacy by mixing it with other, more widely held values:

> Segregationists had always striven to elevate their argu-
> ments above the maelstrom of demagogic racist appeals
> and segregationist police brutality that pervaded the
> South. Their alternate approach attempted to construct
> what they believed to be "respectable" resistance strategies

capable of a wider appeal to those outside the confines of
the region's borders. As a result, they were not left isolated
by the failure of resistance, but rather were brought
seamlessly into the new currents of developing national
conservatism.[34]

This "developing national conservatism" found a home, and success in Texas elections, with the Republican Party. Wright, however, would emerge in the 1970s as a national leader of the Democratic Party that opposed this conservatism and was firmly committed to civil rights.

Conclusion: The Shifting Politics of Race and Property Rights

Review of letters sent by Texans to future House Speaker Jim Wright yield two significant conclusions about race in American and Texas politics. First, a skilled, or possibly lucky, politician like Jim Wright could still navigate the politics of race and federal public policy from a Texas foundation and ascend to the national leadership of the leftward-shifting Democratic Party. Second, Wright's incoming correspondence on race in the 1960s reveals the primacy of private property rights in Texas and American political culture.

Wright, like most Democratic Texas congressmen of the time, was able to avoid serious electoral challenge. The closest he ever came to defeat was in 1980, when he defeated a well-funded Republican challenger 60 percent to 40 percent while Ronald Reagan was carrying the district 52 percent to 46 percent over Jimmy Carter. What is more significant is Wright's rise to leadership in 1976, during a period when liberals and reformers were advancing within the Democratic Party. When he ran for the open majority leader position in 1976, he was a throwback to a different Democratic Party. As a high-ranking member of the pork-barreling Public Works

Committee, he was a defender of advancement by seniority, which had been drastically weakened by reforms after the 1974 election. Wright had a mixed record on civil rights and sought leadership of a party where Southern segregationists were a rapidly shrinking minority.

Wright's voting record in the 1950s and 1960s was only partly what his constituents, or at least those constituents motivated to write letters, wanted from their man in Washington. His support in 1968 of a federally enforced, though weak, right to buy or rent housing irrespective of race cut against the nearly nine in ten respondents who opposed federal intervention on behalf of racial minorities. But that vote on the 1968 Civil Rights Act moved him closer to his non-Southern colleagues. The growing backlash against federal social and economic action was rapidly eroding the Great Society coalition, with support for civil rights legislation dropping from 69 percent in 1964 to 59 percent in 1968 on final passage. Wright and future majority leader Hale Boggs of Louisiana were two of only six of the 294 members who voted on both bills but shifted from opposition to support.[35] This was a case of pre-leadership signaling, showing liberal members of the caucus that Wright and Boggs were joining the pro–civil rights mainstream of the party.

Wright likely would have held his seat if he had continued to vote against nondiscrimination legislation after 1964 but would have been in a weaker position in later leadership contests in a more liberal caucus. The other more coherent strategy, consistently supporting civil rights measures like his colleague Jack Brooks did, would have created more electoral uncertainty. Wright had the benefit of observing how fellow Democratic economic liberals Carl Elliott of Alabama and Frank Smith of Mississippi had lost their seats because of redistricting processes controlled by their more segregationist intraparty opponents. The post–1964 Civil Rights Act electoral record of other Southern urban and peripheral South liberal Democrats was mixed in this period of regional transformation. Charles Weltner of Atlanta survived the 1964 Deep South landslide for Barry Goldwater but lost his seat in 1966. Ross Bass of rural Middle Tennessee won election to the Senate in 1964 but lost his primary for a full term to the more conservative Frank Clement in 1966. Claude Pepper, whose liberalism had cost him renomination to the Senate in 1950, avoided a challenge from the right in his liberal Miami electorate with large populations of Northern migrants, Jewish voters, and racial minorities.

Wright understood that his vote against the Civil Rights Act of 1964 and his roots in the segregationist one-party Texas of the 1950s and 1960s were liabilities in his 1976 leadership race. Combined with his support for the Vietnam War and relative conservatism on domestic issues, Wright's voting record placed him behind two other ambitious Democrats as the party met to select new leadership. The other two major candidates had unimpeachable civil rights credentials. Front-runner Phil Burton, from San Francisco, had voted for all civil rights bills from 1964 forward and was a leader of the reformist group of Democrats that had swelled with the 1974 Watergate landslide. Richard Bolling of Kansas City had an even longer record of pro–civil rights activity as the primary supporter of integration legislation on the powerful Rules Committee. Wright's notes for his speech to the closed-door Democratic Caucus meeting prior to the majority leader election outline his argument on civil rights. He emphasizes his votes for the 1957 Civil Rights Act and every piece of integration legislation from the 1965 Voting Rights Act forward. He explicitly references his evolution on the issue as a Southern liberal.[36]

Wright specifically addressed his prior mixed record on civil rights in a letter to Democratic House colleagues on November 17, 1976, just prior to the majority leader vote. He writes, "I could not pretend to have a 'perfect' record on civil rights" and voted against some bills "for reasons which I thought at the time to be valid but which I no longer believe to be correct." Wright cites his refusal to sign the Southern Manifesto, his vote for the 1957 Civil Rights Act, and his support for all post-1964 integration legislation, stating:

> I am pleased by the fact that I have probably have as good
> and long-standing a record of support for basic civil and
> human rights as anyone from my part of the country
> could be expected to have and survive in the political tur-
> bulent years that are behind us. My record in this regard
> is quite different from that of most of my colleagues from
> the geographic area I represent.[37]

The Texan attempts to diminish the sterling pro-integration records of his rivals Bolling and Burton, writing, "It takes a hell of a lot more courage and conviction for a person from my area to take these public positions than it does for someone from Kansas City or California."[38]

The evidence presented here from Wright's incoming constituent correspondence clearly supports his retrospective evaluation of the political context facing a relatively liberal Southerner deciding whether to support or oppose the 1964 Civil Rights Act. While most House members from the region did vote against the landmark legislation, Wright probably overstated the narrowness of his options. Fellow Texas liberal House member Jack Brooks, then representing a district that included Beaumont and much of rural East Texas, voted for all civil rights bills, including the 1964 legislation, and was consistently reelected. Charles Weltner, representing an Atlanta-centered Georgia district, voted for the 1964 act and was narrowly reelected. But Wright's larger point about his electoral vulnerability on the issue was correct.

Wright's civil rights evolution was just enough to support his narrow election as majority leader. Bolling and Burton had both alienated potential supporters with ideological inflexibility and an unwillingness to cultivate personal relationships. Wright's base of Southerners, conservatives, and committee chairmen enabled him to eliminate Bolling by two votes in the penultimate vote and to best Burton by a single vote for the majority leadership.[39] This narrow victory enabled Wright to succeed Tip O'Neill as Speaker of the House in 1986 and to function as one of the most effective modern legislative leaders until his rapid fall in 1989.

Wright was the last leader of the Democratic Party in Congress to emerge from the coalition of urban liberals and Southern conservatives that dominated the party in the House and often the Senate in the middle part of the twentieth century. When forced to resign over allegations of financial improprieties involving publishing contracts and campaign finance in 1989, Wright was replaced by Tom Foley of Washington State, a liberal in the reformist tradition. Not since Wright have the House Democrats had a leader who was from the South, or from the moderate portion of the party.

The opposition to civil rights legislation and to federal government action in general that emerges from Wright's incoming correspondence reveals one source of this leftward shift in the Democratic Party. The movement of whites to the Republican Party that began on the presidential level in the 1960s would by the 1990s leave the Democrats as a clear minority in Southern congressional elections. Candidates from a state like Texas could no longer count on the support of the dozens of moderate and Southern populist members necessary to advance in House leadership. This shift was evident in the ascension of Nancy Pelosi (D-CA) to the leadership of House Democrats in 2003. A protégé of Jim Wright's 1970s antagonist Phil Burton and representing Burton's old San Francisco congressional seat, Pelosi is firmly anchored on the left end of a left-trending party. When minority leader Richard Gephardt (D-MO) left the leadership to run for president in 2004, Martin Frost (D-TX) began preparing to challenge Pelosi, then the second-ranking House Democrat. Frost, a former Jim Wright loyalist who represented much of Wright's old Fort Worth base, would have created a rerun of the 1976 majority leader race with a challenge to Pelosi from the moderate wing of the party. But after canvassing potential supporters, Frost decided that his chances were so slim he would not even attempt to challenge the California liberal Pelosi.[40]

The opposition to civil rights, which Wright sometimes joined and later repudiated, is often conceptualized as fundamentally about racism and white supremacy. But the prominence of property rights arguments in Wright's incoming civil rights correspondence reveals a different facet of the anti-integration narrative. This data demonstrates the fundamental importance of individual economic rights in the American political tradition. Support for a free market society in which individuals are unencumbered by government regulation was a powerful component of the defense of segregation. This property rights narrative, while idealized and, while ignoring the valid economic rights claims of minorities, allowed supporters of segregation to connect their economic and personal interest with broader egalitarian themes in American politics.

The legislative output of the federal government in the 1960s is even more remarkable considering that some opposition to integration, as seen by Wright's constituents, was grounded in property and economic rights. When President Lyndon Johnson of Texas pushed through the 1964 Civil Rights Act, he was staking his political future and that of his party on a vision of federal government action that ran fundamentally counter to the understanding of American individual rights held by Texans. Even in a then strongly Democratic Fort Worth represented by the relatively liberal Jim Wright, integrating public accommodations and employment was understood as a denial of fundamental individual rights and a carrier of anti-American values:

> I feel that these bills are detrimental to the majority of the citizens of our country and of little consequence to the minority for which they are intended. Communism, welfare states, and Socialism are not my concept of Freedom.[41]

This constituent, writing in July 1963, encapsulates the challenge faced and overcome by Wright in the 1960s: win renomination and reelection while moving along with his party in a more socially liberal direction.

Wright's success in navigating the politics of civil rights in the 1960s stands in contrast to the party that dominates the Texas congressional delegation in the early twenty-first century. Immigration plays a similar role for contemporary Republican politics that civil rights did for Democrats of the 1960s. Much of the party's base opposes progressive reform and sees their social and economic position as being under threat. Republican leaders have not been successful in pushing a reform consensus, as shown by the total failure of Texan president George W. Bush in pushing comprehensive immigration reform through a Congress controlled by his party in 2005. Immigration would later contribute to the surprise defeat of Representative Eric Cantor of Virginia in 2014, since he could not survive a Republican primary while under suspicion of supporting immigration reform. In the 1960s, Wright, while facing similarly strident opposition on social issues, was able to survive as a moderate within a caucus trending away from his constituents, even when they saw his eventual support of civil rights legislation as a threat to their economic liberty and property rights.

1   Civil Rights File, Jim Wright Papers, Mary Couts Burnett Library, Texas Christian University, Fort Worth, Texas (hereafter cited as JWP).

2   JWP.

3   Ronald E. Marcello, "Reluctance versus Reality: The Desegregation of North Texas State College, 1954–1956," *Southwestern Historical Quarterly* 100 (October 1996): 168–82.

4   B. D. Behnken, "The 'Dallas Way': Protest, Response, and the Civil Rights Experience in Big D and Beyond," *Southwestern Historical Quarterly* 111 (July 2007): 27.

5   Michael Barone, Grant Ujifusa, and Donald Matthews, *Almanac of American Politics: The Senators, the Representatives—Their Records, States and Districts 1972* (New York: Gambit, 1971): 801–2.

6   Tony Badger, "Southerners Who Refused to Sign the Southern Manifesto," *Historical Journal* 42 (1999): 521.

7   The NAACP litigation, which Wright was unconnected to, eventually led to the US Supreme Court decision *Sweatt v. Painter* in 1950, ruling that the University of Texas Law School must admit Black people.

8   John M. Barry, *The Ambition and the Power: The Fall of Jim Wright, A True Story of Washington* (New York: Viking, 1989): 52.

9   Robert A. Caro, *Master of the Senate* (New York: Vintage, 2002), 787–88.

10 Badger, "Southerners," 524.

11 Badger, 522.

12 The Eisenhower administration's stronger bill, which was similar to the later 1964 act, could not overcome a Senate filibuster in 1956. The 1957 bill was able to avoid the same fate by subjecting claims of denial of voting rights to jury trial, ensuring continued white control of civil rights policy in the South.

13 Phone calls to offices also serve as a kind of proxy for public opinion, but they have not been preserved in archives.

14 Works by George I. Lovell (on civil rights) and Alan Brinkley (on populist critics of President Franklin Roosevelt) use archival letters to establish mass political attitudes during the New Deal period. See George I. Lovell, *This Is Not Civil Rights: Discovering Rights Talk in 1939 America* (Chicago: University of Chicago Press, 2012); Alan Brinkley, *Voices of Protest: Huey Long, Father Coughlin, and the Great Depression* (New York: Alfred A. Knopf, 1982).

[15] Wright also replied to letters from clearly out-of-district locations (for example Houston or Dallas). This might be related to the fact that he was preparing for another statewide Senate campaign in 1966.

[16] I here assume that a writer in 1964 who, in a general manner, calls for Congress to support or oppose school integration is not specifically commenting on the portions of the 1964 bill that gave the federal government the ability to bring suit on behalf of children in segregated public schools. Infrequently writers would comment directly on that part of the bill, and those letters were included.

[17] JWP.

[18] JWP.

[19] These letter writers do not address the possibility that guaranteeing civil rights might require federal action, including enhanced authority.

[20] JWP.

[21] JWP.

[22] Data drawn from the papers of: Carl Albert (D-OK) and Jeffery Cohelan (D-CA), Carl Albert Center for Congressional Research, University of Oklahoma, Norman, OK; Hale Boggs (D-LA), Tulane University Special Collections, New Orleans, LA; Robert Dole (R-KS), Robert Dole Institute of Politics, University of Kansas, Lawrence, KS; John Dowdy (D-TX), W. R. Pogue Legislative Library, Baylor University, Waco, TX; Florence Dwyer (D-NJ), Kean University Special Collections, Kean University, Union, NJ; Gerald Ford (R-MI), Gerald R. Ford Presidential Library, Ann Arbor, MI.

[23] Ibid.

[24] Ibid.

[25] Ibid.

[26] The attempt to strip Title IV failed 190 to 222, but the bill died in the Senate.

[27] A sample of letters to Cabell 1966–68, drawn from his papers at Southern Methodist University, were 82 percent opposed to civil rights legislation.

[28] JWP.

[29] JWP.

[30] JWP.

[31] JWP.

[32] JWP.

[33]   See Clive Webb, *Rabble Rousers: The American Far Right in the Civil Rights Era* (Atlanta: University of Georgia Press, 2010).

[34]   George Lewis, *Massive Resistance: The White Response to the Civil Rights Movement* (London: Hodder Arnold, 2006), 26.

[35]   The other four members who voted against the 1964 act and for the 1968 act were likely acting on unique factors. Louis Wyman of New Hampshire had lost reelection in 1964 and regained his seat in 1966 and was building a profile better suited to a later statewide run for Senate in 1974. Ellis Berry of South Dakota had been unable to attach an amendment on Native American land rights to the 1964 bill but voted more like a midwestern moderate in 1968. Dante Fascell of Miami emerged from the 1966 redistricting with a relatively liberal district, reducing his electoral vulnerability. John Young of the Corpus Christi area may have been reacting to the growing Latino vote in his district and solidifying his party loyalist status as a member of the Rules Committee.

[36]   Undated notes, Civil Rights File, JWP.

[37]   Majority Leadership Election File, JWP.

[38]   Jim Wright to Robert Dawson, Jim Wright Folder, Richard Bolling Papers, Kansas City Library Special Collections, University of Missouri.

[39]   See Anthony Champagne et al., *The Austin/Boston Connection* (College Station: Texas A&M University Press, 2009), 230–50.

[40]   *Houston Chronicle*, November 9, 2002.

[41]   JWP.

CHAPTER 6

Jim Wright at Home in Fort Worth

JAMES W. RIDDLESPERGER JR.

Fort Worth. Twilight lingers on the plains. It is my favorite time of day—tranquil and unhurried, sweetly sad with faintly fading light but fraught with promise of a morrow.

—JIM WRIGHT'S JOURNAL, JUNE 11, 1972

Weatherford is much the same. Driving the streets, one sees not "housing" but "homes"—each with its own distinct personality, reflecting something of the character of him who built it or him who lives there—so many sites evoking memories that haunt and sweetly burn. God bless the Weatherfords of this world: Theirs is the only permanence. I am a sentimental slob. How empty life would be if I were not.

—JIM WRIGHT'S JOURNAL, APRIL 10, 1972

Jim Wright was a prominent, then dominant, citizen of Fort Worth for the nearly thirty-five years he represented the city in Congress. It is easy to think of him as always having been popular in Fort Worth, but that would give a false impression. Indeed, Wright came to Fort Worth as an outsider, a young man whose ties were to Weatherford, a small town about thirty miles west of Fort Worth. Wright had represented Weatherford in the state legislature and then served as its mayor. He declared as a candidate for the Twelfth Congressional District in 1954 to challenge the power structure of Fort Worth, making a populist appeal that took on Fort Worth's leading citizen, Amon Carter, directly. Carter and other leaders of Fort Worth had a comfortable and positive working relationship with the incumbent member of Congress, Wingate Lucas. Lucas had already served four terms in office and was building seniority in the House of Representatives. Perhaps Lucas envisioned a long career representing the Fort Worth district, like his predecessor Fritz Lanham. Lanham had enjoyed a twenty-six-year run as a member of the US House. But Wright was brash and confident and relished the challenge that confronted him. With high energy, hard work, insight, and talent, Wright took on the Fort Worth establishment and won his election.

Over time, Wright came to be the most powerful political leader in town. He maintained a strong popularity, and he repaid the citizens of Fort Worth by "bringing home the bacon." When he left Congress in 1989, there was barely a corner of Fort Worth where Wright's impact could not be seen. For example, highways, river levees, reservoirs, huge federal military contracts, Carswell Air Force Base, the DFW Airport, and the famous Fort Worth Stockyards had all received funding under Wright's tutelage. Indeed, one political cartoonist famously remarked that Wright brought so much money to Fort Worth that the federal government had to build a Bureau of Engraving and Printing in Fort Worth to print the money coming to Wright's district. In the first congressional session after Wright left, Carswell Air Force Base was scheduled to be shuttered, removing a major employer from Fort Worth. That closure signified the influence Fort Worth had lost with Wright's resignation. It is hard to imagine that Congress would have planned to shut down a major military installation in the home district of the House Speaker.

At the same time, Wright was also a strong member of the Democratic Party, and he had national ambitions from the beginning of his tenure. While he was building loyalty in Fort Worth because of his activities on the Public Works Committee, he also found himself supporting the more liberal national Democratic Party on many issues. As a result, the relatively conservative Fort Worth establishment always had some tension with Wright, even as he built seniority in Congress and used his growing leverage to secure federal resources in Fort Worth.

Developing a Home Style

Like all members of Congress, Wright sought to build and maintain positive relationships among his constituents. Doing so would put him in position to raise money for his campaigns and to head off organized opposition. Texas was a state known for its influence in national politics, and to great measure that was because of the leadership of Sam Rayburn, the Speaker of the House when Wright first went to Congress. Rayburn took great interest in the members of the Texas delegation, and Wright was a willing student. Rayburn argued that the key to Texas influence in Washington was that "we pick 'em young, we pick 'em honest, we send them there and we keep them there."[1] Wright knew that he would need to build relationships in his district, and he set out to do so.

Political scientist Richard Fenno suggested that to be successful, members of Congress have to develop a successful "home style." Wright took to that responsibility with his characteristic high energy and political skill. His success in developing his relationships in Fort Worth was made easier by the favor that Rayburn did for him when he went to Washington. Wright's passion to run for Congress had been fueled in part by his desire to be engaged in foreign policy, and he expressed the desire to be assigned to the House Foreign Affairs Committee by the venerable Speaker. However, Rayburn explained that the Foreign Relations Committee in the Senate was the strong congressional committee on international issues and that what the Texas delegation really needed was a voice on the Public Works Committee. Wright was persuaded to take that slot, and he used it to "bring home the bacon" to his hometown for his entire tenure in Washington and to forge relationships with members of the Texas congressional delegation and with other House members. Ultimately, he used his seat on Public Works as a springboard into the leadership. As Julian Zelizer wrote, Wright understood politics as keeping the folks back home happy, "whether by helping constituents with federal agencies or by directing federal largesse to local businesses to create jobs for the electorate."[2]

Fenno's insight to understanding representation was to envision the relationships that members of Congress develop in four concentric circles of influence: geographic, reelection, primary, and personal constituencies. The broadest circle is that of the geographic district, and it includes everyone who physically resides within the district. The second consists of those who are likely to vote for the Congress members in their reelection bids—mostly members of their political party but also those who simply have an affinity for their representative. The third circle is composed of the primary supporters—those who can be relied on to work for the representative, in primary elections and throughout the term in office. The smallest circle consists of the candidate's intimates—family, close friends, and trusted advisers.[3] Wright understood these differing constituencies and worked hard to maintain his support from all four.

Among Wright's intimates was his monthly lunch club. Wright had many close friends. Some were part of a group called the Loquacious Old Fellows (always abbreviated LOF; the words to characterize the group could change from time to time). Members of that group maintained close ties to General Dynamics and Bell Helicopter, to the *Fort Worth Star-Telegram*, to the city's faith community, to organized labor to raise money, and to key members of the "Seventh Street Gang" business community. From the beginning, Wright leaned on his close friend, Craig Raupe, to organize his relationships in the district. Wright met Raupe when Wright was mayor of Weatherford and Raupe taught political science at Weatherford College, and the two became as close as brothers. Raupe managed Wright's first campaign for Congress and followed him to Washington as his administrative assistant for nine years.

Wright enjoyed support from Weatherford from the beginning of his time in Congress, and while Fort Worth became his home and was the key city in his district, Wright always held a special relationship with the citizens of Weatherford. Among his close supporters were Benjamin Hagman (Larry Hagman's father and Broadway actress Mary Martin's husband) and Fort Worth mayor Willard Barr. He was close to George Mallick. Mallick liked to be close to power—it wasn't that he really wanted anything, he just liked being near power.[4]

Wright had two clubs to raise money: the Wright Appreciation Club and the Wright Congressional Club. Anyone could be a member of those groups if they wrote a check for $200. They met twice a year. One was a serious meeting where there was discussion of issues; the other was more of a public meeting to keep people informed and to perhaps bring a celebrity to speak to the group. These organizations kept Wright in close contact with his primary and reelection constituencies. His oratorical skills always made people want to come hear him speak, and his easy manner with people, remembering names and details about families, quickly made huge numbers of constituents feel as if they had a personal friend in the nation's capital. As Wright gained seniority and as his name became associated with projects that were helping Fort Worth grow, even the business community began to feel more warmly about Wright and to join his congressional clubs.

Wright also used TV and radio extensively and communicated regularly with his constituents, taking full advantage of the franking privilege to send out his newsletter, *The Wright Slant on Washington*, which landed in his constituents' mailboxes regularly. Wright was exceptionally detail oriented and, rather than "staffing out" the writing of his newsletter, he was involved in every stage of its development. In this manner, he was constantly pushing to contact individuals in his geographic constituency and expand his popularity. He was proud of the way he handled constituent mail and was conscientious in answering it. His detailed constituent replies were so edited and messy after multiple corrections that his secretary, Norma Ritchson, often would have to retype them.[5]

Wright was a talented and energetic speaker. Members of Congress shuddered at the thought of having to follow Wright to the podium. He earned a reputation for being perhaps the best orator in Congress. On the occasions when he returned to his district, Wright spent most days speaking to civic groups not primarily making campaign speeches but rather reporting "on national problems and Congressional attempts to solve them." He received dozens of invitations to speak to "luncheon clubs, PTAs [Parent Teacher Associations], veteran's clubs, student bodies, study groups, chambers of commerce—you name it." Wright accepted those invitations readily and worked them to his advantage. In the 1976 edition of his book *You and Your Congressman*, he reported that in one year, during three recess periods when he had been home in his district, he had spoken to 114 such groups.[6]

One of Wright's great skills was learning the names of his constituents and being able to recall them quickly and sometimes over years. Wright had a prodigious ability to learn the names and faces of constituents. He always tried to sit in a public room with his back to a wall. That way, he said, he could see someone advancing toward him and by the time they got to the table, he would be able to remember who they were and their names. As John Barry writes, "He remembered who had married whom and whose grandson was at what college, he knew his district block by block."[7]

An Upstart Upsets the Incumbent

To accomplish his ambition to become a member of Congress, Wright had to defeat an entrenched four-term incumbent, Wingate Lucas, who had the support of the Fort Worth business community and, especially, of the powerful owner of the *Fort Worth Star-Telegram*, Amon Carter. Carter was a tour de force in Fort Worth—an oilman, a philanthropist, and a community leader. Wright's associate Marshall Lynam observed that "in those days, the crusty old publisher wielded such immense political power that it was virtually unthinkable for him to be kicked in the political shins by this obstreperous interloper from Weatherford."[8] Wright threw himself into the campaign with all-consuming energy. He recalled that his strategy included scheduling fourteen-hour days—shaking hands, making speeches, mobilizing his friends, and seeking to appear on television. Wright explained that his opponent, Congressman Lucas, continued to speak ill of Wright, but said Wright, "I haven't got anything against the Congressman except that we both want to be in Congress."[9] Lucas had followed the powerful Fritz Lanham as a representative of Fort Worth. Lanham had been a native of Weatherford, like Wright, and had been from a powerful Texas political family. His father, Samuel W. T. Lanham, had also served in Congress and had been a governor of Texas early in the twentieth century. Lucas had less standing, and though he had the support of the business community, he was not invulnerable to a young, energetic, and talented opponent.

In order to appear on television or in the Fort Worth newspaper, Wright had to get around the fact that both media were owned by Carter. And though Carter favored Lucas, he did not shut off access to the media by Wright. Wright was able to buy a half-hour time on television for $520 (about $5,000 in 2022) and a full-page ad in the newspaper for $974.40 (about $10,300 in 2022). Carter famously only asked if Wright's check would be good before running the ad in the *Star-Telegram*.[10]

After his initial election, Wright rarely drew meaningful opposition in his reelection bids, though he had a well-financed opponent in the 1972 election cycle. In that year, the unpopularity of Democratic presidential candidate George McGovern, a longtime friend of Wright's and fellow B-24 pilot from World War II, gave the Republicans hope that Wright might be vulnerable. Wright defeated his opponent, James Garvey, with nearly 80 percent of the vote.[11] Republicans ran opponents against him several times, but they were not well financed and they never really challenged him in the general election, with the exception of the 1980 election, discussed below. Only once, in 1986, did he even face nominal opposition within the Democratic Party.[12] Wright had developed a high popularity among his constituents and was invulnerable to meaningful challenge.

Perhaps Jim Wright's most difficult campaign for reelection came in 1980. In that election, while Wright had his usual strong support from working-class supporters and union members, he had become more reliably liberal in his voting record after moving into the leadership, and since he was in the leadership, not only did conservatives in Fort Worth oppose him as usual but national Republican organizations did as well, including the Moral Majority and the National Conservative Political Action Committee (NCPAC). While Wright had navigated his way through Fort Worth politics for more than a generation at that point, he had never been terribly popular in the business community. Wright had been a moderate Democrat in national politics, but in Fort Worth, he was known as a liberal. The 1980 campaign promised to be difficult in part because Jimmy Carter had failed to unite the national Democratic Party and Senator Edward Kennedy of Massachusetts had challenged Carter for the Democratic nomination. Meanwhile, Republicans had united behind the affable and popular Ronald Reagan, and Reagan looked to be a formidable candidate in Texas, a state that had been trending toward Republican for more than a decade at that point and during the 1978 campaign had elected its first Republican governor, Bill Clements, in more than a century.

Fort Worth oilman Eddie Chiles, a friend of Wright's until the 1980 campaign, began to run an ad campaign against the power of the national government with the running tag "What are you mad about today, Eddie?" Chiles took out a full-page ad in the *Fort Worth Star-Telegram* after Wright's reelection in 1978 in which, Wright said, Chiles "excoriate[ed] me for my support of Carter" and signed it "Your friend, Eddie."[13] Chiles turned his wrath about big government on Wright and vowed to defeat him for reelection. Chiles bought billboards around Fort Worth with the simple message "Come home, Jim" and branded him as "a socialist." Chiles found a credible candidate to oppose Wright, a former mayor pro tempore of Fort Worth named Jim Bradshaw, and promised $500,000 (about $1,720,000 in 2022) to promote his campaign. Bradshaw quickly enrolled in a school for Republican candidates run by NCPAC, kicking off an aggressive campaign against Wright.[14] Bradshaw had a reputation as "one of the biggest womanizers that ever came down," but Wright refused to use his negative reputation as a political tactic to win the election, saying, "I want to beat him on merit. I don't want this to become a gutter politics and I don't plan to use it."[15]

Wright began to organize against this unprecedented challenge. President Carter came to Fort Worth during the campaign, appearing at Fort Worth's north side Stockyards days before the election. Soon, Wright's supporters found a reservoir of support that surprised even the congressman himself. Wright's focus on casework and bringing public works to Fort Worth had earned him a loyal following, not just among labor Democrats but also among the "people back home." His stature in Congress also worked to his favor; Congressman Bill Gray of Pennsylvania, a close friend of Wright's from Congress, came to Fort Worth to assist in the campaign. Gray, a prominent African American leader from Philadelphia, helped solidify Wright's support in the Black community.[16]

The campaign was a vigorous one, and Wright, who was always in high demand to stump for Democratic candidates across the nation, was forced to spend a great deal of effort at home to secure his own reelection this time. Bradshaw ran a professional campaign against him and was supported in large measure by Chiles and other conservative businessmen. However, Wright's worry was overblown, and Bradshaw's optimism proved unfounded. On election day, Wright received 61 percent of the vote, compared with Bradshaw's 38 percent, and despite support from the Fort Worth business community, Bradshaw had $126,500 of unpaid campaign debt.[17]

Perhaps the biggest surprise of all was that Wright used the campaign to follow the advice of one of his favorite adages that he attributed to Abraham Lincoln: "The best way to defeat an enemy is to make him your friend." Wright reached out to Bradshaw after the election and they became close enough that when Bradshaw died, Wright was invited by his family to speak at the funeral.

Wright and the Business Community

In Fort Worth, there were always people who loved Jim Wright and people who hated Jim Wright. Once, Wright came up for membership in a club, and Fort Worth mayor Bob Bolen had to call Betty Wright and warn her that Wright would not get voted a member.[18] Wright's successor in the Twelfth Congressional District, Pete Geren, remembered that the Fort Worth business community liked Geren better than they liked Wright. Wright had a strong populist streak and strong ties to labor. And as time went by, Wright became involved in national party politics that moved him further to the left than he had been before moving into the leadership. For example, Geren remembered, Wright made the business community angry with his involvement in Central America that was opposed to Reagan's policies. There was a sense that politics stopped at the water's edge and that Wright was interfering. However, Geren remembered, the business community, however much they liked Geren, regretted that he did not wield the political power that Wright had enjoyed.[19]

Wright interceded on behalf of Texas thrifts during the failure of the Federal Home Loan Bank System in the 1980s, and critics of

Wright gave him the name Jim "Money Talks" Wright and argued that his advocacy of Texas Savings and Loans made him a "willing tool of the powerful thrift industry lobby."[20] For his part, Wright argued that he was only communicating with federal officials on behalf of his constituents and was not in any way trying to influence decision-making. Wright was concerned during the mortgage crisis about two things: the Texas economy and key supporters in his district in the savings and loan industry. The S&L crisis could not have come at a worse time in terms of Wright's political fortunes, however. He made calls as Speaker on their behalf, and it gave his critics fodder to criticize him as bringing undue influence on government enforcement.

At a meeting in Fort Worth, Wright's aide and best friend, Craig Raupe, commented, "I looked around and saw some good, reliable businessmen. I also saw some crooks."[21] While Raupe never named some of the questionable characters in attendance, he instinctively understood that the S&L crisis could potentially compromise Wright's reputation. Wright survived the savings and loan issue in 1988, but rumors—never substantiated—that he had tried to wield influence on behalf of unsavory characters gave Republican Newt Gingrich of Georgia an excuse to come after Wright.

Bringing Home the Bacon

Wright's first big role on the Public Works Committee soon after he was elected to Congress was also a bipartisan one. Those were the Eisenhower years, and working across the aisle was not only accepted but mostly expected in Congress. Wright worked with Eisenhower easily, often explaining that he saw Ike as something of a father figure, as Eisenhower was about his father's age. Wright saw cooperation as an opportunity to build the ambitious interstate highway system, and he advocated doing so on a pay as you go basis, largely through the collection of fuel taxes.[22]

Former Fort Worth mayor Bob Bolen remarked in 2013 that

Wright was underappreciated and that his marks remain all over the city: highways, urban development, Bell Helicopter, Lockheed, and DFW Airport, all due to Wright.[23] As a freshman congressman, Wright went to a meeting with Eisenhower regarding interstate highways and proposed a pay-as-you-go system for highways that Eisenhower adopted, so his impact in Congress was early, and it extended far beyond his district.

He worked assiduously on issues about water, advocating for the building of lakes and reservoirs in Texas and levees along the Trinity River to prevent flooding and seeking to reduce water pollution. He had to fight President Richard Nixon on the issue of water pollution, a constant theme of conflict between Nixon and Congress about spending.[24] He strongly supported turning the Trinity River into a canal and bringing barge traffic all the way to Fort Worth and used his influence to keep it on the agenda in Congress. Ultimately, though Wright wielded his influence to the best of his ability, the canal was not funded because the project was considered far too expensive.[25]

Wright sought funding to invest in the dilapidated Fort Worth Stockyards, an area that had once been a thriving part of the city and had fallen into disuse after the heyday of centralized buying and selling of cattle and after the massive Armour and Swift slaughterhouses had shut down. The Stockyards were the source of Fort Worth's nickname "Cowtown" and had been at the heart of developing the Fort Worth Fat Stock Show as a signature event. But they were now mostly vacant and had become something of a ghost town. During the Reagan years, Wright fought hard for a $7.5 million appropriation to rebuild the area and make it a tourist attraction. To the Reagan administration, it was unnecessary spending. "To the administration, it was pork, to Wright, an investment."[26] Eventually, funding was obtained, and the Stockyards began to thrive again. Wright always claimed "that every one dollar of federal seed money had generated eight dollars of private investment."

By 1979, Fort Worth had the highest federal per capita spending of any district in the country.[27] Not only had Wright advanced in his influence within Congress as the powerful majority leader but he also had used that position to attain for his district an impressive list of projects to help the local economy grow. While critics of public works spending often complained about wasteful spending, Wright always reminded them that "one man's pork is another's bread and butter" and insisted that his highest calling as a member of Congress was to bring home to his constituents "the government programs that they had earned and they deserved." As a result, by the time Wright became Speaker of the House, John Barry concluded that "in Fort Worth, Jim Wright was like a God."[28]

Resignation

The end of Wright's career, like its beginning, was partly centered in his home district. He developed political alliances and friendships across his district, including with George Mallick and Carlos Moore. These were his friends, and he was extremely loyal to his friends.

His time in Washington had been productive, but his divorce and some financial setbacks had left him, by the mid-1970s, in precarious financial circumstances. He reported that his finances were "in a shambles."[29] To help with that, Wright wrote a book that might help generate revenue in a way that would be within House ethics rules. Members of Congress were no longer allowed to receive honoraria for the speeches they made because of the appearance of conflict of interest such payments might generate. But they could receive earned income, and many members earned income through royalties that they received from books they had authored. In Wright's case, he gathered previous writings into a little book that was not published by a regular book publisher but rather through the printing company of his friend Carlos Moore. And because there was no huge publishing staff behind the book, Wright received a royalty on each book that was perhaps five times the amount usually given an author. Neither was the book distributed to book retailers across the country; it was available by personal contact with Wright and his associates.

This caused problems with public relations for two reasons. First, the book was sold primarily in bulk and often to groups with whom Wright would speak. They would be distributed to attendees of the speech, and Wright often would sign them after the speech. Wright's critics charged that this practice was an evasion of House ethics rules. Wright admitted that it might appear so but insisted that there was no such intent. He emphasized that book royalties were expressly protected under House rules.[30] He admitted that his staff wanted to sell the book, as did he, and that perhaps such had been a mistake. But importantly, the practice was completely aboveboard and entirely within House rules.[31] Part of the negative publicity also came from the fact that Moore, Wright's friend and publisher, had served time in prison on a conviction for tax evasion. Moore had taken $90,000 dollars from the Teamsters Union. He denied that he had kept the money, claiming instead that it had been political contributions. Moore never revealed where the money had been distributed.[32]

Additionally, Wright entered into a business relationship with George Mallick, a wealthy constituent. Their joint venture was called Malightco and was intended to be a business opportunity that would employ Wright's wife, Betty, who had given up her congressional committee job when Wright became majority leader in 1977. However, it was charged that the business venture was just a thinly disguised plot to distribute money to the Wrights and was never intended to be a real business plan. Wright argued strongly against that, claiming in his resignation speech that in fact the company had been a real business and that Betty had evidence of work she had done to earn her salary. As with Moore, Mallick's reputation caused some of Wright's negative media coverage. Mallick had hoped for funding for the development of the Fort Worth Stockyards, and the fact that Wright had secured such funds gave an appearance that Wright was pushing that development to repay Mallick for his support of Wright. Wright argued that the two activities were unrelated and that it was an obvious need in Fort Worth to redevelop the Stockyards, which for many years had driven the Fort Worth economy and then had declined into dilapidation.

The charges against Wright were in some ways out of character, for he was not known as a member who craved wealth. Unlike many of his colleagues, Wright had never really been inspired by acquisition of money. He tended to dress modestly and to drive modest cars. He was astonished when he was made to appear to be greedy, saying, "I don't care about money. I never cared about money."[33]

And while the charges ended up hounding Wright from office, reporter Mark Miller said, "If we had found any evidence of Wright benefitting improperly, we'd have reported it. We didn't. But there was the appearance of impropriety."[34] Perhaps even more persuasively, Barry, who wrote the authoritative account of Wright's resignation, concluded, "When it was all over I thought Jim Wright had been [treated more unfairly] than any other figure in American political history. No one ever lost more power for less reason."[35]

The ethics controversy soon became part of a "feeding frenzy" in Washington among the media, and many of Wright's colleagues refrained from supporting him. The feeding frenzy argument had, months earlier, resulted in John Tower's defeat as a nominee for defense secretary, and Republicans saw Jim Wright's resignation as a perfect symmetry. Rather than getting an "eye for an eye" in retribution for Tower, they got a "Texan for a Texan." Newt Gingrich himself, having started the process moving, admitted that the ethics investigation against Wright was "never about ethics; it was always about power."[36]

Class at TCU

After his resignation from Congress, Wright moved back home to Fort Worth, choosing to live in his district over remaining in Washington, DC, where he had ascended to the peak of congressional power. Once home, he characteristically threw himself into public life, keeping regular office hours, remaining active in Democratic politics, writing op-ed pieces for the *Fort Worth Star-Telegram*, being faithful in his church attendance, and teaching a course at Texas Christian University. The course was entitled Congress and the Presidents, and it brought his experience in public office to life for his students. He conducted a congressional simulation, forced his students to do an exercise in balancing the budget, and lectured on the presidents with whom he'd served in Washington, from Dwight Eisenhower to George H. W. Bush.

His class really had an impact on students. Wright brought not only a compelling understanding of the institutions of national government but also personal experience as a major actor in government to his classes. And students, of all political stripes, found his class interesting and his tolerance of diverse opinions inspiring:

★ One former student recalled that Wright's class "was one of the most impactful classes I have ever taken" and that Wright took him and some fellow classmates to dinner one evening, where Wright spent much of the evening recalling the day of the Kennedy assassination. As someone who had been an "integral player IN history," Wright's sharing of himself with students left the student "blessed to have spent the time I did with him."[37]

★ Another student offered this reflection: "Jim Wright's class on Congress and the Presidents was one of my most memorable classes at TCU. Given Speaker Wright's decades of service as a representative of Texas on Capitol Hill, and his involvement in many key pieces of legislation in our country, I felt like I had a front-row seat to US political history. As a political science major, I remember it being such an insightful and fun way to learn about the inner workings of the federal government. Through Speaker Wright's personal stories and firsthand experiences, I gained an appreciation for how personalities shaped Washington politics. I recall learning not only about the achievements and agendas of many US presidents and congressional leaders, but also getting a sense of what they were like as people and the personal attributes that made each of them successful, and sometimes not-so-successful, politicians. We got firsthand accounts of major events in US history, as well as learning about Speaker Wright's personal and professional relationships with Washington's elite. The class was taught with plenty of charm, wisdom, and humor, and I am grateful I had the chance to learn from one of Texas's all-time greats."[38]

★ Wright was "very balanced" in his approach to examining politics and would always "appreciate differing opinions" about politics. "He never spoke badly of someone in Congress," appreciating that different points of view made for healthy politics and that different constituencies had different needs from government policies.[39]

★ "Speaker Wright was an incredible professor, mentor, and friend to many TCU students following his time in Congress. I am tremendously grateful for his willingness to teach and mentor those of us who had the privilege of taking his Congress and the Presidents class. As a college student, I had a great interest in politics, and I loved learning about his experiences in Washington and hearing the wonderful accounts of his time representing the people of Fort Worth. As I serve the people of my district in the state legislature, I often reflect on one of his favorite quotes: 'You can disagree without being disagreeable.' As an elected official in the social media era, I'm often reminded of how difficult yet necessary that quote is to live out. The work of our public servants is to help create and build a more perfect union. The views and paths to creating our future may differ, but the end goals are often the same. Speaker

Wright helped me to understand that notion. Although our political views often differed, Speaker Wright was always willing to listen and question me as he shared his own views. I truly enjoyed the opportunity to debate with him about hot topics of the day. I know his legacy will continue to live on through the lives of his many students."[40]

Wright Symposium

Beginning in 2001, Wright presided over a symposium named in his honor at TCU. The first was a symposium on the Texas congressional delegation over Wright's time in office, with one panel dedicated to Wright's career. Wright hosted friends and former colleagues in Fort Worth, including Fred Harris, Martin Frost, Lee Hamilton, David Boren, Bill Richardson, John Anderson, Charlie Wilson, and Jim Baker. He also hosted his two successors in the Twelfth District of Texas, Pete Geren and Kay Granger, along with former Texas state senator from Fort Worth, Wendy Davis. He attended his last symposium only weeks before his death, a symposium studying the legacy of Sam Rayburn on the occasion of the seventy-fifth anniversary of Rayburn becoming speaker. Dee Kelly was a special speaker that day, and the two of them shared memories of a lifetime of Fort Worth politics. They had been frequent competitors, but on this day, they were longtime friends. Wright wrote comments for the event. He was weak, and many thought he would be unable to attend, but he did come in a wheelchair. Though he was too weak to present his comments, he was present when they were read, and he found the energy to greet all in the audience.

Church had always been important to Wright. At one point in his early career, he was even a lay minister at a Presbyterian church in Granbury, before later changing his membership to the United Methodist Church. Had he not gone into politics, he might very well have become a minister. And, at one point, he even related the two careers: "Don't you think a politician is like a minister?"[41] In retirement, Wright was an active member of First United Methodist Church in downtown Fort Worth. He could be found in the pews virtually every Sunday morning and loved reciting the Bible verse of the day in the service when called on, teaching Sunday school classes, and addressing gatherings among the faithful. After the terrorist attacks of September 11, 2001, Wright spoke to a grieving crowd at church, beginning his remarks with Thomas Paine's famous words: "These are the times that try men's souls."

Wright became a regular contributor to the *Fort Worth Star-Telegram* through his op-ed articles. His topics were wide ranging. Of course, the most frequent subject of his columns was politics, and he regularly expressed his long-held views about civility in politics, bipartisanship, and the necessity of compromise, while espousing his long-held progressive values. Other columns ranged from discussing memories of growing up in Texas and memories of family experiences. He also addressed the meaning of life issues and his perspective on the world around him.

During the last twenty years of his life, Jim Wright combated three different cancer scares. First, he had a large portion of his tongue removed because of a growing cancer. He always said that the lucky part of his resignation from Congress was that the cancer was discovered in time. Had he remained in Congress, he would have put off diagnosis. The second cancer surgery removed half of his lower jaw and replaced it with a bone extracted from his leg. As always, he found humor in that too. His friend and former assistant Marshall Lynam sent to him: "Jim, I spent a good part of my life trying to keep your foot out of your mouth and now they've gone and inserted a whole leg in there." Finally, Wright fought prostate cancer.

Wright Recognized at Home

The resignation did not break Wright's bond with his constituents. Polls showed that 81 percent of his constituents would have voted for him again, and that total was 72 percent even among Republicans.[42]

Wright had been the dominant political figure in Fort Worth but had often seen the highest awards given by civic clubs escape him. However, he lived long enough to speak at the Chamber of Commerce breakfast, held on the fiftieth anniversary of the Kennedy speech in Fort Worth the morning before his assassination. Wright was the honoree that day, and a five-minute tribute to his career was presented. In his brief comments, he reflected on his good fortune and said that if he just said thank you to all who had supported his career, he should not have enough days of life to complete the task. He was also honored by the Exchange Club of Fort Worth on May 13, 2014, joining other giants of the community as the honoree earning the title of Fort Worth's Outstanding Citizen. This honor marked Wright's acceptance by the insiders in Fort Worth's business community. Wright had often clashed with that group during his career in politics, but in the end they recognized his stream of golden deeds.

Wright had spent a career trying to develop the economy of Fort Worth. He had earned the respect of the community. And he had made countless friends. His legacy in his hometown was secure. When he left Washington, it had been his primary residence for more than a third of a century. However, for Wright, as the quotes at the beginning of the chapter suggest, there never was a question of where home was. It was in the communities he had represented—in the Texas House of Representatives, as mayor, and then as a member of Congress. His friends were in Weatherford and Fort Worth, and at the end, that was what mattered most.

1   James W. Riddlesperger Jr. and Anthony Champagne, eds., *Reflections on Rayburn* (Fort Worth: TCU Press, 2017), 56.

2   Julian E. Zelizer, *Burning Down the House* (New York: Penguin, 2020), 8.

3   Richard F. Fenno Jr., *Home Style: House Members in Their Districts* (New York: Longman, 1978).

4   Norma Richson, interview by Anthony Champagne and James W. Riddlesperger Jr., Fort Worth, October 1, 2013.

5   Richson, interview.

6   Jim Wright, *You and Your Congressman* (New York: G. P. Putnam's Sons, 1976), 195.

7   John M. Barry, *The Ambition and the Power: The Fall of Jim Wright; A True Story of Washington* (New York: Viking, 1989), 510.

8   Marshall Lynam, *Stories I Never Told the Speaker* (Dallas: Three Forks, 1998), 14; see also Barry, *Ambition*, 51.

9   Jim Wright, interview by Ben Proctor, March 3, 1992, JW Papers, TCU.

10   Jim Wright, *Balance of Power* (Atlanta: Turner, 1996), 31–32.

11   Wright, *Balance of Power*, 227–30.

12   Ben R. Guttery, *Representing Texas: A Comprehensive History of US and Confederate Senators and Representatives from Texas* (self-pub, 2008), 255–88.

13   Wright, *Balance of Power*, 329.

14   Wright, 331.

15   Paul Driskell and Marge Youngblood, interview by Ben Procter, July 8, 1981, JW Papers, TCU.

16   Lynam, *Stories*, 178.

17   Lynam, 186.

18   Bob Bolen, interview by Anthony Champagne and James W. Riddlesperger Jr., Fort Worth, October 1, 2013.

19   Pete Geren, interview by Anthony Champagne and James W. Riddlesperger Jr., Fort Worth, August 19, 2014.

20   Mark Carl Rom, *Public Spirit in the Thrift Tragedy* (Pittsburgh: University of Pittsburgh Press, 1996), 5, 171.

21   Barry, *Ambition*, 219.

22   Barry, 52.

23   Bolen, interview.

24 Wright, *Balance of Power*, 200.

25 J. Brooks Flippen, *Speaker Jim Wright: Power, Scandal, and the Birth of Modern Politics* (Austin: University of Texas Press, 2018), 174–77.

26 Barry, *Ambition*, 89.

27 Barry, 53.

28 Barry, 224.

29 Barry, 55.

30 James W. Riddlesperger Jr., Anthony Champagne, and Dan Williams, eds., *The Wright Stuff: Reflections on People and Politics by Former House Speaker Jim Wright* (Fort Worth: TCU Press, 2013), 263–69.

31 Riddlesperger Jr., Champagne, and Williams, *Wright Stuff*, 273.

32 Charles R. Babcock, "Speakers Royalty 55%," *Washington Post*, September 24, 1987.

33 Barry, *Ambition*, 415.

34 Barry, 534.

35 Jeff Guinn, "A Lion in Winter," *Fort Worth Star-Telegram*, August 26, 2001, 12G.

36 James W. Riddlesperger Jr. and Anthony Champagne, *Lone Star Leaders* (Fort Worth: TCU Press, 2011), 144.

37 John Athon, personal communication via email to Anthony Champagne and James W. Riddlesperger Jr., March 5, 2022.

38 Melanie Harris, personal communication via email to Anthony Champagne and James W. Riddlesperger Jr., March 15, 2022.

39 Joshua Simpson, quoted in Joey McReynolds, "Fort Worth, TCU Say Goodbye to Jim Wright," *TCU 360*, May 12, 2015.

40 Thomas Pressley, personal communication via email to Anthony Champagne and James W. Riddlesperger Jr., July 7, 2022.

41 Barry, 51.

42 Lynam, *Stories*, 266.

43 Exchange Club of Fort Worth Program, "85th Annual Golden Deeds Award Banquet," May 13, 2014.

Jim Wright in conversation with his friend and colleague Martin Frost, Jim Wright Symposium, TCU, October 3, 2003. Frost would later be one of Wright's eulogists, as seen in Chapter 1. *All photos in this gallery are property of the Jim Wright Symposium, TCU, and are used by permission.*

University of Oklahoma President David Boren (center) poses with Betty and Jim Wright, October 15, 2004. Boren, a former US senator and governor of Oklahoma with whom Wright served in Congress, was the keynote speaker at that year's symposium.

Lee Hamilton, who served in Congress from Indiana (1965–1999) and later as vice-chair of the Iraq Study group named by President George W. Bush, acknowledges a standing ovation, with Jim Wright leading the applause, after his speech in the Old TCU Student Center Ballroom, September 18, 2007.

Wright and his colleague former Representative Charlie Wilson pose for a picture at the opening function of the new Brown-Lupton University Union (BLUU), September 3, 2008. Wilson was in the public eye at the time because of the recent release of the movie "Charlie Wilson's War," starring Tom Hanks as Wilson.

Senior Statesman Jim Wright poses before Wright Symposium just outside the
BLUU Ballroom, September 3, 2008.

Wright and former senator and Democratic nominee for president in 1972 George McGovern share a laugh before the 2009 Wright Symposium, February 2, 2010. The two of them had first met as B-24 Pilots during World War II.

Wright in conversation with Texas A&M President John Sharp and Sharp's wife Charlotte before the Wright Symposium, March 20, 2014. Sharp previously served as Texas Comptroller of Public Accounts.

Former Congressmen David O'Brien Martin (R-NY), at left, and Bill Alexander (D-AR), at right, discuss how to restore civility to politics at the 2013 Wright Symposium, February 13, 2012. Alexander would later be one of Wright's eulogists, see Chapter 2.

Wright poses with Jim Riddlesperger at the 2015 Wright Symposium, his last. Riddlesperger read Wright's statement that day, where Dee J. Kelly was the keynote speaker in the Dee J. Kelly Alumni Center on the 75th anniversary of Sam Rayburn becoming House Speaker, March 30, 2015. Wright was weak in body but strong in spirit, just weeks before his death—May 6, 2015.

CHAPTER 7

Jim Wright and the Hurdles of National Leadership

ANTHONY CHAMPAGNE

J im Wright's congressional career is a story of some luck, immense talent, intense ambition, and incredibly hard work. Throughout that career Wright struggled to have a national impact on public policy and in doing so faced one hurdle after another. His career shows the immense difficulty, the sacrifices, the frustrations, and the risks that must be taken to achieve and hold national leadership. More broadly, Wright's efforts to gain national leadership show the difficulty of gaining national political power, the problems of holding that power, and why so few people are willing to undertake efforts to rise to top offices within the American political system. As Congressman Jack Brooks discovered, it is far easier to gain power through the congressional committee structure and the seniority system than it is to become a congressional leader. Brooks told Pete Geren that he had considered going into the leadership, but family commitments made him realize that he never could work as hard as Wright, and so he decided to take the easier route of leadership in committees instead.[1]

Wright was able to achieve his goal. He became Speaker and expanded the power of that position beyond that of any twentieth-century Speaker after the revolt against Speaker Joseph Cannon in 1910. Ultimately, however, well-executed political onslaughts on Wright by Newt Gingrich, whose attacks Wright grossly under-estimated, led Wright to leave the House, telling his close friend and chief deputy majority whip Bill Alexander, who urged Wright to stay in the speakership and fight the charges against him, "Bill, I just don't have the votes."[2] What follows then is a case study of Wright's rise to national leadership, his time in House leadership, and his withdrawal from the political stage.

Entering the House

Wright described his football coach, Robert Harris, as his hero. Harris also taught world history and Wright became interested in studying history, especially the events of World War I. Wright's father had been a captain and infantry commander in the war and admired President Wilson, and Wright became convinced that the Senate had made a grave mistake in rejecting the League of Nations and retreating into isolationism. It was in world history class, ac-cording to Wright, that he decided rather than becoming a football coach, he would go to Congress and contribute to world peace. That goal of his became, according to Wright, a "near obsession."[3]

When Wright was elected to Congress, to pursue his goal he sought an assignment on the Foreign Affairs Committee. He spoke to Speaker Sam Rayburn about getting on that committee, but Rayburn dissuaded him, saying that the committee was of little importance. Years earlier John Nance Garner had served on the committee and had turned down its chair in order to be appointed to the Ways and Means Committee. Later, when Tom Connally began his service in the House of Representatives, Garner apologet-ically put Connally on the committee, explaining to Connally that "it's a minor committee."[4] Rayburn urged Wright to take a seat on the Public Works Committee because, explained Rayburn, there needed to be a Texan on all major committees.[5] Wright acceded to Rayburn's request and remained on Public Works until he became majority leader in the House. Public Works allowed Wright to bring projects to his district, which contributed to his political longevity in the House and allowed him to improve America's infrastructure and to gain support from other congressmen for backing projects beneficial to their districts.

On Foreign Affairs he would have had a much harder time proving his worth to his own district or helping other congressmen with their pet projects. Yet, while on Public Works, he was able to advance his interest in foreign affairs. Wright had a special interest in Latin America, perhaps because of family connections. His maternal grandmother had run a company store on the Mexican border and his father had been in a federalized National Guard unit sent to the border to guard against Pancho Villa's raids. Wright spent time at the Pan-American Exposition in Dallas in 1937, and he had traveled many times to Mexico. As a result, as a member of the Public Works Committee, he took an interest in the construction of the Inter-American Highway, becoming a leading advocate for the road and traveling on it by car in 1957.

In 1960, he was asked by the Eisenhower administration to help with a bill that would authorize construction of the Pan American Health Organization building in Washington, DC. The bill was in trouble because of opposition from isolationist Republicans, Democrats who wanted to embarrass the president in an election year, and a bipartisan group of congressmen who were opposed to foreign aid. Wright contacted members to get their support for the bill and joined in the debate over it. When the bill passed, Speaker Rayburn invited Wright to celebrate in the Board of Education room, Rayburn's famed hideaway office that he used to socialize, discuss policy, and plan strategy. It was there that Rayburn told Wright there was insufficient attention paid to Latin America and that inattention was dangerous to American interests.

Wright was later a supporter of John Kennedy's Alliance for Progress, an effort to bring about economic and social development in Latin America. To Wright, the alliance was a Marshall Plan for Latin America. Wright traveled to Latin America and became an advocate for Father Daniel McClellan's organization of credit unions in Peru, even giving a luncheon for Father McClellan in Washington, where Speaker McCormack not only attended but was impressed by the priest's ideas.[6]

Wright's interest in Latin America and foreign affairs continued throughout his congressional years and culminated in his controversial efforts to secure peace in Central America. It was an involvement in foreign policy by a House leader not seen since Speaker Henry Clay, who also had been deeply interested in Latin America and had been a leading supporter of Latin American independence movements.

In terms of domestic policy, Wright quickly took an active role as a member of the Public Works Committee. He supported water quality legislation that offered state grants for construction of waste treatment centers, and he supported federal regulation of industrial pollution in interstate waters. Most importantly, however, was his involvement in the proposal for a system of interstate highways. President Eisenhower had appointed General Lucius Clay to lead a panel to study creating an interstate highway system. That panel led to a proposal that a ten-year construction program be financed with $24 billion in bonds paid in part by gasoline and tire taxes.

Democrats did not favor the funding proposal, and Wright thought the proposal too costly and too broad. He spoke with Rayburn, who agreed that while the country should go into debt in times of war or depression, it should not go into debt to build highways. Rayburn arranged for Wright and others to meet with Eisenhower, and Wright argued for a highway trust fund to pay for construction rather than to pay for bonds. Eisenhower realized the interstate highway proposal needed Democratic support and he wanted the legislation before the election, so he agreed with

Wright's ideas. The Federal-Aid Highway Act of 1956 provided $25 million in construction using Wright's pay-as-you-go trust fund paid for with higher gasoline and user taxes.[7]

Perhaps Wright's involvement in interstate highway funding ranks as his most important national policy contribution as a member of the Public Works Committee; however, he was involved in much legislation with less breadth than interstate highways but nevertheless of great importance. For example, Wright recalled that in 1958, Senator Lyndon Johnson had a bill that passed the Senate at the end of the session. The bill was an important one that would require a comprehensive study of all Texas rivers. Ultimately that study led to significant water development in Texas. The problem in getting House passage of the bill was that its timing was terrible since the House Committee on Public Works had adjourned. It was not possible to get the committee back in session and there were only a couple of days before Congress adjourned. With considerable effort, Wright was able to poll the committee and get their unanimous agreement. Then he arranged with Speaker Rayburn to be recognized for a unanimous consent request. Problems developed when one member of the Public Works Committee, Harry McGregor, believed that Wright's poll of the committee did not mean he had approval for a unanimous consent request. Wright had to withdraw his request and went to the cloakroom, where he had an argument with McGregor, who Wright believed had broken the agreement. Congressman John Blatnik had to mediate what became a hot-tempered argument, but Wright got an agreement from McGregor. He then got Speaker Rayburn to again recognize him for a unanimous consent request, but when he asked for unanimous consent, Congressman H. R. Gross began asking questions and reserved the right to object. After satisfying Gross, who could generally be depended on to object to such requests, Wright was able to get unanimous consent on his third effort, shortly before the end of the congressional session.[8] Wright's account of his efforts with the bill show that in a crunch, Wright was a congressman who could be depended on. It also showed that Wright had a temper, a perennial problem he had difficulty controlling. Years after he retired from Congress, when asked about that famed temper, he responded that the temper was due to the high stress he was under when in Congress.[9]

Wright was not afraid to oppose powerful persons. During the Johnson presidency, for example, the highway beautification bill was being considered and Wright was the floor leader for the bill. President Johnson took a special interest since highway beautification was a major goal for Lady Bird Johnson. Indeed, Johnson was so invested in the bill that he told Wright, "I don't want to take a step backwards." Johnson said, "We ought to go down with flags flying" because "I believe I'd rather lose fighting."[10] Wright knew that the bill could not pass without changes, but the problem was that officials from the administration kept sitting in on the private deliberations of the committee. When an amendment was proposed, those officials would say that they had to take it up with the White House. Afterward, they would return and report that the amendment was not acceptable. Wright became increasingly irritated with the administration over this behavior, and when the bill was about to come up for consideration, Carl Albert suggested some amendments that he thought would help it to pass. Larry O'Brien, representing the administration, said that he would have to take those amendments up with the White House. Finally, Wright had enough. He blew up and said, "Carl [Albert] and Mr. Speaker [John McCormack], these guys don't have the authority to say anything, and they're not going to agree to any amendment; it isn't their responsibility and so far as I'm concerned, they can sit up there in the gallery and watch us do it. I'm dedicated to passing a bill, and I'm going to accept those amendments that I think will aid in the passage of the bill and no more." The result of Wright's decision was that the bill passed, but Wright noted than Lyndon Johnson was never fully satisfied with the outcome of the bill.[11]

Seeking Higher Office

Wright was an early success as a member of the Public Works Committee, and that success would continue. However, he was driven to advance in politics and that opportunity arose in 1961. Lyndon Johnson had run for both vice president and reelection to the Senate. His dual candidacy was so that he could retain his powerful position as Senate majority leader should he lose the vice presidency. In Johnson's 1960 race for the Senate, he won with 58 percent of the vote against a new face in Texas politics. John Tower had been unsuccessful in a race for state representative in 1954 and had been very active in Republican Party politics but was largely unknown outside of Republican circles. Tower received 41.1 percent of the vote in the 1960 Senate race, an unusually strong showing for a Republican statewide candidate. With Johnson as vice president, however, it was necessary to have a special election in 1961 for the now vacant Senate seat. Tower was again the Republican nominee. Wright was the first to announce, but he was followed by seventy other Democratic candidates. William Blakley was clearly the biggest threat to Wright. He was part of the conservative wing of the Texas Democratic Party and had been appointed by Governor Allan Shivers as an interim US senator when Price Daniel resigned in 1957. In 1961, he was again appointed interim US senator by Governor Price Daniel when Johnson resigned from the Senate. Blakley was fabulously wealthy, unlike Wright, who ran up considerable debt in his campaign. Blakley made the runoff election against Tower, with Wright finishing third. Tower received 30.9 percent of the vote; Blakley, 18.1 percent; and Wright, 16.2 percent. Tower then defeated Blakley with 50.6 percent of the vote to become the first Republican senator from the South since Reconstruction.

Tower ran only after checking with Allan Shivers, the dominant conservative in the state, to make sure Shivers did not wish to run. Tower thought that Blakley had confounded Shivers because Blakley had been viewed as a seat warmer in the interim Senate position who would not run in an election. Tower, however, considered Blakley to be an ideal opponent. He thought he could certainly count on Republican votes since he was the only Republican in the race and he thought he picked up a lot of conservative Democrats when he ran against Johnson in 1960. He also thought he got a lot of dissident Democrats who simply would not swallow Blakley's candidacy. In Tower's view, while Blakley was a "very fine gentleman, . . . he had no political acumen whatsoever—absolutely none! He was not a good candidate, he didn't like crowds, he was not a particularly good speaker." In Tower's view, Blakley's only advantage was money and lots of it.[12]

Wright said that he thought Johnson had been friendly to his candidacy in 1961 but that he did not seek an endorsement from Johnson because Johnson had several friends in the race. Wright said he had thought that by announcing first, he would scare away the other candidates, but obviously he did not frighten away anyone. Wright did think that if Johnson had provided a little help behind the scenes, he would have been elected, because he was very close to beating Blakley. But Wright noted that Johnson did not stick his neck out for him. Johnson's staff was mixed about whom they supported. While Johnson's top aide, Walter Jenkins, supported Wright, Cliff Carter supported Will Wilson, who finished fourth in the race.[13]

Wright was so downhearted with his failure to win the Senate race—and also frustrated by the debt he incurred—that he went to Johnson and asked to be appointed an ambassador, returning, of course, to his original interest in foreign affairs. Johnson refused Wright's request, telling Wright, "You think you're frustrated? Who else in Washington do you think is frustrated?"[14] It certainly did not help Wright's disposition that Johnson told him that all of Johnson's friends and advisers were saying that Wright did not have a chance to win the election.[15]

In 1962, Wright seriously considered running for governor, which might have given him an edge to run for the Senate against

Tower in 1966. However, John Connally announced that he would run, and Price Daniel said he would seek reelection. Connally's and Daniel's candidacies destroyed Wright's chance of being elected governor.[16]

Texas's other Senate seat, however, was up for election in 1964. Liberal Democrat Ralph Yarborough had defeated interim senator William Blakely in the 1958 Democratic primary with 58.7 percent of the vote versus Blakely's 41.3 percent. Yarborough then went on to win the general election, where he received 74.6 percent of the vote. Wright said that he received a call from Lyndon Johnson urging him to run against Yarborough. Wright's biographer, J. Brooks Flippen, wrote that Johnson told Wright that if he ran, "there's a lot I can do for you."[17] Wright also said that shortly after hearing from Johnson, he got a call from the leader of the conservative Democrats in Texas, Allan Shivers, who also urged him to run against Yarborough. Wright admitted he did not know whether it was coincidence or a collaboration between Johnson and Shivers that the two calls came so close together, although Wright smiled, suggesting he thought Shivers and Johnson had consulted with each other. With Johnson's and Shivers's support, Wright no doubt could have run a strong race and may well have beaten Yarborough. Along with being far more moderate in his politics than Yarborough was, Johnson, of course, hated Yarborough, and Shivers did as well.[18] Wright, however, explained that he had no antipathy toward Yarborough and did not consider their political views to be very different. Most importantly, many of his friends and supporters were also friends and supporters of Yarborough's. As a result, Wright said he decided to pass on challenging Yarborough.

Deciding whether to run against Yarborough in 1964 was a considerably more complex decision, however, than Wright indicated. Johnson spoke with Houston Harte, where it was clear that he increasingly worried there would be still another party fight. He described it as a "typical Texas stunt." Connally was trying to get Shivers to run against Yarborough, but Johnson noted that while there was a lot about Yarborough he would change, Yarborough voted with Johnson more than anyone else did in the Texas delegation. Yarborough, claimed Johnson, had become "meek as a lamb" during the Johnson presidency. There were still other prospective opponents who were being discussed—most notably Joe Kilgore and Lloyd Bentsen. Johnson argued that they could not beat Yarborough and, said Johnson, "I damn sure don't want two Republicans up here voting against me." Johnson believed that the only person who could beat Yarborough was Jim Wright, and he could only do it with Johnson's support.[19]

In a phone conversation with Johnson, however, Wright said that he had tried to raise money for a race against Yarborough, but he just could not get the money to do it. Kilgore had been considering running against Yarborough after Shivers decided against a race, but Kilgore had pulled out with Johnson's strong encouragement. Johnson told Wright that neither Kilgore nor Shivers could beat Yarborough but that Wright had a chance. Johnson said that Kilgore had the money but Wright had the votes, and he thought a ticket where Connally was the candidate for governor and Wright was the candidate for Senate would be ideal. Connally, Johnson said, could campaign with his arm in a sling (from his wounds in the Kennedy assassination) and to Wright he said, "Keep your tongue in your mouth." In Johnson's view, that would be a strong ticket against Don Yarborough (a liberal Democrat who had run a strong race for governor in 1962 against Connally) and Ralph Yarborough. He told Wright he would not be against a Connally-Wright ticket and that if Wright lost, Johnson would take care of him, so Wright should not feel that he was gambling anything. He even told Wright that he did not see how Wright could do anything else as a member of the House. The only thing he thought Wright had to worry about was if Connally did not embrace him, Wright would be unable to get "that fat cat money." For certain, however, Johnson said that he was not going to help Kilgore, who would vote against him. Wright, however, was clearly reluctant, telling Johnson that he just could not see how he could do it at this point.[20]

The next day, February 3, 1964, Johnson spoke with Jack Brooks, who told him that Don Yarborough was getting labor support in his race against Connally and that was contrary to what he had been told. There had been an understanding with labor that if Ralph Yarborough got a free ride in his race for Senate, Connally would not face opposition from labor. Kilgore had told Johnson that he would not run against Ralph Yarborough if Johnson objected, and Johnson said that Kilgore was now out of the race, but now Connally was getting challenged by Don Yarborough with labor support and Connally was so mad that he was shaking. Johnson told Brooks, "We ought to get Jim Wright in the race by 10:00 [they were facing a filing deadline] or someone else if they are going to play that way."[21]

A few days later, however, George Brown told Johnson that labor endorsed only Ralph Yarborough and not Don Yarborough. Johnson railed against Kilgore, saying that a Kilgore candidacy for the Senate would not help Connally and that Kilgore was another Tower, who would never vote for Johnson policies on anything. While Johnson called Kilgore "my friend," he said that he "never votes with me." Putting Kilgore in the Senate, Johnson said, was the "worse thing you could do." He claimed it would be like putting the bitter competition in charge because he voted like Shivers. Wright, Johnson added, would have run against Ralph Yarborough, but he could just not get the money. He could not even get prospective donors to return his calls.[22]

Radio broadcaster and businessman Gordon McLendon, then a conservative Democrat and who later changed parties, ran in the Democratic primary against Ralph Yarborough. Even though McLendon brought in famous actors, such as John Wayne, to help his campaigning, Yarborough got 57.4 percent of the vote against McLendon's 42.6 percent. In the general election, George H. W. Bush challenged Yarborough, but Bush did not do much better than McClendon had. Yarborough got 56.2 percent of the vote to Bush's 43.6 percent.

Wright was very interested in the 1966 Senate race against John Tower, however. While there never was personal animosity between Wright and Tower—Wright described Tower as always being a gentleman with him and always being willing to work with him on matters that affected Texas—Tower was much more conservative than Wright and of a different party. Wright spoke with Lyndon Johnson, probably in August 1965, and thought that Johnson would back him in a challenge to Tower. Johnson told Wright, "You deserve to be in the Senate, and I want you to come down here to the White House before we adjourn this session and talk with me about it."[23] In a phone conversation in September 1965, Johnson asked Wright if he had made up his mind about running against Tower. Commenting on Wright's remarkable speaking skills and work ethic, Johnson said, "I don't think you ought to mess around. You can out-talk him and out-work him." There had been talk at that point that John Connally was going to challenge Tower, but Johnson said Connally had told him that he was not going to run. Johnson told Wright that he could help him financially and that if Wright lost, he could give him a job. All Wright had to do, said LBJ, was to "make up your mind, burn your bridges, go full steam ahead." He could, said Johnson, "beat this runt Tower." As with the discussion of the race against Ralph Yarborough, however, Wright noted that he was having trouble getting supporters to commit to contributing to his campaign.[24] Later, when Wright met with LBJ, Johnson had noticeably cooled on helping Wright. He volunteered only to talk to a couple of the twelve or fourteen people whom Wright considered key to his race against Tower. Wright said, "I thought it strange in light of the comments he earlier had volunteered."[25] Johnson's switch in the level of his enthusiasm for Wright's candidacy fits with Wright's description of Johnson: "You never know what Lyndon Johnson is thinking, but you do know that he is two steps ahead of everyone in the room."

Money remained a problem for Wright to run against Tower in 1966, and he attempted to generate funds and support without Johnson's help. He made a television appeal for support and for $10 donations.[26] Immediately after taping that television appeal, he made another run at Johnson to try to gain his support. He went to the LBJ Ranch and talked for an hour with Johnson, where, to Wright's immense frustration, Johnson made it clear that he did not consider it important to replace Tower. Wright made a direct appeal to Johnson, saying, "Mr. President, how much more good could I do you and your program if I were a member of the Senate than I can do you as a member of the House?" Johnson was not the least bit encouraging, responding, "Not a hell of a lot. I'd rather have you than almost any senator, and you can do me more good right where you are than 90 percent of them can do me in the Senate."[27] It was then Wright realized that unless he got a strong response to his television appeal, a race for the Senate was not in the cards because Johnson was not going to be helpful.[28] Wright's appeal to Johnson did not work and his television appeal for support failed. On top of those problems was that he was still in debt $70,000 from his 1961 race for the Senate and he had children about to go to college. Wright simply was in no position to take on another statewide campaign.[29] Johnson's effort to discourage Wright is hard to explain except for the problem Wright had in raising funds for a statewide race. Wright was having trouble raising funds, and LBJ did not want to be Wright's fund raiser. Later, for example, when Waggoner Carr was the Democratic nominee against Tower, Johnson told John Connally he would provide $15,000 or $20,000 to Carr, but Carr was just one of a dozen other candidates to whom Johnson was going to contribute money.[30]

Waggoner Carr, former Speaker of the Texas House of Representatives and the Texas attorney general, was the Democratic candidate against Tower. Carr proved a disappointment as a candidate even though he had held the highest position in the Texas House and had run a successful statewide race for attorney general. Tower substantially improved his victory margin over his 1961 race for senator, receiving 56.4 percent of the vote, compared with Carr's

43.1 percent. In a call to labor leader George Meany, Johnson made it clear that he would have preferred Jim Wright to Carr. Carr, he said, was "not a confederate of mine" like Wright was. It was clear Meany had no great enthusiasm for Carr. He told Johnson that from the perspective of labor, there was not much difference between Tower and Carr, and that labor likely would not take a position in the race. Of course, even though Carr was not Johnson's preference, he would rather Carr in the Senate over Tower, and he suggested that labor should not write Carr off and alienate him from labor like Shivers, Connally, or Daniel. He told Meany that it was better for labor to have a Democrat in the Senate and that while Carr would never support labor on Taft-Hartley, he thought Carr could be persuaded to support labor's position 75 percent of the time. Johnson reminded Meany that he had opposed labor on Taft-Hartley but that labor had "made a Christian out of me."[31]

Johnson got an early report from George Mahon that Carr was not doing well because he was seen as a "colorless" candidate of the administration. In contrast, Mahon reported that the Texas papers were presenting Tower as the "leader of everything good." He was also concerned that the liberal wing of the Democratic Party in Texas would be happy with a Tower victory because that would leave Ralph Yarborough in a position of power in a Democratic-controlled Senate. Johnson agreed with Mahon's concern.[32]

In a conversation with John Connally, Johnson said that he was going to provide Carr with $15,000 or $20,000 in campaign funds. Connally was enthusiastic about Carr and reported to Johnson that he had done a great deal for Carr, though he had not been too open in doing so out of concern that his activities could be used by Republicans against Carr. It was Connally's view that Carr was doing well in the state by mid-October, but he was concerned about attacks on Carr that claimed he was weak and dependent on Connally and LBJ. Johnson said that the only influence in Washington that Tower had was with Barry Goldwater and that it should be argued that Carr was going to Washington to speak for Texas.[33] Connally's enthusiasm was obviously misplaced, with Tower's strong performance and election to another Senate term.

In keeping with Wright's unwillingness or inability to run against Yarborough in 1964, he did not run against him in 1970. But former congressman Lloyd Bentsen challenged Yarborough in the Democratic primary and defeated him with 53 percent of the vote, compared with Yarborough's 47 percent. Bentsen then went on to be elected to the Senate when he defeated George H. W. Bush in the general election with 53.6 percent of the vote, compared with Bush's 46.5 percent. Bentsen had spoken to Johnson, now retired from the presidency, in 1970 about running against Yarborough. Rather surprisingly, Johnson discouraged him from running, telling Bentsen, "Well Lloyd, you know I think a great deal of you. But I watch Senator Yarborough. I still pay attention to politics. Senator Yarborough comes down here every weekend, makes two or three speeches. He has kept his fences mended. You know, he has even sent me commemorative stamps. I guess if he sends me commemorative stamps, he must be sending them to everybody. Lloyd, I just don't believe you can beat Ralph Yarborough." Bentsen replied, "Well, Mr. President, I can't if I don't try. I've made up my mind. I'm going to run."[34]

Bentsen had an enormous amount of money available for the campaign against Yarborough, and he had told Connally in 1968 when Connally asked him if he would like to be governor that he wanted to run against Yarborough instead. He had made a tentative effort to run against Yarborough in 1964, but in one story claimed that he never spoke with Johnson about challenging Yarborough, and for personal reasons that included large debts, he chose not to run.[35] In another story, he claimed that LBJ "sweet-talked" him out of running. Perhaps Johnson did sweet-talk Bentsen, but with Joe Kilgore, Johnson browbeat him out of running. Johnson, of course, was running for president in 1964 and wanted to avoid a messy Texas Democratic primary. With Bentsen against Yarborough in 1970, the race was a head-to-head battle of a conservative Democrat backed by the Connally organization against the liberal wing of the Democratic Party. The campaign by both men was a gutter-level brawl of which neither should have been proud, but Yarborough was defeated.[36] Wright, had he run, would have had much more difficulty because he was unable to raise the funding for such a race that Bentsen had and he could not have presented himself as the conservative alternative to Yarborough.

Tower was up for reelection in 1972, and the Democratic nominee to challenge him was Barefoot Sanders. Sanders was later appointed by President Jimmy Carter and became a highly regarded federal district judge. At the time of his race against Tower, he had served in the Texas House of Representatives from 1953 to 1959 and had unsuccessfully run for the US House of Representatives in 1958 against the right-wing Republican incumbent Bruce Alger. In 1961 he was appointed US attorney for the Northern District of Texas and he served in that office until 1965. He then served as assistant deputy attorney general and assistant attorney general until 1967, when he became legislative counsel to the president. President Johnson nominated Sanders to the US Court of Appeals for the District of Columbia, but Johnson's presidency came to an end before the Senate voted on Sanders, and President Nixon did not renominate him. Sanders had exceptional legal credentials but had only been elected a state representative, and that was in the 1950s. Nevertheless, he ran in the Democratic primary against Ralph Yarborough, who had been defeated in the Democratic primary by Lloyd Bentsen two years previously. Yarborough did exceptionally well in the primary but barely failed to get a majority of the vote. That threw Yarborough into a runoff primary against Sanders, and Sanders won with 52.1 percent of the vote. Sanders went on to challenge John Tower, who got 53.4 percent of the vote versus Sanders's 44.3 percent.

Wright knew that had he decided to run against Tower, Sanders would not have made the race. However, Wright again decided he would not run even though he thought he could have beaten Tower.

Wright described Sanders as having "unfeigned boyish charm," and a writer described him as having the appearance of "Tom-Sawyer-Grows-Up hiding an acute lawyerly intelligence."[37] In spite of Sanders's remarkable personal charm, however, Wright did not think Sanders could win.[38] The election was in 1972, with a race between Richard Nixon and George McGovern. It was a terrible year to be a Democrat running for office.

If the Senate Is Unattainable

At the end of 1971, Wright was fifty years old and he was realizing that he was not able (and was less willing) to achieve his goals. He wrote, "Maybe just in the past year have I really acknowledged that I won't ever be president. Conceivably I've known it subconsciously for several years but only in this year have said it to myself and you know? It's kind of a relief! . . . I'm no longer willing to pay the price I once would gladly pay for escalation up the political ladder."[39]

Wright was well aware of his exceptional ability as a public speaker, but he wrote, "The power of my oratory is no longer irresistible as it well nigh was." He still thought that he was a better public speaker than anyone else in Texas, but he did not think he looked as good on television as he had when he ran for the Senate—"when I came so very, very close to winning"—in 1961. Wright then explained his biggest problem in not advancing to the Senate. He wrote, "I'm not willing to humble myself, to go hat in hand to the fat cats and beg for money." He also wrote that he was "unwilling to go through the sheer physical torture and mental torment of a statewide campaign." Explaining further why he was reluctant to try again for the Senate, he wrote that he was experiencing "a sort of personal conservatism [that] creeps in with middle age." He was comfortable where he was, and he was accumulating seniority and thus gaining power in the House—something that, he wrote, was a "crutch that I once vowed never to embrace." Overall, he was unwilling "to venture boldly and risk the relative security (financial and otherwise) of my present job."[40] He may have thought that he, unlike Barefoot Sanders, could beat John Tower, but it was clear from his diary entry that he was no longer willing to try.

Wright was also worried about money. He wrote, "My finances are a shambles," and he thought he had been foolish to have "so long ignored them and let them drift." When he was thirty years old, Wright wrote, he was rich, but at the age of fifty, "I'm driving a ten year old car, owe so God-awful much money that I'll need luck to pay it off."[41]

Wright remained torn over his love for his congressional work and his financial difficulties. In early 1972, on the seventeenth anniversary of the first State of the Union address that he attended, he wrote that he felt "something akin to shock" that he had spent about a third of his life in Congress. Significantly, he expressed great satisfaction with being in Congress in spite of his financial struggles. He wrote, "Has it been worth it? To me, yes. In terms of personal satisfaction, I know of no other career which could as well have served my needs. I hope I haven't been too selfish in pursuing it as the expense of financial security for my family."[42]

Still, in early 1972, Wright seemed to undergo a down period in his life. Bob Casey, Graham Purcell, and Wright spoke at a Texas Press Association breakfast and almost missed their flight. Wright wrote that they got on the plane with only about five minutes to spare. It caused him "to ponder this hurried, harried pace which can shatter my tranquility and make my insides churn like the thrashing innards of a clothes washing machine. Time was when the emotional excitement of close connections and cliff-hangers impacted their own stimuli of satisfaction in the sense of consummate utilization of time. No more! A pace of constant crisis takes its toll."[43]

Still, he was torn between seeking a more financially secure and less hectic life or staying in Congress. Just days after his near-missed flight, he spoke at the annual banquet of the Limestone

Institute. It was an audience of about five hundred, with about fifty of the audience being members of Congress. Wright spoke about a key Public Works Committee item, the national highway program. He thought his speech was not one of his best speaking efforts but still was quite good, and he received a standing ovation and praise from his congressional colleagues. Overall, he was quite pleased and noted, "My seemingly insatiable thirst for public appreciation was ministered to."[44] It was probably the next night that Wright and his wife, Betty, went to the annual dinner of the National Women's Press Club. Senator Frank Church and Henry Kissinger were the speakers and Wright wrote that he was envious of them and admitted that they both did well. However, Wright kept thinking that he could have done a better job than Church, even though others thought Church had given a good speech. Wright confessed, "The truth is that I'm still jealous because Frank got the nod to make the keynote speech at the National Democratic Convention in 1960."[45] That was an event that took place twelve years earlier and it was still troubling Wright. Wright realized how absurd that was, writing, "Isn't that a sad commentary?" Betty made it clear that she thought Wright had gone overboard in his need for public attention. She told him, "Jim, can you not be happy unless you're the center of attention every night?" Wright confessed that he was happier and more satisfied when "I can throw myself wholly into an effort, sublimating self and concentrating only on outcome."[46]

It was not long before Wright was provided the opportunity to get his finances in order and lessen the hectic pace of his life, though it would mean leaving elective politics. He and Betty had dinner with Phil and Olive Tucker and during dinner Phil "made a very attractive proposition—financially more attractive and more tempting than any I've received in the past few years." Phil was a lobbyist for the Outdoor Advertising Association and wanted to retire. He offered Wright the job and even offered to let Wright delay taking the job until the end of Wright's likely forthcoming congressional term. It was a chance for Wright to resolve his financial problems. Wright wrote that he liked being in Congress and got great satisfaction from his work, but he wondered if he could afford to stay in spite of his enjoyment of the work. However, he expressed fear that he would be "thoroughly miserable as a 'Legislative Representative.'"[47] He had his chance to make money and have a less hectic life, but he concluded that he was not going to give up a public life even if it meant crushing debt and constant crises.

Bob Bolen noted that Wright, as a senior member of the Public Works Committee, could do a great deal regarding highways, urban development, and industries important to Fort Worth, such as Bell Helicopter, Lockheed, and DFW Airport. Wright, however, wanted more. If the Senate (and later the presidency) was not achievable for him, he wanted a leadership role in the House. In 1970, Jack Brooks asked Wright to take his place as zone whip. That zone was the Texas delegation, where Wright would be responsible for trying to corral votes for the leadership. The job was the lowest rung in the leadership ladder of the House.[48] However, Carl Albert of Oklahoma was becoming Speaker, which was another advantage to Wright because he was on good terms with Albert and other members of the Oklahoma delegation, most notably Ed Edmondson, who was one of Wright's closest friends.[49]

In early 1973, at a Texas delegation breakfast, Wright was endorsed for the position of majority whip, and failing that, the position of deputy whip. Wright was pleased and wrote that he had not asked for that endorsement. He realized that John McFall was presently the deputy whip and had been promised the majority whip position, but five days later, Tip O'Neill announced that Wright would be deputy whip.[50] As deputy whip, Wright was an important figure in the leadership and was close enough to Speaker Albert that he was able to urge Albert to retire when Albert's drinking became a major problem.[51]

Moving Up in the Leadership

With Carl Albert's retirement, Tip O'Neill moved up the leadership ladder from majority leader to Speaker. John McFall was the majority whip and ordinarily would have been in position to be elected majority leader. Scandal stood in his way, which opened up the possibility for others to grab the leader's position. Phillip Burton of California jumped into the race, as did Richard Bolling of Missouri. Wright was a latecomer to the race. He said that O'Neill had told him that being majority leader would not require more work than being on Public Works did—Wright commented that it was a statement that was clearly untrue, but it led Wright to believe that O'Neill wanted him as majority leader. Nevertheless, Wright admitted that O'Neill was such a skilled politician that he may have said similar things to others. In contrast, Bolling thought O'Neill backed him because Eddie Boland, O'Neill's closest friend in the House, backed Bolling.[52]

It was likely around this time that Lanny Hall asked Wright if he was going to run for majority whip, and Wright told him that he did not want to be whip, that he preferred staying on Public Works and becoming its chair. However, said Wright, he might have a shot at majority leader.[53] McFall, after all, was in a scandal; Burton had made a lot of enemies, including O'Neill; and Bolling was arrogant—a man who did not suffer fools and tended to think most others were. Wright was late in the majority leader's race, but he was right; he did have a chance.

Wright staff member John Mack believed the majority leader race was an "anybody but Burton" race. Burton, said Mack, was simply "a bully." Mack said that Burton threatened members and described a situation when Norman Mineta was in the chair and Burton was drunk. Burton went to the chair and ordered Mineta to do what he wanted even though it was contrary to procedure. Seeing trouble coming, Mack went to California congressman George Miller, who was close to Burton and was a very large man, and Mack persuaded

Miller to get Burton away from the Speaker's rostrum before Burton created a scene.[54] Even Miller, who described Burton as his mentor, said that Burton "was very loud and gregarious and pointed and direct" and that "he could really . . . make people upset and mad."[55] It was an event in 1972 that led to an irreparable break between O'Neill and Burton, even though O'Neill thought Richard Bolling, Wilbur Mills, and Burton the three most knowledgeable members of the House. The break came after a Democratic fundraising dinner in a bar at the Beverly Hills Hotel. Burton was drunk and kept using a profane term that offended O'Neill. When Burton failed to respond to O'Neill's caution about using the word, O'Neill told him, "Curb your tongue." That led Burton, according to O'Neill, to go "berserk" and want to fight. Before Burton was restrained, he threatened O'Neill, saying, "I'll never forget this. I'll never forgive you. I'll run against you." O'Neill recalled, "That's where the break came, and there was a terrific coolness."[56]

John McFall was a Californian, like Burton, and was well liked. He was also whip and was therefore on the third rung of the ladder of leadership behind the Speaker and the majority leader. But he was not going to win the race for majority leader because he was engulfed by scandal. He had received $4,000 from Korean lobbyist Tongsun Park and had put the money in his office account. It was alleged that he used the money for interest-free loans to pay his California taxes, buy his daughter a car, and help pay her college tuition.[57]

Richard Bolling had been a protégé of Sam Rayburn's, but he was also the architect of some of the major reforms in the House. He had long had dreams of being in the leadership. On November 19, 1961, the day after Rayburn's funeral, Bolling had announced that he would run for majority leader, which forced Carl Albert to announce his candidacy as well.[58] Albert quickly sewed up that race, and Albert and Bolling developed a good working relationship, so much so that Bolling believed Albert would get the Oklahoma delegation to support him for majority leader. Bolling's files have a note that Albert "said he would do everything short of endorsing me out loud" and another note saying that "Carl A. said he might try to dissuade Wright."[59] Wright, however, said that Albert did exactly the opposite: Albert encouraged Wright to run.[60] Bill Alexander stated that Bolling had leadership ability and was a very strong personality, but that "his time had passed." His strongest supporters in the House had retired or had died.[61] John Barry best described Bolling's problem: "His biggest opponent was his own ego, for his brilliance was more than matched by his arrogance."[62]

Bolling and Burton thought Wright could not win for three reasons: Wright had the support of the oil and gas lobby (after all, he was a Texan), and both men were claiming that Wright was in oil's pocket; Wright had voted against the 1964 Civil Rights Act; and, finally, Wright did not have the unanimous support of the Texas delegation.[63]

Wright thought the Korea scandal would stop McFall and did not think Bolling could win. In John Mack's view, O'Neill certainly preferred Wright to Burton, although O'Neill would have been happy with Bolling. Wright did have several advantages, however: he was on Public Works, he was a Southerner, and he had the big Northern cities led by Mayor Daley.

One problem that Wright had entering the race is that he did not have the support of the entire Texas delegation. Bob Eckhardt and Jack Brooks supported Phil Burton, although Paul Driskell said, "Brooks apologized one hundred times for voting for Burton" and Wright always responded, "You committed even before I announced."[64] What was less known than Burton's support by the two Texans was that California congressman Leo Ryan, later killed by members of Jim Jones's cult in Guyana, supported Wright for majority leader.[65]

A major advantage for Wright was that he was a Southerner, which provided regional balance since Speaker O'Neill was from Massachusetts. In spite of two Texans backing Burton, Wright still had the support of the bulk of the Texas delegation. He also had the support of the Public Works Committee, which was a committee that allowed him to do favors for many congressmen over the years and especially allowed him to gain the support of the major Northern cities, most notably Chicago and New York, since key urban legislation went through that committee. What more than anything won the majority leadership for Wright, however, was described by John Barry: "Most important in this race was Wright himself. Wright would devote everything in his soul to this race. Meticulously, attending to each detail, he would exploit every resource available to him, exhaust himself as well as those around him. . . . He kept in personal touch, personal control of his campaign. . . . He poured himself into his effort, asking members one by one for support. By summer recess he had sat down privately with 165 colleagues."[66] Wright had an enormous capacity for work. He was a driven man and that was the fundamental cause of him gaining the majority leadership.

A Driven Man

Wright may have been stymied in his efforts to advance to the Senate, but that did not lessen his remarkable energy and work ethic. People who knew him and worked with him frequently commented on Wright's enormous capacity for work. John Mack, for example, stressed Wright's incredible schedule. He recalled that Wright wanted to have a working breakfast at the Capitol at 6:30 in the morning, although Mack finally convinced him to breakfast at 7:30 instead.[67]

Steve Charnovitz had been a congressional fellow in Wright's office. Charnovitz wrote some speeches for Wright. For speeches, Wright wanted one-half of a legal page with large print. Charnovitz also did some policy work for him, especially dealing with international trade, but Wright did not have a policy shop in his office. Wright was his own policy man. Charnovitz noted that Wright read extensively, although sometimes he did not finish what he was reading because of time pressures. He spoke with lobbyists and other members, however, and gained information that way as well. Charnovitz was especially impressed with Wright's ability to remember what he had read and heard. He saw Wright accurately recount information and statistics on numerous occasions completely from memory. Wright, he said, could hear a trade association presentation in the morning and without taking notes use that information in a speech in the afternoon. Especially when Congress was in session, Wright kept a hectic schedule. He was always working and so did not spend a lot of time on the floor. Wright kept his daily schedule on an index card, and he would add meetings to the card during the day. He would run from meeting to meeting, frequently having two meetings scheduled at the same time. As he was going from one meeting to another, Charnovitz would brief him. At the same time, he would be interrupted by both Democrats and Republicans, who all wanted a moment of his time.[68]

Wright was so busy when he was in the leadership that he viewed congressmen who interrupted his day as interfering with his plans. There were always members who wanted to see him and thus interfered with his schedule. He would get upset with the interruptions and say that he had no time to see people. Staff member Kathy Mitchell would then remind him, "How do you turn down someone you have known for twenty-five years?" At that point, of course, Wright would accept the need to be interrupted. Mitchell said Wright was so busy that it was a struggle to get him to take time off to see a doctor and that it was nearly impossible to get him to go to the dentist.[69] In fact, Wright said that had he not resigned from the House, he would have died, because as Speaker he did not have time to see a doctor. After he resigned, he went to a doctor, who diagnosed a spot on his tongue as cancer, requiring removal of part of his tongue.

John Barry wrote that Wright was "inaccessible" and "distant." Wright rarely was on the floor of the House, and, wrote Barry, "When he did appear he quickly grew annoyed at the members who would line up to see him, to invite him to their fund-raiser, to ask for a vacant room down the hall from their office, to ask him to have a word with the Rules Committee about making an amendment in order. He complained, 'I'll be talking to one member, and someone else will come and interrupt as if I was just passing time, as if we weren't talking about something important.'"[70] While Wright did not spend a lot of time on the floor of the House, certainly far less than did Tip O'Neill, that did not mean Wright was out of touch with what was happening on the floor. Just as Sam Rayburn had D. B. Hardeman as his eyes and ears on the floor, Wright had John Mack, who performed the same function for him. Mack said that Jack Brooks told him that his job was to "act like a fly on the wall," and Dan Rostenkowski told him that he needed to be able to look at members talking on the floor and instinctively know what they were talking about.

Unlike O'Neill, who, like Rostenkowski, was "a drinking, dining, back-slapping ward politician, Wright was not. Wright was working, giving speeches, giving testimony." O'Neill functioned as a kind of guidance counselor and usually had an open-door policy.[71] O'Neill allowed "discussions to take place and would gently direct discussions toward an outcome. Wright wanted to lead and direct an outcome rather than work toward a consensus like O'Neill."[72] In short, Wright was too busy to engage in the social interactions with the members that characterized O'Neill as Speaker. One of Wright's longtime staff members compared him to Lyndon Johnson in the sense that "he was busy all the time—always was." Wright, she said, "worked constantly."[73] The result of Wright's failure to schmooze with the members as O'Neill had explains why Jim Chapman noted that Wright was respected, but unlike O'Neill, he was not loved.[74] Wright did make some effort to socialize with the members: he had dinners at his home with members; he had cordial relationships with many members and some senators; he had close friendships with some senior members, such as Ed Edmondson, Graham Purcell, and Jack Brooks; and he had close friendships with some younger members, such as Mike Andrews and Martin Frost.[75] However, his friendships were limited; senior members like Richard Bolling hated him, and John Dingell never regretted that Wright left Congress.[76] Younger members, in general, chafed at Wright's leadership, which they thought too firm.[77]

There were situations where if Wright was not in attendance, he would send John Mack to relay what was going on. Mack would go on golfing trips with O'Neill, Bob Michel, and Rostenkowski in order to provide information to Wright about what was being discussed.[78] Wright was not a golfer and thought golf a waste of time, but sometimes when O'Neill and Rostenkowski would go to play golf in Palm Springs, Wright said he would go just to find out what they were discussing and what sorts of deals they were trying to make.

Wright did prepare almost all of his speeches. While he used speech writers from time to time, they never lasted long, and he tended to tear up their drafts and prepare the speeches in his own way. Dorothy Beard commented on Wright's memory, which she described as "phenomenal." She said she saw time and again how he could rely on information that he had memorized. Once, she said, he flawlessly delivered a convention speech from memory when the teleprompter was improperly set.[79] Bob Bolen recalled that he and Wright visited an African American church when they were campaigning and that Wright was called on to speak. Wright spoke for fifteen to twenty minutes, quoting from the Bible at great length and giving the entire speech with no notes.[80]

Unlike Tom Foley, who had a large staff and was not interested in details of legislation, Wright was detail oriented and had a relatively small staff. Wright disliked being surrounded by staff and tended to only have one staff member with him at a time.[81] A longtime staff member, Kathy Mitchell, recalled that in Wright's early days in the House, he had a five-person staff; when he was Speaker, he had a staff of thirty to thirty-five. Like others who worked with Wright, she recalled that he was "always on the go." She, like John Mack, recalled the early-morning working breakfasts and that he would go into the night with multiple meetings and receptions.[82]

The Challenges of Leadership

Everyone Was New to Their Jobs

One of the problems facing the O'Neill-Wright leadership in the early days of the Carter administration was that everyone was new to their job. Frank Moore was assistant to the president for congressional liaison in the Carter administration. He stated that there was a great deal of criticism of Carter because he did not glad-hand, had not been in Congress, was new to Washington, and brought in new people from Georgia. But Moore noted that there had been a huge influx of new congressmen, known as the "Watergate Babies," who did not come through party ranks and were undisciplined. They did not owe anyone and believed themselves to be independent actors. Coupled with a huge new group of congressmen was Tip O'Neill as a new Speaker. Then Jim Wright was a new majority leader, who had won by only one vote in a "bruising, bruising three-way fight." The majority whip was also new. None of the leaders were sure of themselves and their jobs. The Speaker looked out over about 150 new members of Congress who were wanting to end the seniority system and were demanding to elect their own committee chairs. They were deposing committee chairs, such as Bob Poage on the Agriculture Committee. Moore added, "And you're supposed to be leading this group, and you look out and see all these people are overthrowing people you've served with for thirty years. You see them, you know, pushed off to the side; you become a little concerned about your own fate."[83]

The Young Rebels

Jim Wright commented that O'Neill was especially concerned that Richard Gephardt, Tony Coelho, and other leaders among the younger members of Congress were plotting to overthrow the leadership, just as committee chairmen such as Wright Patman and Bob Poage had been overturned. Wright kept advising O'Neill,

"Just let them try; they don't have the votes." Still, such disloyalty by those who were key members of the Democratic Caucus had to be a cause for concern. John Mack noted that Gephardt and several Watergate Babies strategized about overturning the leadership in meetings that were held in Coelho's house. Mack, like Wright, was aware that O'Neill remained terribly concerned about their meetings, but Mack had a spy in the meetings and was kept informed about everything that was said. Wright was well aware that the plotters did not have the votes to mount a successful challenge to the leadership. Nevertheless, Wright and O'Neill had many conversations about the disaffected young members.[84]

The Loss of the South

Another major topic of conversation between O'Neill and Wright was Democratic losses in the South. It was those losses that led Wright to become involved in the House special election that occurred after the resignation of Northeast Texas Democratic congressman Sam Hall. Hall was approached by Phil Gramm and asked if he would be interested in being a federal judge. Hall was interested, although convinced that there was no way he could be appointed a federal judge by Ronald Reagan. Gramm, however, used his influence to get Hall the appointment, which opened Hall's congressional seat. Gramm then recruited Edd Hargett, a former quarterback for Texas A&M who played professional football, to run for the seat. Gramm also provided substantial financial backing for Hargett's race. Since the election was a special election, it was an all-party race with seven candidates, and Hargett was the only Republican. Hargett got 42 percent of the vote, followed by 30.2 percent for Jim Chapman. Wright decided that it was time to stop Republican inroads in Texas, and he, along with Lloyd Bentsen, started raising money for Chapman's campaign. With that financial support, Chapman was able to win with 51.1 percent of the vote. With Wright as majority leader and about to become

Speaker, he was able to give Chapman important committees, which, of course, strengthened Chapman's position in his district and ensured a Wright loyalist on key committees. Chapman was put on Steering and Policy and on Public Works and Transportation. Chapman said that he wanted to be on the Banking Committee, but he realized you went on the committee that Wright wanted you to go on. Wright stopped the Republican onslaught in that Texas district, but he could not stop the steady gains the Republicans were making in the rest of the South, and unfortunately for Wright, the fewer Democratic representatives from the South, the less the need for a Southerner like Wright to represent the interests of that region in the House.

The bulk of the conservative wing of the Democratic Party in the House, commonly known as Boll Weevils, were from the South and were led by Texas congressman Charles Stenholm. Just as the Watergate Babies were rebellious against the leadership, the Boll Weevils were also a problem. On one occasion, Stenholm even challenged O'Neill for the Speaker's position because the Boll Weevils did not believe they were getting a fair share of the better committee assignments. Stenholm said that while he saw his support drop from twenty to thirty votes to five or six, O'Neill did meet with him and agree to be more solicitous of the Boll Weevils' interests. Wright, Stenholm said, understood that Stenholm had to be conservative from his district or that a Republican would be elected. O'Neill understood as well, and on one occasion, when Stenholm was almost kicked out of the Democratic Caucus, both Wright and O'Neill defended him, saying that without Stenholm, a Republican would be elected. Wright even campaigned for Stenholm, and Stenholm said that Wright was not a negative force in his district, even as a leader of the national Democrats, in part because of Wright's remarkable speaking ability. Wright, said Stenholm, was the best extemporaneous speaker he had ever seen.[85] Wright, nevertheless, believed that the Boll Weevils were making a mistake: even if they voted with the Republicans, eventually the Republicans would still try to take them down. It seemed like a problem that Democrats could not solve. The Boll Weevils had districts that prevented them from voting like national Democrats, and by voting with Republicans, they would either eventually change parties or would be defeated by Republicans.

The Phil Gramm Debacle

Phil Gramm ran against Lloyd Bentsen for the Senate in 1976 and was defeated, but in 1978 he was elected to the House of Representatives. Gramm coveted a seat on the Budget Committee, but after he had been in office only two months, he challenged the House leadership and almost succeeded in getting a balanced budget provision approved by the House. In 1980, he tried to pass an unsuccessful substitute to the Democratic budget that would have increased defense spending and cut social programs. However, Gramm continued to push for a seat on the Budget Committee, and with Wright's help was able to get on the committee. Wright claimed that one of the reasons for putting Gramm on the committee was to keep an eye on him.[86] Gramm was also accused of reneging on a promise that he made to Wright, Jim Jones, and other Democratic leaders that he would have a more cooperative working relationship with the Democratic Party. Such a promise certainly seems to have been given. Wright received a letter from Gramm that said:

> I was gratified and honored that the Steering and Policy Committee nominated me for a position on the Budget Committee. I want to thank you for your support, which was essential in my effort to obtain the nomination.
>
> I hope that my work on the Budget Committee will always merit the confidence you have shown in me. I will work diligently to assure the Democrats in the House are presented budget resolutions they can enthusiastically support on the Floor and at home in their districts.

> While I have strong views on the necessity of
> balancing the budget and opinions about how that goal
> should be achieved, I intend to be a responsible member
> of the Budget Committee. I will work hard to perfect the
> budget in committee and during Floor debate, but as a
> member of the Committee I will support final passage of
> the budget.[87]

Another Texan helped by Wright also betrayed him—Kent
Hance was elected to the House in 1978 and Wright put him on
the Ways and Means Committee, again with a commitment that
he would argue Wright's position within the committee and then
support the committee's decision. Both Gramm and Hance became
key supporters of the Reagan administration's budget and tax bills.[88]

Gramm bore the brunt of Wright's anger for the betrayal.
Hance, he said, simply had such a great sense of humor that it was
hard to stay angry with him. And Wright thought Hance really
did not want to bolt but that "he just couldn't withstand the pressures from his district." While Hance was "just weak of character
and easily persuaded, and doesn't have much force of conviction
and really meant to do the right thing," Gramm, Wright thought,
"just deceived me deliberately." Wright considered Gramm to be
"an intelligent man, but he is insatiably ambitious. His appetite for
publicity is voracious" and he "is never going to be satisfied to be
part of the team effort."[89]

Wright was asked if Gramm's and Hance's betrayals hurt him
as majority leader, and Wright responded that he was hurt personally and that it made him feel he was ineffective as a leader. He
added that he thought their betrayal hurt him with liberals in the
caucus and that it subjected him "to a certain amount of scorn or
pity" and that liberals "may feel that I am not a very strong leader
because I can't deliver any greater percentage of the Texas delegation."[90] Elsewhere, however, Wright wrote that Gramm's "blatant
open split with the Democrats has made me look a bit like a fool."[91]

Wright, of course, was hurt badly by their betrayal—these two men were Texans and both were put on prime committees because of Wright's efforts on their behalf. There is little doubt Wright was blamed for not exercising due diligence in pursuing those two appointments—and for sending Gramm on a path that would lead him to becoming a Republican senator from Texas.

There Is Not Enough Time

John Barry wrote that while Wright's daily schedule generally listed a half dozen receptions, he rarely went to them. Instead, members would invite him, and he would tell them, "Have my secretary put it on my schedule." When he would not attend, John Mack would tell them that the reception was on his schedule, but something came up at the last minute and Wright could not attend.[92] The suggestion was that even though Wright was in the leadership, he was a no-show at events such as receptions important to the members. That was not actually how Wright operated. Just as during the day he often had two meetings scheduled at the same time, he tried to pack more receptions into his evenings than he could attend. One example of him overcommitting is noted in his diary: "It is Tuesday night. I've been to five receptions since 6:30 . . . for Steed, Ammerman, Eckhardt, Sharp and Udall—an average of 15 or 20 minutes at each place. There were seven on my card tonight. Couldn't make the other two, which were downtown. All seven were slated from six to eight o'clock."[93]

Though Barry wrote that Wright rarely attended evening receptions even though he accepted invitations to them, elsewhere he provides a sense of Wright's workday. Wright was picked up by his driver at 6:15 a.m. and immediately began reading memos and checking the papers. A staff member said he read five papers a day. He had an early appearance on the *Today* show. Then he went to his regular breakfast staff meeting. At 10:00 he had a Democratic Caucus meeting and at 10:30 he had to be at the White House for a leadership meeting with the president. At 11:30 he had a regular leadership meeting, followed by a press conference. At noon, Wright convened the House and then for a half hour had a meeting and had his picture taken with six small groups. Then he went to lunch with the Texas delegation. Afterward, he had to deal with nonbudgetary issues and his staff wanted decisions from him. Then at 2:30 he was needed on the House floor. Frank Carlucci, the new national security adviser, had an appointment with him and he was busy and had to keep Carlucci waiting. At 3:30 there were members wanting to see him on the House floor. O'Neill had practically lived on the House floor or on one of the couches in the cloakroom while a colleague presided and where he was almost always available to the members. Wright went back to his office, where Bill Gray briefed him on a development. Then his staff wanted to meet with him. Then members lined up for just five minutes with him. At 5:00 p.m. representatives from General Dynamics, a key business in his district, had a reception in the Speaker's dining room and Wright had to put in an appearance. After that he had four receptions for colleagues on his schedule. That night when he went home, the *Washington Post* did a Style section piece on him and Betty. That was his typical workday—twelve to fourteen hours a day. He would often work until 10:00 or 11:00 p.m., sometimes even later, and then fall asleep watching television.[94]

Wright was also busy campaigning and raising money for House colleagues. Although Wright's *Washington Post* obituary described his public speaking as "stentorian" and showing a relish for "folksy aphorisms and jokes," he was a popular speaker on the political hustings.[95] In fact, he was the backup speaker for Hale Boggs, where, if Boggs had been unable to go, Wright would have gone on the ill-fated plane trip to Alaska where Boggs and Nick Begich died on a political campaign trip.

———————

Pushing Too Hard

Wright pushed to centralize power in the Speaker's hands in ways unseen since the speakership of Joseph Cannon prior to the 1910 revolt against his power. Clearly, Republicans were opposed to a powerful Democratic Speaker. After all, James Baker noted, Wright "was a partisan and a damn good one," who was "as stubborn as a Brahma bull."[96] Democrats disliked his heavy-handed approach. Wright established deadlines for legislation that upset the members and he tightened the rules. He challenged the traditional jurisdictions of committees. He gained control over key committees. There was grumbling that he did not consult with members but dictated to them. There were also complaints from liberals that he compromised too much. Although there was strong support for sessions to be Tuesday through Thursday, Wright scheduled sessions on Fridays and Mondays. Perhaps the most significant criticism of Wright was that he insisted on tax increases even though it was widely believed to be a losing position for Democrats, who saw Walter Mondale go down in defeat in part because he advocated for increased taxes.[97]

The breaking point for Wright was the budget reconciliation bill in 1987. A loose agreement on the bill was made to cut spending and raise taxes, but Republicans wanted spending cuts and tax increases to occur simultaneously. The Boll Weevils agreed to support the reconciliation bill provided its welfare reforms were taken out, and Wright agreed to allow that in a rules vote preceding the final vote. Liberals, however, took the position that Wright had promised that the welfare reforms would be in the final bill. Wright was caught in conflicting promises and decided that the rules vote would go forward with the reforms included. That led to successful opposition from the Boll Weevils, and a second vote was scheduled with welfare reform deleted. Wright wanted a second vote immediately, but a second vote could not occur on the same day, so Wright ordered Congress adjourned and immediately reconvened, creating another legislative day and a chance for a second vote. Republicans were outraged and at the end of the vote, Wright was one vote short. Wright kept the clock running beyond the normal fifteen minutes for voting while Jim Chapman was persuaded to switch his vote in Wright's favor. Wright won, but Republicans almost rioted. Liberals resented the pressure he had put them under, and conservatives felt distrustful of him. Wright knew his victory had been costly and he had trouble sleeping.[98] Wright had gone too far, and it was at this point that one could argue his opponents gained the upper hand.[99]

Wright did not initially pay attention to the charges brought by Newt Gingrich—Gingrich was not a power in the House but rather a backbencher who took pleasure being a thorn in the side of O'Neill, Wright, and the Republican leader, Bob Michel. Gingrich was initially seen as leading a one-man crusade against Wright, but with Common Cause urging an ethics probe into sales of Wright's book *Reflections of a Public Man*, the ethics charges against Wright gained steam, and what followed was a steady drip of allegations against Wright and a media frenzy of unfavorable publicity. One problem was that Wright did not have a high opinion of lawyers and, unlike O'Neill, did not have counsel as majority leader or as Speaker. Another problem was that when the ethical charges started, Wright simply would not listen to advice. Jack Brooks tried numerous times to advise Wright on dealing with the allegations, and that irritated Wright, who finally exclaimed, "I have seen all of Jack Brooks I want to see."[100] Senior Democrats were irritated by Wright's leadership because by his efforts to centralize power in the Speaker's office, he was weakening the power of the committee chairmen. They saw Tom Foley as a more desirable person for Speaker since Foley was a caretaker with no agenda, unlike Wright who wanted to change things.[101] Wright was not the back-slapping politician that O'Neill was. While he had friends among the younger members, he did not cultivate them, and they chafed as well under Wright's demands. Wright became a target for Republicans when John Tower was defeated for secretary of defense. The mantra became "A Texan for a Texan." His efforts toward a Central American peace also angered Republicans, who saw him as interfering with executive control over foreign affairs. With the decline of the Southern Democrats, there was less need for a Texan in the leadership. In fact, with Wright's resignation as Speaker, the Austin-Boston pattern of Democratic leadership in the House came to an end.

After Wright resigned as Speaker, he spoke with the *Washington Post* and provided a superb summary of his career as a national political leader: "I was probably obsessed with the notion that I have a limited period of time in which to make my mark upon the future and, therefore, I must hurry. Maybe I was too insistent, too competitive, too ambitious to achieve too much in too short a period of time, and anyway I couldn't have changed."[102]

1   Pete Geren, interview by James Riddlesperger Jr. and Anthony Champagne, August 19, 2014.

2   Bill Alexander, interview by James Riddlesperger Jr. and Anthony Champagne, October 18, 2011.

3   James Riddlesperger Jr., Anthony Champagne, and Dan Williams, eds., *The Wright Stuff* (Forth Worth: TCU Press, 2013), 8.

4   Donald C. Bacon and Anthony M. Champagne, *Nicholas Longworth: The Aristocrat Speaker* (Lanham, MD: Lexington Books, 2021), 68.

5   James W. Riddlesperger Jr. and Anthony Champagne, *Lone Star Leaders* (Fort Worth: TCU Press, 2011), 137.

6   Jim Wright, *Worth It All* (Washington, DC: Brassey's, 1993), 8–32.

7   J. Brooks Flippen, *Speaker Jim Wright: Power, Scandal, and the Birth of Modern Politics* (Austin: University of Texas Press, 2018), 110–12.

8   James C. Wright Jr., oral history by Joe B. Frantz, Lyndon Baines Johnson Library, June 30, 1969, I-21–I-23.

9   For several years after he retired from Congress, James Riddlesperger and I would go to lunch with Wright from time to time and talk with him about his congressional career. He was very open in these conversations and, for example, willingly spoke of his reputation for being hot-tempered. Where it is mentioned in the text that Wright made a comment, it is from these luncheons.

10 Telephone conversation #13214, sound recording, LBJ and Jim Wright, July 24, 1968, 9:55 a.m., Lyndon Baines Johnson Library.

11 Wright, oral history, I-34.

12 John G. Tower, oral history by Joe B. Frantz, Lyndon Baines Johnson Library, August 8, 1971, I-8.

13 Wright, oral history, I-30.

14 John M. Barry, *The Ambition and the Power: The Fall of Jim Wright; A True Story of Washington* (New York: Viking, 1989), 53.

15 Wright, oral history, I-31.

16 Flippen, *Speaker Jim Wright*, 149–50.

17 Flippen, 163.

18 John Tower put it mildly when he said, "There was certainly no love lost between Ralph and Lyndon, that was always apparent." Tower, oral history, I-13.

19 Telephone conversation #1448, sound recording, LBJ and Houston Harte, January 20, 1964, 10:15 p.m., Lyndon Baines Johnson Presidential Library, University of Texas at Austin (hereafter LBJL).

20 Telephone conversation #1869, sound recording, LBJ and Jim Wright, February 2, 1964, 9:15 p.m., LBJL.

21 Telephone conversation #1863, sound recording, LBJ and Jack Brooks, February 3, 1964, 8:35 p.m., LBJL.

22 Telephone conversation #2082, sound recording, LBJ and George Brown, February 14, 1964, 12:20 p.m., LBJL.

23 Wright, oral history, 42.

24 Telephone conversation #8803, sound recording, LBJ and Jim Wright, September 1, 1965, 9:25 a.m., LBJL.

25 Wright, oral history, 43.

26 Barry, *Ambition*, 54.

27 Wright, oral history, 44.

28 Wright, oral history, 44.

29 Wright, oral history, 44.

30 LBJ Recording of Telephone Conversation, WH Series, 10962, LBJ and John Connally, October 16, 1966, 8:52 p.m., LBJL.

31 LBJ Recording of Telephone Conversation, WH Series, 10230, LBJ and George Meany, June 14, 1966, 10:32 a.m., LBJL.

32 LBJ Recording of Telephone Conversation, WH Series, 10629, LBJ and George Mahon, August 22, 1966, 11:14 a.m., LBJL.

33 LBJ Recording of Telephone Conversation, WH Series, 10962, LBJ and John Connally, October 16, 1966, 8:52 p.m., LBJL.

34 Lloyd Bentsen, oral history by Michael Gillette, Lyndon Baines Johnson Library, June 18, 1975, I-4–I-5.

35 Bentsen, oral history, I-4.

36 Al Reinert, "The Unveiling of Lloyd Bentsen," *Texas Monthly*, December 1974.

37 Jim Wright, diary, December 30, 1971, Jim Wright Papers, Mary Couts Burnett Library, Texas Christian University, Fort Worth, Texas (hereafter cited as JWP); Al Reinert, "The Unveiling of Lloyd Bentsen," *Texas Monthly*, December 1974.

38 Jim Wright, diary, December 30, 1971, JWP.

39 Jim Wright, diary, December 30, 1971, JWP.

40 Jim Wright, diary, December 30, 1971, JWP.

41 Jim Wright, diary, December 30, 1971, JWP.

42 Jim Wright, diary, January 6, 1972, JWP.

43 Jim Wright, diary, January 22, 1972, JWP.

44 Jim Wright, diary, February 2, 1972, JWP.

45 Jim Wright, diary, February 3, 1972, JWP.

46 Jim Wright, diary, February 3, 1972, JWP.

47 Jim Wright, diary, August 8, 1972, JWP.

48 Bob Bolin, interview by James Riddlesperger Jr. and Anthony Champagne, October 1, 2013.

49 Flippen, *Speaker Jim Wright*, 205; Kathy Mitchell, interview by James Riddlesperger Jr. and Anthony Champagne, May 24, 2013. Mitchell considered Edmondson to be among Wright's closest friends, as did Norma Ritchson. See Norma Ritchson, interview by James Riddlesperger Jr. and Anthony Champagne, October 1, 2013.

50 Jim Wright, diary, January 3, 1973, JWP; Jim Wright, diary, January 8, 1973, JWP.

51 Ritchson, interview.

52 Flippen, *Speaker Jim Wright*, 255.

53 Lanny Hall, interview by James Riddlesperger Jr. and Anthony Champagne, November 1, 2013.

54 John Mack, interview by James Riddlesperger Jr. and Anthony Champagne, May 23, 2013.

55 "Phillip Burton as described by Rep. George Miller," C-Span clip of Q&A with Rep. George Miller, June 8, 2014. Bill Alexander described Burton as having a "jolly ruthlessness" about him. Alexander, interview.

56 John Aloysius Farrell, *Tip O'Neill and the Democratic Century* (Boston: Little, Brown, 2001), 390–91.

57 Anthony Champagne et al., *The Austin/Boston Connection: Five Decades of House Democratic Leadership, 1937–1989* (College Station: Texas A&M University Press, 2009), 236–37.

58 Champagne et al., *Austin/Boston Connection*, 156.

59 Jim G. Bolling to Richard Bolling and Gillis Long, August 2, 1976, Richard Bolling Papers, University of Missouri-Kansas City Special Collections and Archives.

60 Jim Wright, interview by Ben Procter, Jim Wright Papers, TCU, April 26, 1992, 16.

61 Alexander, interview.

62. Barry, *Ambition*, 19.

63. Barry, *Ambition*, 25.

64 Paul Driskell, interview by James Riddlesperger Jr. and Anthony Champagne, January 23, 2015.

65 Driskell, interview.

66 Barry, *Ambition*, 22–23.

67 Mack, interview.

68 Steve Charnovitz, interview by James Riddlesperger Jr. and Anthony Champagne, May 24, 2013.

69 Mitchell, interview.

70 Barry, *Ambition*, 110.

71 Driskell, interview.

72 Mack, interview.

73 Ritchson, interview.

74 Jim Chapman, interview by Anthony Champagne, May 29, 2013.

75 Charnovitz, interview.

76 Charnovitz, interview; Geren, interview.

77 Mack, interview.

78 Mack, interview.

79 Dorothy Beard, interview by James Riddlesperger Jr. and Anthony Champagne, May 22, 2013.

80 Bolin, interview. Wright explained to Bolin that he memorized a few speeches to use just in case he was unexpectedly called on to speak at an event. On one occasion at a lunch with Wright, James Riddlesperger Jr. and I experienced a remarkable example of Wright's exceptional memory. Sam Rayburn's early mentor, Congressman, and later Senator, Joseph Weldon Bailey was mentioned. Wright proceeded to recite from memory Bailey's speech against his political opponents who tried to impeach him. Rayburn

had recited the speech to Wright decades previously. To this day, it is the most remarkable memory feat ever witnessed by Riddlesperger or myself.

81   Charnovitz, interview.

82   Mitchell, interview.

83   Frank Moore, oral history by Martin Elzy, Jimmy Carter Library and Museum, July 30–31, 2002, 30. Burton was seriously thinking about again challenging Wright for majority leader until the 1978 elections. See Flippen, *Speaker Jim Wright*, 281–82.

84   Mack, interview.

85   Charles Stenholm, interview with James Riddlesperger Jr. and Anthony Champagne, September 10, 2015.

86   Richard Fly, "Gramm's Opposition to Budget Angers Colleagues," *Dallas Times Herald*, April 12, 1981.

87   Phil Gramm to Jim Wright, January 8, 1981, JWP.

88   David S. Broder, "Diary of a Mad Majority Leader," *Washington Post*, December 13, 1981.

89   Jim Wright, interview by Ben Proctor, July 2, 1981, Jim Wright Papers, TCU.

90   Wright, interview.

91   Broder, "Diary."

92   Barry, *Ambition*, 147.

93   Wright, diary, October 18, 1977, JWP. Of course, his schedule involved more than receptions. He was in great demand for speaking. Staff member Norma Ritchson said it was not at all unusual for Wright to give seven speeches in a day. Ritchson, interview.

94   Barry, *Ambition*, 153–54.

95   Timothy R. Smith, "Jim Wright, House Speaker Who Resigned Amid an Ethics Investigation, Dies at 92," *Washington Post*, May 6, 2015.

96   James Baker, interview by James Riddlesperger Jr., April 27, 2012.

97   Flippen, *Speaker Jim Wright*, 358–59.

98   Flippen, 359–60.

99   New York Republican congressman David O'Brien Martin thought Wright made a huge mistake in keeping the vote open on that bill. He said that it allowed Newt Gingrich to say, "This is how they [Democrats] treat us" and

it gave influence to Gingrich among House Republicans. Martin thought events in the House would have taken another direction—a more positive one—had it not been for that vote. David O'Brien Martin, interview by James Riddlesperger Jr. and Anthony Champagne, October 18, 2011.

[100] Driskell, interview. Ralph Yarborough, for one thought, Wright too defensive over Gingrich's charges. He wrote, "Let him be bold as a lion, not a whimpering kitten." He much preferred Jack Brooks's advice for Wright to take a more aggressive stance in responding to Gingrich's attacks. Ralph Yarborough to Jack Brooks, June 8, 1989, Jack Brooks Papers, Briscoe Center for American History, Austin, Texas.

[101] Geren, interview.

[102] Smith, "Jim Wright."

Photo of Wright at his desk on Capitol Hill early in his career. Wright became famous for his excessively cluttered desk.

Wright leans over to talk with one of his most important mentors, Speaker Sam Rayburn at a 1956 fundraiser in Fort Worth. This photo features two House Speakers whose careers spanned from 1913–1989 between them (Rayburn 1913–1961, Wright 1955–1989).

Speaker Wright swears in future Speaker Nancy Pelosi, June 9, 1987. With Pelosi is her family, including her father Thomas D'Alesandro Jr. (seated in a wheelchair), who had served in Congress from 1937–1947 and later as mayor of Baltimore, Maryland. This picture features two speakers whose careers span from 1955–present (Wright 1955–1989, Pelosi 1987–present). *Photo courtesy of Congresswoman Pelosi's office.*

Speaker Jim Wright takes oath of office, January 6, 1987.

After being elected House majority leader in 1977, Wright worked closely with President Jimmy Carter (at left) and Speaker Thomas P. "Tip" O'Neill (center).

"I THINK IT'S A SIGNAL THEY'VE ELECTED A SPEAKER OF THE HOUSE. OFFHAND, I'D SAY IT'S JIM WRIGHT."

Fort Worth *Star-Telegram* cartoonist Etta Hulme foreshadows Wright's election as Speaker with a caricature of the Capitol Dome sporting Wright's signature bushy eyebrows. *Fort Worth Star-Telegram. Used by permission.*

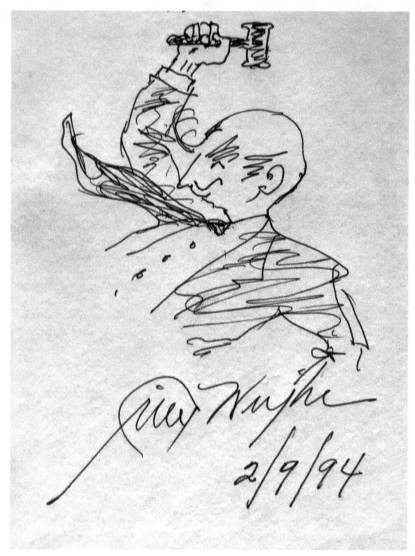

Jim Wright draws a whimsical sketch of himself wielding the Speaker's gavel and attaches his signature.

Speaker Jim Wright addresses the media regarding a drought relief bill. In the background are Congressmen Bill Gray (PA) and Morris Udall (AZ).

Four Speakers of the House. From left, Thomas P. "Tip" O'Neill (1977–1987), Carl Albert (1971–1977), Jim Wright (1987–1989), and Thomas Foley (1989–1995).

CHAPTER 8

Jim Wright and Foreign Policy

CARRIE LIU CURRIER

S cholars of foreign policy are interested in studying both macro- and micro-level factors that help explain the behavior of countries in the international arena. At the core is the question of conflict and cooperation, with realists and liberals offering opposing perspectives on whether peace is possible. Realists take a somewhat pessimistic view of the international system and assume that countries are in constant competition with one another and exist in a Hobbesian state of nature in which life is "solitary, poor, nasty, brutish, and short."[1]

Realists assume countries are guided by power, self-interest, and fear of domination by others, making war inevitable, even as it is not desirable. In contrast, liberalism offers a worldview in which peace is possible, power is not measured in military might alone, and the study of domestic actors makes a difference. The focus is on cooperation, human progress, interdependence, and the spread of democracy. Liberalism argues that economic and social issues matter.[2] Although this debate regarding war and peace is centuries old, with Thucydides's account of power politics in the *History of the Peloponnesian War* marking the birth of realism and Enlightenment-era works like Immanuel Kant's *Perpetual Peace* advancing liberalism, it is still useful for framing foreign policy in the contemporary period.[3]

In the context of the United States, the realist perspective is embodied by decision-makers like Theodore Roosevelt and Henry Kissinger, both of whom embraced the pursuit of power politics and emphasized the need for self-interest in an anarchic world. Liberalism, meanwhile, is associated with Woodrow Wilson, who promoted internationalism at the end of World War I and advocated for capitalism, democracy, and institutionalism. At the core of Wilson's approach was an emphasis on peace and diplomacy, where institutions served as one way to facilitate greater cooperation. It is also important to note that in international relations, realism and liberalism are more complex than their association with the terms *hawks* and *doves* when it comes to US foreign policy. The mindsets and worldviews that are associated with realism and liberalism are not limited to questions on the use of force.[4] The larger issues include thinking about how our world is structured and how different levels of analysis can provide insight on solutions to global problems.

The idea of examining a problem from multiple vantage points, or levels of analysis, has its roots in Kenneth Waltz's influential book *Man, the State, and War* (1959).[5] Waltz offers a framework to examine the causes of war by introducing three images: the system, the state, and the individual. The images address factors found in the international system itself (the system), the various elements within a country that guide its foreign policy (the state), and the key individuals who help construct that foreign policy (the individual). At the systemic level we examine the environment external to a country, such as geopolitics, alliances, intergovernmental organizations, and international law. At the state or domestic level, factors like public opinion, regime type, domestic institutions, parties, and the military industrial complex can all influence a country's foreign policy. And, finally, at the individual level we identify the key decision-makers and the psychology of decision-making. In the end, we can formulate a comprehensive view of how we reach certain policy outcomes.

Using these theories and concepts of international relations, this chapter examines Jim Wright's contributions in US foreign policy. While it is impossible to capture the many ways Wright was able to influence foreign policy over the thirty-four years he served in political office, there are a few key areas of his time as majority leader and Speaker of the House that deserve further consideration. His most distinguished accomplishments include his role as the first American to give an address on Soviet television, his role in Middle East peace, and his role in the Central American peace process. Each of these events will be examined considering the theoretical framework shaping the US worldview as well as using the systemic, domestic, and individual levels of analysis.

The Road Less Traveled

Jim Wright's interest in foreign affairs grew out of his youth. Wright came of age in the post-WWI and pre-WWII years and had a "lifelong interest in aviation and foreign policy."[6] When Pearl Harbor was bombed, he was in his third year of college and decided to enlist in the Army Air Corps to join the war on Fascism, which eventually took him to the South Pacific. Like many of his generation, Wright felt a strong sense of nationalism, which grew into a deep moral commitment to democracy and peace.[7] When the war ended, many returning young veterans viewed public service as a way to give back to their country. The global landscape had changed, the Cold War was beginning, and politics was a good entry point to start making a difference.

When Wright entered politics in his twenties, he could not have envisioned a thirty-four-year career that would span some of the most contentious times in US political history. His political career, starting with his time in the state legislature, then as mayor, and eventually in Congress, may have seemed more focused on local and domestic issues, but Wright's real passion was in international politics, and specifically the pursuit of international peace. When he eventually arrived in Washington, he was eager to get involved in foreign affairs. He wanted the opportunity to work with others to pursue peace and to defend the freedoms that the United States was both built on and was working to spread throughout the rest of the world. However, when Wright met with Speaker Sam Rayburn and indicated his preference to be part of the Foreign Affairs Committee, he was forced to set aside his foreign interests and was encouraged to serve on the Public Works Committee instead. Rayburn was interested in creating balance across committees for the Texas members of the House, and foreign affairs was considered more the Senate's arena. Rayburn convinced Wright that he would "help colleagues in the Texas delegation" best by serving on the Public Works Committee.[8]

Once on the Public Works Committee, Wright worked on highly sought-after infrastructure spending that helped him build networks among members in the House, eventually helping him get elected as majority leader in 1976.[9] One way he was able to use his position on Public Works to expand into the realm of foreign affairs was through America's interstate highway system. In 1956, the Public Works Committee passed legislation to connect the United States coast to coast by means of interstate highway. This vision went further, to Latin America, with the creation of the Pan-American Highway, which established roads to link the entire Western Hemisphere. The road would eventually connect North, Central, and South America for nineteen thousand miles, with just a small sixty-six-mile lapse in the rainforest, known as the Darien Gap. The Pan-American Highway was more than just a road—it was part of a greater sense of Pan-Americanism. Meant to strengthen peace and cooperation, the highway fit with Wright's general values as well as with his growing personal interest in Latin America. Wright took a few congressional trips to Panama over the years to help solidify some of this work, which enhanced his interest in Latin America more generally. He even attended the Foreign Service Language Institute for a time to learn Spanish, a language he saw as strategically important to the United States and he believed would "help him contribute more effectively."[10]

Although Wright's talk with Rayburn had moved him in a different direction from what he'd planned, he never lost his desire to be involved in the international policy realm. The events of his time helped solidify his deep moral commitment to democracy and peace, and for him foreign policy and domestic politics were often intertwined. Later this would create tension for Wright under different presidents. Where Wright saw the role of Congress in foreign affairs as a partnership, the executive branch under Nixon and Reagan saw things differently. By examining the three foreign affairs issues involving the Middle East, the Soviet Union, and Central America outlined previously, we can see why it is important to study these issues from different levels of analyses when examining individual actors like Jim Wright and his impact on key foreign policy events.

The First Stage of Middle East Peace

In addition to the challenges presented by Cold War alliance structures that pitted the US and Soviet spheres of influence against each other, international relations in the 1970s were also complicated by various regional geopolitical issues. One of the most contentious issues, and arguably among the most difficult to address on a global scale, involves how religion and nationalism intersect. Nowhere is this more apparent than in the Middle East and North Africa, where deep-rooted religious cleavages and contested territorial claims have led to conflict in the region.

At the systemic level of analysis, it is clear to see that geopolitically, Israel serves in a precarious physical location, surrounded by Arab countries. In addition, the sovereignty claims of Israel over Jerusalem and the significance this territory holds to both Arabs and

Jews affect countries beyond the immediate region. The alliance structures in place have put the United States in a unique position as an ally to both Israel and Egypt, who have competing interests in the region. That position creates important opportunities for the United States to help broker more peaceful relations among countries it considers its allies. Geopolitics, alliance structures, and fears of regional instability explain why the Middle East holds a special place of significance both then and now.

Domestic-level factors of importance within a country's governing apparatus include public opinion and feelings of nationalism. The strong sense of national identity that a citizenry embraces can greatly affect the way a country chooses to pursue various policies. Moreover, how various government institutions work with one another is also important. In the United States, the president is primarily the voice of American foreign policy. However, in some cases, "Congress may challenge the president's supposed monopoly on foreign policy," and this can result in "congressional foreign policy entrepreneurs."[11] At this time, Speaker Tip O'Neill's philosophy on Congress's role in foreign policy was that formal working missions by members of Congress to countries abroad "enhanced the capacity of Congress to deal with foreign problems."[12] In other words, Congress had a role to play, even in the early stages of formulating foreign policy. When institutions and the individuals who hold those government positions are in sync, it can be beneficial to achieving desired policy outcomes.

Generally, in matters of foreign policy, executive branch leaders are the ones emphasized, but given how complex country negotiations can be, and depending on the climate offered within a country as outlined above, the scope of individuals of interest can widen to include other key actors. While Jim Wright, House majority leader at the time, was not specifically in a foreign policy role for the United States, his importance to US political institutions and the opportunities it afforded him make him relevant to examine at the individual level of analysis.

Wright had an amicable relationship with President Carter, a man he felt he "knew at a deeper, personal level," and their similar worldviews, based on Wilsonian ideals of peace and cooperation, built a level of trust and admiration between them.[13] Without question, President Carter was the chief architect in the Camp David Accords, leading to the first formal peace agreement between Israel and any of its Arab neighbors. This meeting at Camp David was arguably the "greatest deed Jimmy Carter performed while in office" and one where, Wright said, "I've never felt better about any role I ever performed in my life."[14] Before that meeting could occur, several factors had to come together, and Wright found himself both in the right place and at the right time to help broker those early stages.

When Wright organized a congressional trip to Egypt and Israel in November 1977, he could not have known that the leaders of those two countries would soon open a door for negotiations. Israeli Prime Minister Menachem Begin was a Zionist, and Egypt's President Anwar Sadat was a devout Muslim and staunch nationalist. Nothing about their backgrounds indicated that they would be open to meeting at any point soon. But on November 9, 1977, two days before the American delegation was planning to arrive in the region, Sadat announced the lengths he would take to achieve peace with Israel, stating he was "even willing to go to the Knesset and discuss [peace] with them."[15] On the US delegation's visit with Sadat in Egypt a few days later, Wright was aware that an invitation to Jerusalem from Prime Minister Begin to President Sadat was coming, and he took the opportunity to ask President Sadat if he would go. Sadat replied in the affirmative: "Whenever the invitation arrives, I will be ready to go."[16] As the American delegation moved on to Israel, they, too, soon discovered the Knesset was extending a formal invitation to Sadat, which was quickly accepted. Wright recalls how the US delegation had prepared to leave ahead of this historic meeting, but that their Israeli hosts insisted they be present for the visit.[17] While this initial meeting did not have any formal measures determined, it did a lot to build trust and to lay the foundations of peace between the two neighbors. Wright admired Sadat for his passion to achieve peace.[18] These were values Wright wholeheartedly embodied during his entire career in politics. Wright said, "I have always identified, since the beginning of my interests in political activity, with the dream of Woodrow Wilson for a peaceful world."[19] As the first steps on the road to the Camp David Accords, it was clear to all that this was a historic moment. Journalists recall, "To those of us watching, it seemed as if the notion of family and personal friendship had overcome the barriers of nationality and nationhood."[20] Moreover, Wright's role as the leader for this American delegation brokering the first messages and witnessing these first interactions would leave him strategically positioned as a host to Sadat and Begin on their visits to the United States, as well as serving in an informal counseling role to President Carter regarding the two parties and further peace negotiations.[21]

Wilsonian values regarding peace and the desire to create a better world that extends beyond nationalism to forge a global identity that values the ability to communicate with and command respect from one another can be seen in each of the key actors in this case. Carter, Begin, Sadat, and Wright all placed emphasis on those core ideas and worked to move the people around them away from assuming the natural order of hostilities in a realist's world.

A Thaw in the Cold War

Looming over the Middle East peace process and other important global events of the time was the rivalry between the United States and the Soviet Union during the Cold War. During this time, there were several tests to the relationship between the United States and the Soviet Union that had the potential to destabilize the entire global order. At the systemic level it could be argued that power politics still reigned supreme, with the two superpowers concerned about preserving their self-interests in an uncertain world. Given that tensions were already running high between the two countries, the potential for a security dilemma to develop into all-out war was not impossible to imagine.[22] In a security dilemma, focusing on one's security by building defensive capabilities breeds insecurity and quickly leads countries into an arms race. For realists, an arms race can come to an end when one country thinks they have the upper hand and goes on the offensive, attacking first to avoid being taken by surprise when they have less relative power.

This type of thinking is dangerous with conventional arms but is even more so when one or both countries have nuclear weapons, which both the United States and the Soviet Union possessed. The escalation of conflict from a cold war to a hot war could lead to mutually assured destruction and global annihilation. The bipolar structure of the international system truly created an us-versus-them mentality. The Soviet invasion of Afghanistan tested the buffer zone that divided the Soviet sphere of influence from the Western sphere and represented a growing danger that Communism would start creeping into other parts of the world. When the United States boycotted the Moscow Olympic Games in 1980, the Soviets responded by boycotting the 1984 Olympics in Los Angeles. Tit-for-tat measures were continually taken by both sides to demonstrate that neither country wanted to look soft to the other.

At the domestic level of analysis, regime type is one factor to consider when examining why countries have conflict with each other. The Communist authoritarian regime of the Soviet Union was in sharp contrast with the democratic principles guiding the United States in their actions both at home and abroad. Democracies naturally have more input from various actors, whether from formal government institutions or through public opinion. The tensions that can exist between different branches of government are also something to consider, and in the cases examined here, competition existed between the executive and legislative branches regarding in whose domain foreign policy belonged. While Congress has an oversight and funding role in international affairs, some presidents, like Nixon and Reagan, tried to promote a stronger presidency role. These domestic concerns involving separation of powers and checks on authority are some of the benefits to a democratic system, even though they can lead to internal conflict.

The overarching worldview from the United States was still shaped by a superpower mentality, what Michael Mandelbaum identifies as the third age of American foreign policy. According to Mandelbaum, American foreign policy has been driven by ideological goals and the use of democratic processes for developing and operationalizing decisions. Again, one is reminded of the liberal notions embraced by Wilson that American foreign policy should be associated with promoting American values such as peace and democracy.[23]

Democracy, and how it serves as a pillar for American values, is the thread that transcends the different levels of analyses. At the individual level, there are several important actors, but three will be examined more closely in this case: Mikhail Gorbachev, Ronald Reagan, and Jim Wright. In 1985, Gorbachev became the general secretary of the Communist Party of the Soviet Union after the death of Konstantin Chernenko. His decision to introduce glasnost (political restructuring) and perestroika (economic opening) would forever change the world by reforming that nation's political and economic systems and eventually leading to the disbanding of the Soviet Union. Without Gorbachev and his reform-mindedness, Wright's visit to the Soviet Union and the tension this created with Reagan would not have followed.

Ronald Reagan viewed the Soviet Union as an adversary, a view that represented the realist tradition. His reference to the Soviet Union as "the Evil Empire" in a 1983 speech not only demonized the Soviet Union but also blamed them for the escalating arms race between the two countries.[24] Essentially, Reagan used the dichotomy of good against evil—another way to represent the us-versus-them mentality and to focus on power politics. In addition, Reagan's views on the presidency and its relationship to Congress were not the same as Carter's, with Carter more clearly having adopted liberal Wilsonian views. While Carter saw Congress as a partner to the presidency and was comfortable sharing information, Reagan and those around him wanted to strengthen the presidency and did not see a role for Congress in foreign affairs. This difference between the two administrations sets up conflicts between the legislative and executive branches in terms of information sharing and oversight.

It is here that Jim Wright offers an important counterbalance to Reagan and his ideas on the Soviet Union. Wright was more reflective of liberalism and the notions of interdependence and co-operation that were embraced by Wilson. Reflecting on his study of World War I, he wrote: "The Senate had bungled it badly for all of us by rejecting the League of Nations. If nations could talk out their problems, I reasoned, we wouldn't have to kill each other."[25] Wright was a student of Wilson's speeches and he "heartily embraced" Wilson's views that foreign policy should focus on peace and democracy.[26] Moreover, while Wright had always remained interested in foreign affairs, he was finally able to embrace these interests when he ascended to House leadership, and his leadership in foreign policy became exceptional for a member of the legislative branch, even for a Speaker.

Although much of the focus on the thawing of the Cold War publicly rests on the shoulders of Reagan and Gorbachev, the groundwork for the thaw begins with Wright's visit to the Soviet Union with a House contingent in April 1987.[27] This group, led by Speaker Wright, was "the highest-ranking US Congressional group ever to visit the USSR," and the visit was an important opportunity for dialogue and the exchange of ideas.[28] At the time, Gorbachev was still somewhat of an unknown, and Wright was anxious to see what he was all about. When Wright arrived in Moscow, he met with top Kremlin leaders, including Gorbachev, for two hours. However, he did not want to restrict his meetings to just government officials, and like a true politician from the democratic tradition, he wanted to be able to interact with regular people, which included a request to visit a dairy farm.[29] Reaching out to the average person was important to Wright, and in his diary, he reveals that his beliefs and values about finding common ground were deeply embedded in his psyche. In 1972 on a visit to Leningrad, he wrote, "I get the feeling that the people themselves are not so very much different, inside, than are our people."[30] Later he wrote, "One recalls here that the Soviet Union, like the United States, is a highly pluralistic society, perhaps culturally much more so because it is less mobile. I wish it were possible for me to take a month and visit small towns and the countryside. I'd like to know these people better and learn what makes them tick. I have the feeling that their individual inner aspirations are not widely different from our own."[31] Reaching out from the grassroots level was important to Wright, and the visit was structured to reflect those values.

One of the most notable features of the 1987 visit was that Wright, at the invitation of Soviet leaders, addressed the Soviet people in a televised speech, becoming the first American ever to appear unedited on Soviet TV. Wright was tapped for this honor not because he was the head of the delegation but because he had written "A Letter to Ivan" in 1958 where he envisioned peace between the two countries. Rather than continuing down a path toward a security dilemma and arms races, Wright wrote a letter to an imaginary Soviet citizen named Ivan, appealing to the two people's common desires to better their respective populations by redirecting "guns" spending to "butter" spending.[32] In the letter, he embraced the idea that the Soviet Union was not an enemy to the United States and that perhaps its people were not so different from the average American citizen. This letter was one of many reasons Wright was the perfect person to extend an olive branch on behalf of the United States.

In fact, during Wright's visit with Kremlin officials, they made it clear that the Soviets were interested in making steps toward cooperation. This in-person meeting was proving to be a big first move in breaking down misperceptions, and the immediate impact these personal interactions had on both sides could be seen by all those present. One of the largest issues of concern was the escalating arms race between the two countries. On the visit, Wright appealed to the Soviets that a nuclear arms race was "pointless" and that they should work together on disarmament.[33] Upon his return to the United States, Speaker Wright stated: "We think this moment in history presents the best opportunity we have had in the past 50 years to produce an agreement, mutual and verifiable, on reduction of arms."[34] Walls were not coming down yet, but tools were being shared to start chipping away at the bricks. Wright's views on cooperating, making peace, and negotiating reflected Wilsonian liberalism and were the same ideals that would be the hallmark of his legacy.

The address Wright gave on Soviet television was essentially an updated version of the Letter to Ivan, in which he reached out to the average Soviet citizen and appealed to them as fellow global citizens, with one important addition. In the televised version, Wright encouraged Soviet citizens to reach out and write him a personal letter, one of the most democratic moves one could make, and if they did so, he would not only personally reply but also would send them a lapel pin of an intertwined US and Soviet flag. The pin was a symbol of the peace and cooperation he envisioned for their combined futures and was another way he put Wilsonian ideals back into foreign affairs.

This outreach, presented on Soviet primetime television, would result in nearly 2,500 letters from Soviet citizens. Those who wrote to Wright clearly saw his message of peace and working together to achieve a common goal. One letter Wright received stated: "We, Soviet people, want to live in peace with all peoples of our small and very fragile Earth."[35] They "pray that Americans try to show less supremacy and hopes that they will learn more about the Russian people."[36] Wright truly reached into the hearts and minds of the Soviet citizenry, where letters he received noted "the sincerity and passion of [Mr. Wright's] word" and said: "I have come to the conclusion that it would be great if you were in R. Reagan's position."[37] Dimitry Bonder, a tenth grader, added: "Like other young citizens of our country, I discovered a second [different] America represented by you."[38] Wright moved the citizenry so much that they felt compelled to write to him, and this connection began to break down the hard, realist talk that was portrayed by other top American officials. The values Wright embodied and his grassroots approach to diplomacy were a welcome contrast to the rhetoric embraced by the executive branch of the US government. Individuals make a difference, and the micro level matters.

Central America as the Last Dance

The effects of the Cold War were not limited to the relationship between the United States and the Soviet Union, and the Cold War involved several other countries that represented battlegrounds for US and Soviet influence. Conflict over the global spread of Communism and the erosion of democracy were some of the driving forces of engagement by both superpowers in different parts of the developing world. Geopolitically, the United States was more isolated from many global conflicts than the Soviet Union was, and it did not have to worry about spillover effects in the same way the Soviet Union did. However, Latin America held strategic significance to the United States, and the United States, given its geographical proximity to the region, watched events there closely. The lessons learned from the security dilemma of the Cuban missile crisis, the global alliance structures in place, and the role of geopolitics all set the stage at the systemic level for a major foreign policy challenge.

International issues like the hostage crisis in Iran, the Soviet invasion of Afghanistan, and the fear of Communism spreading to Latin America were all affecting the American foreign policy apparatus at the domestic level. Within the United States, as previously mentioned, there were growing tensions between the executive and legislative branches. Under these conditions, "the role of party leader becomes especially important during divided government, as the speaker becomes a natural counterpoint to the president."[39] During the 1980s, the Iran-Contra Affair would tarnish Reagan's leadership and create low approval ratings, the Democrats would retake the Senate in 1986 to create a Democratic Congress to counterbalance a Republican president, and Reagan's second term would make him a lame duck president. All of this set the stage for conflict between the two branches of government.[40] Institutional tension and the role of public opinion were key domestic-level factors that set up the events to follow regarding negotiating peace and ending the conflict in Central America. In addition, the role of elections and party politics is important to examine. Elections in both Nicaragua and El Salvador were watched carefully with the hope that democratic elements would be upheld and that the voices of the people could facilitate real change within the countries and put an end to conflict. Later, when the Sandinistas postponed elections, they altered the level of trust that US policy was based on. These domestic-level elements had consequences affecting how the different countries approached their negotiations.

Within Latin American countries, another factor was the role of nationalism, and particularly how countries might view unwanted external intervention. Countries like the United States came with their own political baggage, and while some might want to emulate US policies, the line between being seen as a model versus being seen as imposing ideas from the outside was tricky. Nationalism, and the rejection of imperialism, was also an element relevant to many Latin American countries at the time. Countries like Chile, Peru, Mexico, Costa Rica, Guatemala, El Salvador, and Nicaragua all held varying degrees of distrust for countries like the United States, given some of the ways covert operations were being utilized in the region.[41]

During his presidency, Reagan worked hard to prime the American public with the Communism versus Democracy imagery, repeatedly linking Nicaragua to Cuba as the source of training for Nicaraguan fighters and trying to scare the public into seeing Nicaragua as Marxist.[42] Arguably, Reagan wanted support for aggressive intervention in Central America, and framing the issues in this way could help his agenda. It was clear that the idealism principles found with presidents Kennedy and Carter had changed, and Reagan was more interested in relying on "the CIA and other intelligence agencies."[43] However, Congress did not see it the same way and early on voted against supporting any "military or paramilitary operations in Nicaragua."[44] Reagan's approach to the situation was to adopt a power politics stance, eventually authorizing covert operations to achieve his policy objectives. The use of covert operations would eventually be seen as "driving a wedge between branches of government" and undermining US interests in the region.[45] Since Reagan was never convinced that elections in Central America would truly be democratic, he discounted the possibility that democracy could take root without outside intervention. It was clear throughout that he felt the use of covert operations, economic pressure, and harsh rhetoric was the only way to go.

As we look at how individuals can have an impact on foreign policy, Reagan's heavy-handed power politics approach to conflict represents one route. However, one could argue that hardline tactics were pushing countries away from the United States rather than toward it. Another way to approach conflict is to think more collaboratively about how one can help mediate among disputing parties, build trust among the actors involved, and use existing institutions or structures to create the right environment for cooperation. From the US perspective, the goals were to quell conflict, to help instill democratic values and institutions, and to counter the rise of authoritarianism and the spread of Communism in the developing world. However, it would take individuals who were peace minded and interested in brokering an agreement rather than those invested in strong-arming locals into accepting an agreement if there was any chance to end conflict in the region.

Jim Wright's importance to Central American peace is undeniable, and when he became Speaker, he was able to expand the speakership role more solidly into foreign affairs. Wright was not trying to grab power from the president, and his actions would end up offering a counterbalance to the more hawkish approach adopted by the White House at the time. Wright explained he was attempting to "reassert and reaffirm the historic role of Congress in the foreign affairs of the country."[46] He also would later reflect that his only regret in the peace process was that he had "not been able to properly communicate with the White House [his] desire to work with them and not against them."[47] At the core of his approach was a refocusing of politics on institutions and the shared responsibilities between Congress and the presidency and the role of individuals to serve the interests of those institutions and the country at large. In this case, the goal was to avoid Central American states from leaning toward Soviet and Marxist influences and to encourage peace and a democratic constitutional form of government. Reagan saw the move differently, suggesting that Wright was interfering or usurping power and that Congress did not have a role to play in foreign affairs.[48] Wright's critics even went as far as to suggest that Wright had broken the law in negotiating directly with foreign leaders.[49] However, it is clear that the differences that existed between Reagan and Wright, and the way those tensions materialized in domestic politics, could have led to an entirely different outcome in the negotiations for peace.

In terms of the situation in Central America, Wright had developed expertise in Central American issues over the years, and his interest and experience were noticed by President Carter. Carter asked Wright to visit Nicaragua on several occasions to help sort out conflicting information and to ensure the government was making progress on human rights. Prior to a visit in June 1980, Wright managed to save an aid package that was on the chopping block by proposing an amendment that would require the Nicaraguan government to report to Congress their progress on human rights as a condition of that aid.[50] The amendment was essential for setting a positive tone to the delegation's visit and was an economic olive branch that demonstrated the United States' commitment to helping the governing junta in Nicaragua. Wright's approach to the region consistently drew on Wilsonian ideals regarding the possibilities for peace and the importance of international institutions. He was not interested in having the United States work alone or be seen as imposing ideas from the outside but instead wanted to "call on that organization [the OAS] which had been created for that express purpose" of helping Latin American countries resolve conflicts.[51]

The situation in Central America had become volatile for many reasons. The United States was mired in scandal over supporting the rebel Contras against the Sandinista government. El Salvador wanted other countries to stop aiding Marxist guerillas at its borders. The Guatemalan government was under attack by rebels, with refugees flooding into neighboring countries. Honduras had become a training ground for Nicaraguan rebels aided by the United States. And each of these countries, including Costa Rica, was being affected by the surrounding conflicts and feared spillover effects and threats to the fragile democratic structures in place.[52] The United States's role was not entirely external, with a clear hand in trying to guarantee those governments would be democratic and not left leaning.

While the details of the conflicts in these countries are beyond the scope of this chapter, the negotiation of peace is central. In particular, the important issues to examine are how the individual level of analysis matters in the negotiation of Central American peace and, more specifically, Jim Wright's role in the negotiations. Wright's worldview stood in contrast with the perspective and policies President Reagan was trying to forward, and Wright's work behind the scenes was instrumental in achieving the peace accord that would eventually lead to a cease fire and to democratic elections in Nicaragua.

As we examine the impact individuals have on the policy process, one of the first elements is to understand the individual's worldview. In this case, the liberal notion that peace is possible is an important starting point. Wright's goal was to make peace in the region, and he achieved this by trying to take the use of force and covert activity off the table in exchange for dialogue. When one approaches a situation assuming conflict is inevitable, your adversaries cannot be trusted, and negotiation is worthless, then you do nothing to facilitate peace. However, Wright actively worked against this realist mindset, supporting the Boland Amendment in 1983, which prohibited the use of funds to support covert or military action to overthrow the Nicaraguan government. Instead, he led several diplomatic missions to Central America and engaged in personal outreach to Central American leaders like Daniel Ortega, José Napoleón Duarte, and Óscar Arias Sánchez to facilitate peace talks among them. In the aftermath of the Iran-Contra Affair, it would take an enormous amount of effort to rebuild some of the trust lost, and Wright was ready to step up to the challenge. Reagan focused on his own popularity among right-wing members of Congress by promoting the Contras and didn't "really have any faith in the Sandinistas."[53] However, it was Wright who reached out to Ortega and the Sandinistas and argued that the Sandinistas were "willing to negotiate with the Contras so long as the Contras will stop making war against them, or so long as the United States will stop financing the war against them."[54]

Wright's history as a statesman and peace builder allowed him to focus on the greater goal of peace. In fact, his role in the peace process and the conflict it created with Reagan, in spite of its enormous success, was arguably a factor leading to the premature end to his political career. Wright wanted to bridge the executive gap, work across the aisles to help foster bipartisanship, and show a unified front between Congress and the White House in the various negotiations. He helped draft the Reagan-Wright plan in 1987, which took force off the table and was an effort to rebuild trust in the region. The plan was a six-point process of reconciliation between Nicaragua and El Salvador, with the region's countries signing on to ensure they would not aid any groups who were trying to overthrow the government of a neighbor.[55] The hard work Wright put in behind the scenes to work with Ortega toward developing an agreement all parties could uphold was not well received by Reagan. Reagan snidely referred to it as the Wright-Ortega plan, demonstrating unfounded hostility toward an agreement that was moving them all closer to peace.[56] While Reagan wavered in his support for the proposal, Wright never lost sight of the goal and continued to support Central American leaders.[57]

Wright did not seek glory for his role; rather he worked behind the scenes because he understood what was needed to accomplish peace. He knew his adversaries, recognizing that the Central American leaders had to make a deal look good at home with their domestic populations and not have it be seen as dictated by an external power.[58] Wright explained that "it is infinitely better that they [the Central American countries] now have embraced this democratization plan and this reconciliation plan, and each of them has signed it and committed himself and his country to fulfill it and carry it out. Thus, it isn't being forced upon them by the United States."[59] The trust those leaders had in him helped Wright achieve the impossible, convincing the Sandinistas to accept Cardinal Miguel Obando y Bravo to serve as a go-between despite their dislike of Obando. Wright's experience in the region, the integrity he brought to his negotiation role, and his political savviness made him an honest broker. Costa Rican president Óscar Arias would eventually get the Nobel Peace Prize for his leadership in perfecting the plan set out by Wright. And President George H. W. Bush would later tell Wright that peace in Nicaragua would never have happened without Wright's involvement, but Wright would get no other prominent accolades for his role.[60]

In the end, Wright managed to help end the conflict in Nicaragua in 1988 by leading a compromise to end the US-financed war between the Sandinistas and the Contras. His approach led to constructive talks among the five Central American countries and eventually to democratically held elections. While his first foray into Central America was the Pan-American Highway project, Wright was now building new roads to help connect Central America with the United States so that the regions could truly be good neighbors rather than be seen as different entities.

A Commitment to Peace

As conflict continues to plague international relations across the globe, it is easy to fall back on the realist idea that despite not *wanting* war, war is simply inevitable. If one adopts that mentality, then the efforts to pursue peace seem fruitless and war becomes a self-fulfilling prophecy—war is inevitable. From the systemic, to the domestic, to the individual levels of analyses we can clearly see that the outcome we reach has many paths to get there. We must look at the world's problems from multiple vantage points while not losing sight of the fact that individuals matter, and their world-views matter. If it were not for Wilson's ideals on peace and the pursuit of American democratic values, we might be looking at a very different world from the one we see today.

Jim Wright is one of many influential political figures important to the study of Cold War conflicts, but more importantly he is a key piece to understanding peace processes and negotiations in those conflicts. While we often spend time in American history examining our failures where conflict occurs and then evaluating what we did wrong, we do not spend enough time looking at the successes, where peace is negotiated and where conflict is avoided. Wright's thirty-four-year career in the House and a lifetime of political involvement may have ended prematurely, but the hallmarks of his legacy in foreign affairs live on today and remind us that individuals and the philosophies that guide them matter quite a bit in the study of foreign policy. Moreover, the limitations on the speakership that Wright faced when it comes to foreign policy are no longer the same today. Subsequent Speakers have become more assertive in the foreign policy arena, and the foundations for this path were laid by Jim Wright. Wright's pioneering work in the realm of foreign policy is a good lesson that the right mindset can give peace a chance.

1   Thomas Hobbes, *Leviathan*, First Avenue Classics ed. (Minneapolis: Lerner, 2018), 130.

2   Elizabeth Matthews and Rhonda Callaway, *International Relations Theory: A Primer* (Oxford: Oxford University Press, 2017), 75–77.

3   See Immanuel Kant, *Perpetual Peace: A Philosophical Sketch* (Konigsberg, Germany: F. Nicolovius, 1795), and Thucydides, *History of the Peloponnesian War*, ed. M. I. Finley, trans. Rex Wilson (New York: Penguin, 1972).

4   Stephen Walt, "Hawks, Doves, and Realists," *Foreign Policy*, July 28, 2010.

5   Kenneth Waltz, *Man, the State and War: A Theoretical Analysis* (New York: Columbia University Press, 1959).

6   J. Brooks Flippen, *Speaker Jim Wright: Power, Scandal, and the Birth of Modern Politics* (Austin: University of Texas Press, 2018), 9.

7   Ginger McGuire, daughter of James Wright, interview by Carrie Liu Currier, April 16, 2022.

8   Jim Wright, *Balance of Power: Presidents and Congress from the Era of McCarthy to the Age of Gingrich* (Atlanta: Turner, 1996), 40.

9   Flippen, *Speaker Jim Wright*, 11.

10   Wright, *Balance of Power*, 186.

11   Jordan T. Cash, "'The Voice of America': The Speaker of the House and Foreign Policy Agenda-Setting," *Polity* 53, no. 4 (2021): 666; Ralph G. Carter and James M. Scott, "Taking the Lead: Congressional Foreign Policy Entrepreneurs in US Foreign Policy," *Politics and Polity* 32, no. 1 (2004): 34–71.

12   Wright, *Balance of Power*, 298.

13   Wright, 267.

14   Wright, 297.

15   President Anwar Sadat's speech to the People's Assembly, November 9, 1977, Cairo, Egypt, https://sadat.umd.edu/sites/sadat.umd.edu/files/Excerpts%20from%20a%20Speech%20to%20the%20People's%20Assembly.pdf.

16   Marshall L. Lynam, *Stories I Never Told the Speaker: The Chaotic Adventures of a Capitol Hill Aide* (Dallas: Three Forks, 1998), 124.

17   Wright, *Balance of Power*, 303–4.

18 Jim Wright, interview by Ben Procter, October 30, 1981, Jim Wright Papers, Mary Couts Burnett Library, Texas Christian University, Fort Worth, Texas (hereafter cited as JWP).

19 Jim Wright, interview by Ben Procter, March 17, 1985, JWP.

20 John Martin, "An American Journalist Looks Back: Sadat, Begin, and the Palestinians: The Gamble that Helped Spawn a 40-Year Peace," *Viewpoints* 122 (December 2017): 4.

21 Wright, *Balance of Power*, 306–7.

22 The security dilemma is when two actors distrust the motivations of other actors in their pursuit of security and perceive a country's efforts to fortify their defense as offense. Country A works on building its defensive capabilities because they are in continual fear of domination by others, but in doing so, country B sees these efforts to enhance defense as an indication that they are preparing for war. Hence, country B must invest in its own defensive capabilities to avoid being seen as vulnerable or unprepared for an eventual attack.

23 Michael Mandelbaum, *The Four Ages of American Foreign Policy* (New York: Oxford, 2022). For discussion of Mandelbaum's ideas, see Thomas Friedman, "The Ukraine War Still Holds Surprises. The Biggest May Be for Putin," *New York Times*, June 7, 2022.

24 Ronald Reagan's "Evil Empire" speech to the National Association of Evangelicals, March 8, 1983, https://www.reaganlibrary.gov/public/archives/textual/topics/evilempire.pdf.

25 Wright, *Balance of Power*, 25.

26 Wright, 152.

27 Eighteen colleagues accepted the Speaker's invitation to go to Moscow, including majority leader Tom Foley, majority whip Tony Coelho, and five Republicans, including Dick Cheney. For more on those in the delegation, see Lynam, *Stories I Never Told the Speaker*, 90.

28 Lynam, *Stories I Never Told the Speaker*, 91.

29 For more on the story of the dairy farm visit and how it fell short of expectations, see Lynam, *Stories I Never Told the Speaker*, 91–94.

30 Jim Wright, diary, December 6, 1972, JWP.

31 Jim Wright, diary, December 8, 1972, JWP.

32 The guns-versus-butter debate represents a conflict over appropriations, whether more money should be spent on the military (guns) or social welfare programs (butter).

33 Andrew Mangan, "Hundreds of Letters Pouring into Speaker's Office from Soviet Union," Associated Press, May 13, 1987.

34 William J. Eaton, "Best Chance for Arms Pact—Wright: War Is 'Common Enemy,' Visiting Speaker Tells Soviets," *Los Angeles Times*, April 19, 1987.

35 Evgueniy Andryushchenko to Jim Wright, April 20, 1987, JWP.

36 Galina Arkhipovna to Jim Wright, 1987, JWP.

37 Dimitry Bogdanov to Jim Wright, April 24, 1987, JWP; O. Ganye to Jim Wright, April 22, 1987, JWP.

38 Dimitry Bonder to Jim Wright, May 10, 1987, JWP.

39 Cash, "Voice of America," 672.

40 Cash, "Voice of America," 682.

41 Jim Wright, *Worth It All* (New York: Brassey's, 1993), 38–39.

42 Wright, *Balance of Power*, 416.

43 Wright, *Worth It All*, 37.

44 Wright, *Balance of Power*, 421.

45 Wright, *Worth It All*, 37.

46 Jim Wright, interview by Ben Procter, May 31, 1987, JWP.

47 Jim Wright, interview by Ben Procter, March 31, 1988, JWP.

48 Ginger McGuire, daughter of James Wright, interview by Carrie Liu Currier, June 27, 2022.

49 John Barry, "The House of Jim Wright: How a Short-Lived Speakership Made Congressional Gamesmanship the New Normal," *Politico*, May 7, 2015.

50 Wright, *Balance of Power*, 415.

51 Wright, 422.

52. James Lemoyne, "Central American Peace Accord Goes into Effect," *New York Times*, November 6, 1987.

53 Jim Wright, interview by Ben Procter, August 23, 1987, JWP.

54 Jim Wright, interview by Ben Procter, August 23, 1987, JWP.

55 Wright, *Balance of Power*, 464.

56 Wright, 471.

57 Ben Proctor, "Jim Wright," in *Profiles in Power: Twentieth-Century Texans in Washington*, ed. Kenneth E. Hendrickson Jr., Michael L. Collins, and Patrick Con (Austin: University of Texas Press, 2004), 248.

58 Barry, "House of Jim Wright."

59 Jim Wright, interview by Ben Procter, August 8, 1987, JWP.

60 Ginger McGuire, daughter of James Wright, interview by Carrie Liu Currier, June 27, 2022.

61 Cash, "Voice of America," 689.

Majority Leader Wright grasps hands with Israeli Prime Minister Menachem Begin as part of the Middle East peace process, 1980.

Wright greets Egyptian President Anwar Sadat as part of the Middle East peace process, 1980.

Wright greets Costa Rican President Óscar Arias in his quest for peace in Central America, 1989.

Wright (left) and his wife Betty speak to Soviet leader Mikhail Gorbachev on a 1987 trip where Wright became the first American to address the Soviet people live on television.

Etta Hulme portrays Speaker Wright as the power behind President Reagan in navigating the swamps of Central America while trying to negotiate peace in the area. *Fort Worth Star-Telegram. Used by permission.*

CHAPTER 9

Speaker Wright in the Spotlight: Political and Party Leadership on the National Stage

DOUGLAS B. HARRIS

J anuary of 1988, Speaker Jim Wright was preparing to offer the national Democratic response to the last State of the Union address that Ronald Reagan would give as president of the United States. To be on the national stage was certainly a significant accomplishment for Wright, a one-time mayor of Weatherford, Texas, and the son of a traveling salesman. That night Wright's role was to be "the Speaker of the US House of Representatives" and the standard bearer for the Democrats celebrating their legislative achievements in the first session of the One-Hundredth Congress. His task was to deliver a message that could help the party offer a viable alternative to Reaganism and win the White House in the upcoming election year.

The straight-to-camera televised address was famously the Great Communicator Reagan's forte. To be sure, Speaker Wright was, by this time, no mere novice in national media work. He had spent a decade as House majority leader, not only doing the inside work of legislative leadership but also preparing for media moments like this one. Throughout his career, Wright was reputed to be an outstanding floor speaker, and he was atypically media savvy for a politician of his age and era. But Reagan was one of the all-time greats, a former actor seemingly tailor-made for the television era of American politics. House Democrats had been studying Reagan's media performances at a party message retreat when one leadership communications staffer concluded, "We just don't have that kind of talent in our party right now."[1] Of course, reaching that conclusion said more about Reagan's skills and likability than it did about Jim Wright or, for that fact, about Tony Coelho, Dick Gephardt, or any of the other Democratic voices at the time.

Translating Wright's speaking skills honed on the House floor and his Texas style for a national audience took some work. Many seasoned politicians of the era were, like Wright, still learning the ins and outs of television, including having to figure out the basics— what to wear, where to look, etc.—of making their appearances watchable and making their messages connect with a national audience. Media preparation notes—suggestions from staff—written on Speaker Wright's schedule offered the Speaker some telling advice on his appearance:

Items to Bring with You Monday for Evening Telecast

★ Dark blue suit with vest

★ Light blue or light gray shirt

★ Several ties

★ Dark shoes—not boots.[2]

This and other aspects of the overall preparation—which included practice runs of the response with Democratic consultants weighing in on presentation and message—reflected the high stakes of being on the national stage with the end of the Reagan era in sight.

For all of Reagan's strengths, by the late 1980s, it seemed to be more Jim Wright's moment on the national stage. As Speaker, Wright was off to a momentous start in 1987. With Reagan term-limited and in the lame-duck period of this second term,

Wright had been driving the national agenda from the purview of the House speakership, and Reagan, hampered by the Iran-Contra scandal and with Republicans having lost control of the Senate in 1986, was waning in influence. Asked during the Speaker's daily press conference that morning if the Democrats' message would be "that the Reagan era is over," Wright would admit only, "that might be sort of an undertone" and instead insisted that the messaging would be put more in a "positive sense rather than a negative sense. We're saying that the Congress has assumed its responsibility. In cases where the President fails to provide leadership, the Congress fills the need."[3]

For two and half years in the speakership, Jim Wright would be one of the two or three most powerful political figures in the United States of America. Nevertheless, for Wright, taking center stage and going toe-to-toe on national television with the Great Communicator president—not once but twice in this format—must have been one of the high points of a political career that saw him interact with every president since Dwight D. Eisenhower. It was also a symbol of just how potent Wright's leadership had become. In a real way, Wright had been preparing to lead the national Democratic Party for decades, and now he was riding high and was in the national spotlight.

Front Row Seat: Jim Wright's View of Leadership

Wright had had a front row seat to national leadership since he first came to Congress in 1954, during the midterm elections of Dwight Eisenhower's first term. Going to the US House of Representatives in the mid-twentieth-century Congress—what many political scientists call the "textbook Congress"—meant that Wright's first exposure to national politics was at a time when there was a considerable amount of cross-party cooperation and compromise, when committees were prominent in legislative decision-making, and when Congress was on the whole quite focused, domestically, on problem-solving and policymaking on bread-and-butter issues like transportation and economic prosperity, allowing some cautious expansions of the New Deal state in the Eisenhower years, and, in foreign policy, building consensus to fight the Cold War.[4] Although race relations and the push for civil rights would continue and McCarthyite tactics would divide and undermine America's consensus resolve to fight the Soviets, broad agreements could still bridge party divides in America, particularly where congressional leaders and presidents chose to cooperate.

Just as notable is the fact that Texas was prominent in national politics when Wright first went to Congress. Upon Wright's election, the House and Senate minority leaders—Texans Sam Rayburn and Lyndon Johnson—were poised to become Speaker and Senate majority leader, respectively, upon the beginning of the Eighty-Fourth Congress. Moreover, Democrats' majority status, which would be uninterrupted throughout the entirety of Wright's thirty-five years in Congress, would also turn over committee gavels to several prominent Texans in the Eighty-Fourth Congress and in subsequent decades. For Texas as much as any other state, national leadership was part of the career path of representatives and senators in the second half of the twentieth century, owing not only to the seniority that Texas Democrats would accumulate during that time but also to Speaker Rayburn, who was skilled at spotting talented young members of Congress and mentoring them.

Sam Rayburn, Speaker for seventeen of the twenty-one years from 1940 to 1961, looms large. Wright was among Rayburn's many protégés and was a self-described devoted friend and admirer of the Speaker.[5] In Wright's view, Rayburn was "the greatest lawmaker in the history of this nation."[6] More to the point, Rayburn was the model from whom Wright "formed [his] basic concept of a Speaker's function: He saw national needs and made things happen. Under his guidance, the legislative branch fulfilled a role more creative than passive, initiating much of the domestic agenda during the Eisenhower presidency, when one party held the White House and the other led in Congress."[7] Although Wright observed that his own leadership style "wasn't consciously imitative" of Rayburn's leadership style, Wright's approach to working with members was, he reflected, "founded in things I had heard from Sam Rayburn."[8] Additionally, Rayburn's longtime alliance with majority leader John McCormack of Massachusetts, known as the Austin-Boston connection, would serve as an example to Wright of how to balance the Democratic Party's Southern base with its more liberal Northern and Western contingents.[9]

Another of Rayburn's protégés had ascended as high as any could. Lyndon B. Johnson, whom Rayburn promoted in Democratic circles and "treat[ed] like family," had left the House for the Senate in the 1948 elections and was the Senate Democratic leader throughout the Eisenhower years.[10] Although he fell short of winning the Democratic presidential nomination in 1960, Johnson was, of course, added to the 1960 ticket alongside John F. Kennedy, tragically becoming president upon Kennedy's November 1963 assassination.

Wright had known Johnson since before Wright came to Congress, and Johnson would promote Wright's career, even encouraging him, for example, to run for the Senate in 1966.[11] Wright, who at one point in time had harbored his own presidential ambitions, admired LBJ and frequently spoke of him in glowing terms. Johnson, Wright said, "was the last twentieth-century president to have a huge, romantic vision of what this nation should be and a passion to goad and guide two hundred million fellow countrymen to fulfill that vision."[12] Wright marveled, as many have, at LBJ's persuasive techniques and legislative mastery, once calling him the "[twentieth] century's most skilled practitioner of compromise."[13] But Wright also celebrated what he thought were the less well known facets of Johnson, including a "fabric of fundamental beliefs that made him tick . . . convictions so intense that he steadfastly refused even to consider trading on them for political advantage."[14] Admiring Johnson, especially it seems for these qualities, Wright concluded, "President Johnson was a strong, complex personality. He was by far the most persuasive man I have known, much more so in an informal setting than on television or in a prepared speech. He was a mixture of many things—prudence and daring, sophistication and simplicity, gravity and humor, frugality and extravagant generosity. . . . Whatever else he had, he *did* have convictions and—pardon the expression— guts."[15]

For a man who would build his career in legislative party leadership, it is difficult to imagine two more skilled models and mentors than Sam Rayburn and Lyndon Johnson. To a large extent, it was out of their example that Jim Wright would chart his own path.

Center Stage: Rising to Leadership in the House

Most ambitious members of Congress have to decide at some point in their careers if they will seek power inside the institution through the committee system or through party leadership. Although he had achieved some influence through the House Committee on Public Works, Jim Wright had ambitions to be on the national stage that could not be met with that committee's focus on transportation and infrastructure projects. Wright, likely inspired by Sam Rayburn's and Lyndon Johnson's examples, had ambitions for the center stage of American politics—party and national leadership.

After nearly two decades in the House, Wright would get his chance. When Boston's Tip O'Neill was running for majority leader in 1973 against Floridian Sam Gibbons (a result of the disappearance of Representative Hale Boggs of Louisiana in a plane crash in Alaska in late 1972), there was some speculation within the Texas delegation about a potential Wright candidacy, an early sign at least of Wright's growing reputation. But Wright was unlikely to challenge O'Neill, who, in the end, was such a prohibitive favorite that even Gibbons dropped out. Wright, instead, entered the leadership by being appointed one of three deputies in the House Democrats' whip structure. According to O'Neill, Wright's appointment was at John McCormack's suggestion. Calling O'Neill, the former Speaker (and Rayburn lieutenant) McCormack said, "The party has always had a special Boston-Austin connection. . . . Now that you're in the leadership, I'd like you to tell Carl Albert that I would appreciate it if he would keep the Boston-Austin axis going."[16] The message was clear: McCormack was pushing Jim Wright for leadership.

As one of three deputy whips (and all of those under a chief deputy in John Brademas of Indiana and the whip, John McFall of California), Wright was on but a bottom rung of the leadership, but his stock was on the rise. And he clearly had bold ambitions not just for himself but for the Congress. Early in 1973, in the face of decades-long congressional acquiescence to presidential leadership, Wright communicated his vision of Congress-centered national leadership in a letter to O'Neill, the new majority leader:

> To my way of thinking this whole process is backward.
> The congressional leadership should announce the goals,
> establish the program, introduce the bills, give out the
> press release, fashion the policy. Let the President do
> some reacting. Let's not wait for him to be the first to
> propose. Let's assume the initiative ourselves. Congress
> could keep a left jab in his face all of the time. Let's keep
> him off balance for a change.[17]

By 1975, Speaker Carl Albert had appointed Wright to head a task force to draft the House Democrats' policy program to counter President Gerald Ford's domestic policy aims.[18] Albert also appointed Wright to a media-oriented task force, chaired by Brademas, that was designed to promote the House Democrats to the media and the public.[19] Wright's inclusion in both of these groups was meant to provide coordination between the policy and communications arms that the House Democratic leadership was developing. It was also an early sign of how agendas emanating from the House of Representatives would become more public, media creations in the future.

Speaker Albert's retirement in 1976 put majority leader Tip O'Neill on a glide path to the speakership, leaving the majority leader's position open. Under normal circumstances, majority whip McFall might be expected to ascend to the empty chair, but he was facing a stiff challenge from up-and-coming fellow Californian Phil Burton, who was a liberal favorite as chairman of the Democratic Caucus. Indeed, with McFall embroiled in scandal, the race seemed really to be one between Burton and longtime leadership aspirant Dick Bolling of Missouri. Wright believed that O'Neill (who out of loyalty was officially backing his whip McFall) had tacitly given him encouragement to run in a face-to-face meeting. Moreover, the fact that Dan Rostenkowski, a very close friend of O'Neill's, had encouraged Wright to run and was backing his candidacy seemed to indicate that O'Neill would be happy to see the Austin-Boston alliance continue with Wright as his majority leader.

In announcing his campaign for majority leader in 1976, Wright included in a letter to his colleagues a two-page document entitled "The Responsibilities of the Majority Leader as I View Them"[20] outlining his complex view of a party leader's role as a representative of his party. He wrote that the majority leader:

> must be <u>advocate</u>, <u>conciliator</u> and <u>innovator:</u>
>
> 1. The Majority Leaders is first of all an <u>advocate</u>—a communicator, a persuader. He is the primary spokesman both to and for his colleagues. It is his duty to verbalize and articulate the policy of the majority, to present and defend it. He has the responsibility to mobilize broad support for the legislative program—first among his colleagues and then among the public.
>
>   To do this, he must understand the membership. He must be 'bone of their bone, flesh of their flesh'. . . .
>
> 2. The Majority Leader also is a <u>conciliator</u>—a mediator, a peacemaker. . . . Even when patching together a tenuous

majority, he must respect the right of honest dissent, conscious of the limits to his claim upon others. . . . His work is performed among equals, and he must not for a moment lose sight of that fact. . . .

3. Finally, the Majority Leader must be on occasion an <u>innovator</u>. While it is not his primary function to make policy, he often is present at its making. He should be sufficiently thoughtful and creative to contribute to it.[20]

Viewed this way, Wright thought the appropriate leader's role was to be the representative of the House Democratic Party and its members. Indeed, in all of its complexity, Wright's view that a leader must be "bone of their bone, flesh of their flesh" but that he or she also has "responsibilities" to advocate, conciliate, and innovate strikes a tone reminiscent of Edmund Burke's famous view of representation, as does Wright's statement that "in consultations with the Speaker, or in meeting with the President," the majority leader "owes them not only his loyalty but his very best judgment."[21]

More than just a mere "agent" or servant of the party's membership, the party leader must represent them (and the party as a whole) in a more complete understanding of what representation really means. In this way, the leader provides service to members but also actual leadership, including being out in front of their present wishes and preferences and looking out for their longer-term interests. In courting his colleagues' vote, Wright described the role as "part evangelist, part parish priest, and every now and then part prophet."[22]

Now the stuff of legend, Wright's successful bid for the majority leadership position represented an epic struggle of ideology, older versus younger members, and personality.[23] Leadership races are conducted by a multiple-round, single-elimination process whereby: a candidate must win a majority; if no candidate wins a majority on the first round, the lowest vote-getter is eliminated and voting proceeds to another round; the process continues until one candidate wins a majority. After the first round of balloting, Burton was in the lead, with Bolling second, Wright third, and McFall finishing last. With McFall out, the second ballot produced a surprise with Wright jumping to second place, besting Bolling by just two votes. And the head-to-head against Burton was even closer, as Wright, thought to be the most conservative candidate in the race, beat Burton by but one vote, 148 to 147.

After barely winning that race, Wright served as the House Democratic leader for a full decade under Speaker O'Neill before O'Neill retired at the end of the Ninety-Ninth Congress in 1986. The outcome made Wright Speaker O'Neill's number two, thus extending the Austin-Boston alliance for another decade and putting Wright on center stage of American national politics and, importantly, on the leadership ladder to ascend to the speakership.

Showtime: Wright as Leader in Opposition

Throughout his early career, Wright worked hard to forge relationships and demonstrated his deep appreciation of the House as an institution (an attitude learned from Rayburn) and a recognition of the value of compromise that both Rayburn and Johnson represented as model mentors. These values served him well during his period when he rose to prominence in House circles and through his long decade as House majority leader during Tip O'Neill's speakership.

The Austin-Boston alliance, initially represented by Speaker Rayburn and majority leader John McCormack, who were first paired as such in 1940, seemed to face its greatest test under Speaker O'Neill and majority leader Wright during the Reagan years. The regional balancing represented by the alliance was challenged, especially, by Reagan's popularity in the Southern states and his consequent success in picking off the votes of conservative Democrats to pass his budget and tax bills in 1981. Key among Reagan's opposite-party allies were Texans Phil Gramm, Kent Hance, and Charles Stenholm, all of whom were Democrats who supported key administration initiatives in that first Reagan-era Congress (the Ninety-Seventh Congress) and the first two of whom would soon become Republicans. More broadly, the Democrats' "solid South" was waning, and with the loss of its most conservative members, the net effect was that the party was becoming less internally divided and more decidedly liberal.

Wright, who had been reputedly the most conservative of the 1976 majority leader candidates and the Southern anchor of the Austin-Boston alliance, was now the representative of a party that was becoming less Southern and was moving to the left. With only about one-third of the House Democratic Caucus hailing from a Southern state in the 1970s into the 1980s, the job of the Southern half of the alliance was shifting. To be sure, courting that third of the party was essential to winning votes in most Congresses, but as the Congressional Black Caucus grew in importance and represented important Southern constituencies, courting the South became less an effort at ideological balancing than it had been when the alliance began.

Because the Democratic Party was becoming more programmatic and left leaning, members expected their leadership to be so as well. "Bone of their bone" and "flesh of their flesh," Wright became a potent critic of Reagan and was ever loyal to Speaker O'Neill and the Democratic Caucus's efforts to challenge the administration and to speak up for the party and its policy commitments.

Seeing Congress as an equal partner in the separation of powers and a source of national leadership, Wright took to his role as a top Democratic voice countering Reagan. For example, when asked by a reporter how he could influence votes on Reagan's 1981 budget cuts, Wright detailed a strategy to alert the public to the impacts of the cuts to student loans, nutrition programs, welfare, and Social Security: "I try to communicate the facts to Members and as I am doing now to the press, so that people will communicate to their Members what is in the bill. . . . I can't believe that once the American people understand what the draconian cuts are that are being advanced in this resolution, that they will support it."[24]

Wright had a quick wit and sometimes sharp elbows when he would trade barbs with the administration, particularly on a matter that he cared about, like the budget deficit. Wright had long been leery of Reagan's promises regarding deficits. When, in the summer of 1982, Reagan proposed a constitutional amendment for a balanced budget (which was sure to fail given the supermajorities needed for the Constitution's amending process), Democrats thought it merely a public relations gesture designed by Reagan to seem, rather than to be, serious about deficit reduction. Playing a lead role, Wright called the effort "show biz" and "razzle dazzle." He said, "At a time when the nation needs serious economic leadership, Mr. Reagan offers us a Hollywood extravaganza as devoid of serious meaning as a Bugs Bunny comedy."[25]

For Wright, this was not mere posturing for the cameras but a conviction that the Reagan program that increased defense spending and cut taxes would not be able to close the budget deficit. Indeed, behind the scenes in closed-door meetings of the Democratic Caucus, he said essentially the same thing as he had said to the press and the public. Reflecting on the 1981 Reagan budget and tax votes, he told the caucus in 1986:

> We are in one heck of a mess and we are in that mess
> because we have listened to Ronald Reagan. Too many of
> our Members voted for that shabby 1981 tax cut. That
> thing takes $135 billion out of the Treasury every year.
> That is why we have got the shortfall. That is why we
> have got the deficit. . . . So we have added more to the
> national debt in 6 years than all of our ancestors added,
> all put together. . . . Does this bill [the 1986 tax reform
> bill] add to the national debt over the period? It does
> unless we have the guts to face up to it next year to raise
> the revenue and do the things we say we believe in.[26]

When Tip O'Neill announced his retirement after a decade in the speakership, it quickly became clear that Wright, a loyal lieutenant during the Carter and Reagan years, would succeed him. If Sam Rayburn's influence had helped Wright to advance to leadership and to balance out O'Neill's northeastern liberal side of the Austin-Boston alliance, it would be Lyndon Johnson's example that would win out in Wright's calculations and approaches now that he was at the top.[27] With a fire to achieve policy aims that he had been cultivating his whole career, Wright emulated LBJ's policy drive, his deep sense of the convictions that could guide a policy agenda, and, above all, the guts that he had so admired in President Johnson.

The wind was at the Democrats' sails when Wright became Speaker. Although few doubted that the Democrats would keep their House majority after the 1986 elections, they also picked up enough Senate seats to take back control of that body for the first time in Reagan's presidency. Speaking to the House Democratic Caucus in the wake of the election, Wright said that the result "means that the legislative branch—with united leadership in the House and the Senate—can renew its rightful role in this 100th Congress as a prime initiator of policy."[28] By taking the initiative, Wright believed that he was "doing the institution of the House a service to uphold its relative influence in the balance of power . . . to demonstrate the Congress could govern."[29] By contrast, he thought that Reaganism had proved itself to be flawed—more PR than good governance. Looking back years later, Speaker Wright expressed his belief that Reagan's administration was "selling the public a lot of shabby goods."[30]

Now armed with the power of the speakership, Wright would seek to implement the Congress-centered vision of policy and political leadership that he articulated to Tip O'Neill as early as 1973. According to political scientist David Rohde, it was clear that Wright, as Speaker, "believed that the House should produce a program, not just individual bills, and saw it as his task to coordinate that program."[31] Moreover, Speaker Wright used the various tools of the House Democratic leadership—scheduling, the whip system, the power of bill referral and the committee system, and the floor-scheduling and floor-amending prerogatives of the House Committee on Rules—to forward that agenda. Wright was ambitious, driven, and policy oriented. Moreover, he was seasoned and skilled. Journalist John M. Barry observed that Wright excelled at "controlling the pathways of power" in Washington and "was willing to use them in ways unlike anyone since fellow Texan and onetime friend Lyndon Johnson."[32]

Wright surely believed, too, that his path was better for the country as the mounting size of the deficit was evidence that the administration could not govern with America's long-term interests in mind. Looking back at Reagan's historic presidency and the Reagan Revolution's aims to downsize the domestic parts of the national government and to build national strength abroad, the inconsistencies of the Reagan project are evident. Among other shortcomings, the great incompleteness of Reaganism— with its simultaneous promises to enhance military defense, decrease domestic spending and taxation, *and* reduce the budget deficit—was the administration's inability to reconcile the mathematics of it all in ways that would, in fact, bring the budget into balance. This would be the part of Reaganism that George H. W. Bush would be left to address and would be among the things for which Bush would be savaged by conservatives on the right like Newt Gingrich and Pat Buchanan. And this is one of the chief things that Wright, late in the Reagan era, would try to take on as Speaker.[33]

Playing on the highest national stage of his career, Wright prepared to give his first response, as Speaker, to a Reagan State of the Union speech in 1987. As he would again in 1988, Speaker Wright enlisted the help of pollsters and communications professionals. In planning, Wright had told his consultants that he had four main points, including "(1) Democrats have their act together; (2) Democrats know what's important and will accomplish it; (3) Democrats will not be a junior partner in this process; (4) the Democratic Congress and the people want the same important things."[34] In the day following the address, Geoffrey Garin of Peter D. Hart and Associates (who had helped Wright to prepare) praised Wright's performance. Garin wrote:

> The content of your talk was right on target, both in tone and substance. Without being unduly harsh, you did an excellent job of calling the Administration to task for the difference between its rhetoric and its record. More importantly, you put the Democratic Party on the current course for the future by seizing the initiative on the key issues on the nation's agenda.[35]

For Wright, the key issues included the budget deficit, and he felt that he had Reagan on the ropes by mid-1987. In circulating poll numbers to his House Democratic colleagues, Wright observed that "the crack in the Teflon is growing wider. Little by little, the American people are beginning to realize that Ronald Reagan is the principal architect of the budget deficit."[36] A month later, Reagan gave Wright the opportunity to press this advantage when the White House went on offense on the deficit by criticizing Wright and Democrats on the subject. Already armed with an argument more than half a decade in the making at this point, the Speaker's response was blistering:

> It is disappointing and somewhat pathetic that the President last night chose to try to divert attention from the apparent lack of any real accomplishment at the [budget] summit by replaying his tired old diatribes against Congress and former President Carter.
>
> The budget crisis is of Mr. Reagan's own making. The way out is by making hard choices—not by gimmickry, promises of future action, or tinkering with process as a substitute for policy. . . .

> Mr. Reagan has had seven opportunities to present a
> balanced budget to Congress. He has never once chosen
> to do so, and this raises obvious questions of his sincerity
> in calling for a constitutional amendment to require fu-
> ture presidents to do what he had been and still remains
> unwilling to do.[37]

When Reagan made a speech at the Jefferson Memorial the following month touting a program to preserve "essential economic
freedoms," which included as a "centerpiece," again, a constitutional
amendment to balance the federal budget, Wright responded by
decrying the "insensitive priorities and grossly excessive borrowing
of the Reagan Administration."[38] The Speaker then sought to poke
holes in the background image messaging for which Reagan was
so famous while pressing his long-standing image on the Reagan
deficits. Wright said:

> Thomas Jefferson believed in balanced budgets. He
> insisted that "It is incumbent on every generation to pay
> its own debt as it goes." And what Jefferson said, Jefferson
> meant! During each of his eight years in office, the reve-
> nues added to a national surplus.
>
> Mr. Reagan is responsible for piling on more public
> debt than all of his predecessors combined—from George
> Washington through Jimmy Carter.[39]

Of course, the budget deficit is but one example of Wright's
broader agenda, which included, too, legislative action on clean
water legislation, trade and competitiveness, homelessness, welfare
reform, a catastrophic health bill, and a savings and loan rescue.[40]
Wright had an ambitious agenda; he held votes on those items and
used those votes to press the Democratic case against the administration and House Republicans. Looking back, Speaker Wright
took pride in the fact that "we didn't lose a single vote in my first
year as Speaker."[41] As press reports came in touting the One-Hun-

dredth Congress's accomplishments, Wright sent the clippings along with a "Dear Colleague" letter that celebrated "the most productive legislative cycle in more than two decades"—an overall record, he said, "of results rather than mere rhetoric."[42]

By the end of his administration, Reagan was reeling, too, from the Iran-Contra scandal, the revelations that the administration had traded arms for hostages in an effort to help the Nicaraguan Contras. Not only was Wright against many of the foreign policy aims of the administration but he also was one of many who objected to the administration's sidestepping of congressional prerogatives in foreign policy. Knowing that this conflict "poisoned the well with Republicans and some in the Administration," Wright admitted that his views on Central America were "utterly irreconcilable with the views of [Caspar] Weinberger, Ronald Reagan, and [Oliver] North."[43] For his part, Reagan and Republicans in Washington objected to Wright's outsized role and arguably his overstepping when he was negotiating a peace plan in Nicaragua (first on behalf of the administration and later more independently). The administration's objections led to a firestorm of negative coverage for Wright in the Washington press.[44]

Such conflicts between Wright and the executive—in both domestic and foreign policy—would continue into the Bush administration, though the Speaker and the new president made an early effort to find common ground. In the days following Bush's 1988 election victory over Michael Dukakis, Wright sent a congratulatory telegram but, at Bob Strauss's urging, followed up with a personal phone call to the president-elect, which led to a private meeting between the two in Wright's office, where they seemed committed to finding common ground, not only on Bush's "kinder and gentler" domestic policy agenda but also on foreign policy, including the area of Central America that had been so contentious during the Reagan years. With Bush telling reporters of his "great respect for the Congress and a great personal respect for the Speaker," Wright was impressed and relieved by Bush's friendly and open attitude toward cooperation, especially when compared with the "years of hard-fought battles and harsh recriminations . . . in opposition to most of President Reagan's domestic agenda."[45]

Still, divided party control of government is bound to produce conflicts, and there were serious disagreements between the two. Not able to resist a swipe at Republican efforts to soften the party's image after two terms of Reagan, Wright got off a good line in his response to Bush's first State of the Union address when he said, "A kinder, gentler America? That's old time Democratic religion. We embrace it enthusiastically."[46]

To be sure, Wright might have proved a formidable foil to Bush's presidency. As a Texan, he could demystify some of the Connecticut-born president's claims to Southern-ness. As a policy-oriented and already policy-accomplished Speaker, Wright would have sharpened the line of attack that Bush lacked domestic policy focus and vision. But it was not to be, as Wright would resign just four months into the Bush administration. When allegations about Wright came to light regarding a business relationship and a book deal he had made, Newt Gingrich and the National Republican Congressional Committee (NRCC) sought to make Wright "a significant liability" to Democratic candidates by elevating the story in the press and testing television campaign spots. In defense of the Speaker, Democratic Congressional Campaign Committee (DCCC) chairman Beryl Anthony circulated recent news articles on the NRCC's plan "to make Speaker Jim Wright 'Target No. 1' in 1990."[47] For their part, the NRCC admitted behind the scenes that their "interest in Wright is motivated by the fact that no other issue is moving the congressional electorate" in the GOP's favor.[48] As events unfolded, "the combination of the facts, the press, and the Republican . . . strategy consumed Wright in May 1989," and he announced his resignation in a floor speech on May 31 of that year—accomplished, to be sure, but diminished by events and consumed, in part, by his own ambitions as LBJ had been, sooner than he had expected.

Conclusions

In a 1970 book called *Congress and Conscience*, then congressman Jim Wright wrote a chapter grandly entitled "Legislation and the Will of God." Repeatedly quoting scripture and expounding, with self-deprecating humor and personal reflection, on the challenges of doing what's right in Washington, Wright observed:

> About the best that a good Congressman can reasonably hope for is to leave a decent footprint on the sands of progress. If he has done a good job, he will know, when he leaves Washington, that he has helped thousands of his constituents with their individual problems. He will have the satisfaction of realizing that he has accomplished some worthwhile things for his district. Perhaps he will rejoice in the fact that some of his ideas have become a permanent part of a major piece of legislation.[49]

Jim Wright, it seems, had always been good at the representative part of the job. His years on the Public Works Committee and his intensive attention to district concerns helped him to build a steady reelection base back home that would afford him the flexibility to achieve his national aims. When running for reelection in 1986, Wright's campaign worked up a radio advertisement that purported to have a person call the congressman's office to order a pizza. When met with confusion, the caller delivered the campaign's punchline message: "Everybody says Jim Wright delivers!"[50] The same was likely true in Washington, where his Democratic colleagues found him solicitous of their needs and representative of their aims.

As it turns out, Wright was no *average* congressman. He was a party leader, a national voice, and a sparring partner with presidents. He had decided long before even attaining the speakership that he would seek to emulate Sam Rayburn and Lyndon Johnson in bolder efforts to make his mark on national politics. Rayburn was an example of how to build a long career in Washington—by gaining the confidence of colleagues, representing constituents back home, and rising through the ranks of leadership. But if Rayburn was the more proximate model for much of Wright's career, in the end, it was Johnson that Wright emulated as Speaker. Exhibiting the "guts" he admired so much in the president, Wright climbed high, burned bright, and ultimately brought his own career to an end amid the kind of controversy that taking risks and making things happen sometimes engenders.

1   Author interview with anonymous House Democratic Communications staffer. Here and throughout this chapter references are made to documents uncovered in the archived papers of congressional leaders. The collections cited herein include: the Jim Wright Papers, Mary Couts Burnett Library, Texas Christian University, Fort Worth, Texas (hereafter cited as JWP); the John Brademas Papers, Office of University Archives, Elmer Holmes Bobst Library, New York University (JB); the Carl Albert Collection, Carl Albert Congressional Research Center, University of Oklahoma (CAC); Records of the House Democratic Caucus, Manuscript Division, Library of Congress, Washington, DC (HDC); the papers of minority leader Robert H. Michel at the Everett McKinley Dirksen Congressional Research Center, Pekin, Illinois (RHM); the Tip O'Neill Papers, Special Collections, John J. Burns Library, Boston College (TPO).

2   Wright, daily schedule, January 25, 1988, Folder "Jim Wright Schedules 1988," Box RC 1/25, 3/19(a)2, JWP.

3   Transcript of Speaker's Daily Press Conference, January 25, 1988, Folder "Speaker's Press Conferences," RC Box RC 19/8, 19/13, 18/25, JWP.

4   See Chester J. Pach Jr., "Dwight Eisenhower: Domestic Affairs," UVA Miller Center, Dwight D. Eisenhower: Domestic Affairs | Miller Center; Douglas B. Harris, "Dwight Eisenhower and the New Deal: The Politics of Preemption," *Presidential Studies Quarterly* 27 (Spring 1997): 333–42.

5   Jim Wright, *Balance of Power: Presidents and Congress; From the Era of McCarthy to the Age of Gingrich* (Atlanta: Turner, 1996), 17.

6   Jim Wright, "In Memoriam: Sam Rayburn," in *The Wright Stuff: Reflections on People and Politics by Former House Speaker Jim Wright*, ed. James W. Riddlesperger Jr., Anthony Champagne, and Dan Williams (Fort Worth: TCU Press, 2013), 15–18.

7   Jim Wright, "Challenges that Speakers Face," in *The Speaker: Leadership in the US House of Representatives*, ed. Ronald M. Peters Jr. (Washington, DC: CQ Press, 1994), 222–46.

8   Henry Sirgo, "Wright, Jim oral history interview," April 10, 1998, *Edmund Muskie Oral History* Collection, 416, http://scarab.bates.edu/muskie_oh/416.

9   Anthony Champagne et al. *The Austin-Boston Connection: Five Decades of House Democratic Leadership, 1937–1989* (College Station: Texas A&M University Press, 2009).

10   D. B. Hardeman and Donald C. Bacon, *Rayburn: A Biography* (Lanham, MD: Madison Books, 1987), 236–38.

11   J. Brooks Flippen, *Speaker Jim Wright: Power, Scandal, and the Birth of Modern Politics* (Austin: University of Texas Press, 2018), 87, 89, 176.

12   Jim Wright, "LBJ's Tapes Reveal Human Side of Presidency," in *The Wright Stuff: Reflections on People and Politics by Former House Speaker Jim Wright*, ed. James W. Riddlesperger Jr., Anthony Champagne, and Dan Williams (Fort Worth: TCU Press, 2013), 64–67.

13   Jim Wright, LBJ Distinguished Lecture at Southwest Texas State University, October 16, 1984, James Wright: LBJ Distinguished Lecture Series: Texas State University (txstate.edu).

14   Jim Wright, *You and Your Congressman* (New York: Putnam, 1976), 106.

15   Wright, *You and Your Congressman*, 110.

16   Tip O'Neill with William Novak, *Man of the House* (New York: Random House, 1987), 226; Champagne et al., *Austin-Boston Connection*, 185–86.

17   Jim Wright to Tip O'Neill, January 19, 1973, F "Jim Wright's Legislative Suggestions for 1973," Eleanor Kelley Files, Box 8, TPO.

18   See Jim Wright to Carl Albert, January 27, 1975, Legislative Files, 94th Congress, Box 220, F14, CAC.

19   Jim Mooney to Brademas, "Re: Task Force on Communications," June 5, 1975, Folder"Information Task Force" Leadership Files, JB.

20   See Champagne et al., *Austin-Boston Connection*, 230–31; Matthew N. Green and Douglas B. Harris, *Choosing the Leader: Leadership Elections in the US House of Representatives* (New Haven: Yale University Press, 2019), 122–24; John M. Barry, *The Ambition and the Power: The Fall of Jim Wright; A True Story of Washington* (New York: Penguin, 1989), 16, 20.

21   James C. Wright, "The Responsibilities of the Majority Leader as I View Them," July 27, 1976, Campaign Files Box 20, Folder 75, CAC. In his 1774 speech to the electors at Bristol, Burke said, "Your representative owes you, not his industry only, but his judgment; and he betrays, instead of serving you, if he sacrifices it to your opinion"; Edmund Burke, "Speech to the Electors of Bristol," *The Founders' Constitution*, Volume 1, Chapter 13, Document 7, University of Chicago Press, http://press-pubs.uchicago.edu/founders/documents/v1ch13s7.html.

22 Wright, "Responsibilities of the Majority Leader."

23 Several accounts of this race are in print; see Champagne et al., *Austin-Boston Connection*, 219–50; Green and Harris, *Choosing the Leader*, 118–38; John Jacobs, *A Rage for Justice: The Passion and Politics of Phil Burton* (Berkeley: University of California Press, 1995), 296–327.

24 Wright speaking at the Speaker's [O'Neill] Daily Press Conference, May 1, 1981, Folder 11-1 Press Conference Transcripts, January–June 1981, Press Relations, Box 11, TPO.

25 Gillis Long and Geraldine Ferraro caucus talking points, October 1982; Jim Wright speaking at the Speaker's daily press conference, July 1982, Folder "Budget Constitutional Amendment on Balanced Budget, April–July 1982," Press Assistant Files, Box 16, TPO.

26 Jim Wright Address to the House Democratic Caucus, Caucus Minutes, September 17, 1986, pp. 21–22; Box 25-F 7 "100th—17 Sept. 1986," HDC.

27 Among Wright's competitors for the speakership was his one-time key supporter in the race for majority leader, Dan Rostenkowski, who cited Wright's advantages in the leadership ladder's patterned succession whereby Democratic majority leaders were likely to ascend to the speakership. Rostenkowski ultimately dropped because "he could not muster the votes to overcome Wright"; Jacqueline Calmes, "The Hill Leaders: Their Places on the Ladder" *Congressional Quarterly Weekly Report*, January 3, 1987, 6.

28 Jim Wright's comments to the House Democratic Caucus, December 8, 1986, Folder "1986 Press Release," Box RC1/17(b), JWP.

29 Jim Wright, interview by Douglas B. Harris, July 28, 2000.

30 Wright, interview.

31 David W. Rohde, *Parties and Leaders in the Postreform House* (Chicago: University of Chicago Press, 1991), 106.

32 Barry, *Ambition*, 4–5.

33 It was the first of four policy problems that Jim Wright cited in "Challenges that Speakers Face," 223–38. They were: "a budget deficit, a trade deficit, a growing social deficit, and a threatened constitutional crisis arising from the Iran-Contra revelations," 223–24.

34 Michael Sheehan Associates, Memorandum [to Speaker Wright], January 23, 1987, no folder, Box 3-43, JWP.

[35] Geoffrey D. Garin to Speaker Jim Wright, January 28, 1987, Folder "State of Unions," Box 3-43, JWP.

[36] Jim Wright to Democratic Colleagues, May 12, 1987, Folder "Democrats 1987/88," Box 18-13, JWP.

[37] Statement, "Jim Wright Responds to Reagan Diatribe on Budget Statement of Jim Wright," June 16, 1987, Folder "Budget," Box Budget Commission, JWP.

[38] See Gerald M. Boyd, "Reagan Vows to Alter Budget Process" *New York Times*, July 4, 1987; "Statement by Speaker Jim Wright/Jim Wright's Response to Reagan's Economic Agenda," July 3, 1987, Folder "Speech, Budget," Box Budget Commissions, JWP.

[39] "Statement by Speaker Jim Wright/Jim Wright's Response to Reagan's Economic Agenda," July 3, 1987, Folder "Speech, Budget," Box Budget Commissions, JWP.

[40] For a list of Wright's priorities and vote outcomes, see Rohde, *Parties and Leaders*, 110.

[41] Jim Wright, interview.

[42] Jim Wright, "Dear Colleague" letter, October 26, 1988, Box 18-12, JWP.

[43] Wright, interview.

[44] See Steven S. Smith and Mark Watts, "The Speaker and Foreign Policy," in *The Speaker: Leadership in the US House of Representatives*, ed. Ronald M. Peters (Washington, DC: CQ Press, 1994), 107–34, 118–21. Wright gave his side of the story in *Worth It All: My War for Peace* (Washington, DC: Brassey's, 1993).

[45] Jim Wright, *Worth It All*, 218–220.

[46] Jim Wright's Response to George H. W. Bush Address, February 9, 1989, Box National Affairs, JWP.

[47] Beryl Anthony, Dear Colleague Letter, April 4, 1989, Box 17-99, JWP.

[48] Joe Gaylord (NRCC) to House Republican Leadership Staff, October 18, 1988, Folder "Kehl, D. Legislative Republican Party – House (1)," Staff Files, David Kehl Files, Box 12, RHM. For a more extensive consideration of this effort, see Douglas B. Harris, "Sack the Quarterback: The Strategies and Implications of Congressional Leadership Scandals," in *Scandal! An*

Interdisciplinary Approach to the Consequences, Outcomes, and Significance of Political Scandals, ed. Alison Dagnes and Mark Sachleben (New York: Bloomsbury, 2014), 29–50.

[49] Jim Wright, "Legislation and the Will of God," in *Congress and Conscience*, ed. John B. Anderson (New York: J. B. Lippincott, 1970), 23–50, 28.

[50] Radio Ad Copy, October 22, 1986, Box 1-22, JWP.

President Kennedy addresses an early morning crowd in Fort Worth, November 22, 1963. Wright is on the far left of the photo, beaming. To Kennedy's right in the photo are Texas Senator Ralph Yarborough, Texas Governor John Connally, and Vice President Lyndon B. Johnson.

President Lyndon Johnson talks with Congressman Wright on a trip to Fort Worth, May 29, 1968. Johnson speaks to TCU commencement at the new Daniel Meyer Coliseum and announces his support for what became the 26th Amendment—lowing the voting age from twenty-one to eighteen.

Wright at the 1968 Democratic Convention in Chicago where the party would nominate Hubert Humphrey for president.

Wright poses with President Nixon as they cooperate on passage of legislation.

Wright poses with Presidents Ford (left), Carter (center), and Nixon (right) on the occasion of Hubert Humphrey's memorial, January 15, 1978.

Majority Leader Wright talks with President Carter in the Cabinet Room in the West Wing of the White House.

Wright offers President Reagan his opinion. In the background, from left, are Senator S. I. Hayakawa, Alan Cranston, Lloyd Bentsen, unknown, and Senator Strom Thurmond.

President Ronald Reagan delivers his State of the Union Address January 25, 1988. Vice President George H. W. Bush and Speaker Wright are in the background. *Photo from Ronald Reagan Presidential Library.*

The President and Speaker with their wives, 1989. From left: Barbara Bush, President George Bush, Betty Wright, Speaker Jim Wright.

CHAPTER 10

"A Man of My Word": Speaker Jim Wright in Historical Memory

★

J. BROOKS FLIPPEN

Asked late in life what he wanted the world to remember of him, former Speaker of the House Jim Wright paused in thought. It was important for people to remember him as a successful public servant whose accomplishments stood the test of time, Wright replied, but most importantly history should record him as "a man of my word."[1] It was an understandable sentiment; Wright had, after all, been the first Speaker ever to resign amid personal scandal, a man whose reputation had been fodder for national media outlets and had helped galvanize political partisanship. The old lion in winter simply wanted vindication in the eyes of history.

This, of course, was a tall order. As Wright undoubtedly appreciated, history is fickle. It is dynamic, constantly revised. It sees the past from the perspective of the present, ensuring not the consensus the old lion wanted but sustained debate.[2] Wright was a complex man living in complex times, and he left his mark on decades of policy and politics—all of which affect the present. Historical debate is inevitable. History will find much to praise as it constantly revises Wright's legacy, but criticism is assured as well. It is the nature of the

225

beast for leaders such as Wright. In the end, Jim Wright left not one but many legacies—and many open to debate.

For some, Wright will forever be old "snake oil," in the words of former Virginia Republican congressman William Whitehouse.[3] He will never lose the taint of scandal, always the poster boy for Democratic corruption. Others may recall him as the exemplar of a privileged, elite Congress, always willing to pass rules for others but not themselves. Such views are undoubtedly here to stay, much to Wright's chagrin. For one, they fit a Republican narrative of Democratic corruption cultivated since the Truman administration. Well-funded and well-oiled political machines controlled Democratic legislators, GOP campaigns had long stressed. In the words of Truman decades before Wright's 1989 resignation, "When a leader is in the Democratic Party he is a boss; when he's in the Republican Party he is a leader."[4] Democrats did their part to keep the narrative alive. From Louisiana's flamboyant Huey Long in the 1930s, to Chicago's Richard J. Daley in the 1950s, to the "Koreagate" and "ABSCAM" scandals in the 1970s, Democrats provided ample ammunition. Even the Wilbur Mills–Fanne Foxe escapades in Washington's Tidal Basin in 1974 contributed, if adding a degree of both levity and sadness.[5] It all led, Republicans consistently argued, to one inescapable conclusion: Congress—long dominated by Democrats—was a cesspool. In this narrative Wright fit well. He was simply another example, a symptom perhaps, of a broader problem.

The charge resonates among Republicans today. Democrats are corrupt elites, bending it all to their advantage. Such populist fury animates the party base in the age of Trump, an age when social media and political Machiavellianism dovetail effectively.[6] Wright's scandal will undoubtedly remain fodder for the partisan political cannons. In a political culture where ideology often outshines facts, Wright will undoubtedly continue as an easy target. As much as Wright had hoped for vindication, any truth to the charges or countercharges will be less relevant than the impressions the allegations leave. This was a kind of legacy Wright feared but one that some Americans in the future will undoubtedly share.

Wright's scandal might sound familiar, if not quaint, to future historians. The ethics charges—those so upsetting to Wright—included Wright's acceptance of improper gifts from a friend, Fort Worth developer George Mallick, who had business before Congress. Mallick had even hired Wright's wife, Betty, in a do-nothing job and had given the Wrights a car and a rent-free condominium. Wright also had surpassed the congressional limit on honoraria for speeches with bulk sales of his book. Not true, countered Wright: Mallick was a longtime friend who had no business before Congress; the work Betty did was real; there was no evidence of any attempt to violate House rules or profit personally; many in Congress had done similarly. With a special prosecutor appointed, the entire debate festered in the news. New cable television and talk radio magnified criticism. Partisanship reigned.[7] It all precipitated a more confrontational personal politics and, in the end, the demise of the collegial, club-like congressional politics in which Wright had thrived.

Just before Wright's resignation, Republicans claimed that Democrats had slandered Supreme Court nominee Robert Bork. Just afterward, Democrats cried that the accusations against Wright were simply retribution. As charges and countercharges flew, the infamous House Post Office scandal of 1992 broke, reinforcing the very historical context that Republicans depicted and that hardly aided Wright's legacy.[8] In fact, it was only nine years before Republican Newt Gingrich, Wright's chief nemesis and an emerging master of the art of slander, resigned in his own scandal, a victim of the hostile political environment he had helped cultivate. In the years since Watergate, well over 250 members of Congress—Republicans as well as Democrats—have been involved in public scandal.[9] There is certainly grist for the historical mill. Future historians, even those operating from a less partisan perspective or less anxious to assign blame, may cast Wright as part of this devolution of the nation's political culture.

History will surely note all the factors at play in Wright's sad affair, from the political posturing that followed the launch of C-SPAN in 1979 to the elimination of the Fairness Doctrine in 1987. The emergence of talk radio, bipartisan ambition, and tactics that included Republican operatives searching through trash will all get their due. Wright may not always fare well. His driving ambition and willingness to push the envelope—whether regarding legislation, congressional rules, or his own finances and life—are indeed part of his story. His willingness to consolidate and wield power underscored not only his many accomplishments but also the enemies he made. His demands for strict coordination and tight deadlines worked, but in a world of oversized egos and burning ambition he ruffled feathers.

Through his powers of purse and appointment, Wright commanded. He quietly stretched the rules to their breaking point if it meant getting what he wanted. Once in a critical omnibus 1987 reconciliation bill, Wright kept voting open past deadlines by claiming that a member was running late. In fact, his staff was lobbying the recalcitrant legislator in an adjacent cloak room, infuriating Republicans. It worked—the bill passed —even as Republicans decried the "bush league" maneuver and planned their revenge.[10] Wright, history may conclude, helped foster the very political culture he protested and that eventually cost him his political life.

Wright certainly lamented the new politics, even as his name may be tied to it. In his resignation speech Wright proclaimed, "When vilification becomes an accepted form of political debate, when negative campaigning becomes a full-time occupation, when members of both parties become self-appointed vigilantes carrying out personal vendettas against members of the other party, in God's name that is not what this institution is supposed to be about." Wright offered himself as "propitiation for all this season of bad will," his resignation a sacrifice for the Congress of old.[11] It was poignant speech, worthy of its own small place in Wright's legacy. As the Republican moniker "snake oil" implied, many on both sides of the aisle will remember Wright as one of the best orators in the institution's history. In the words of one scholar, his resignation speech was a rhetorical case study in seeking redemption.[12] Alas, Wright's plea was not to be. Today there is too much profit in personal destruction, financial as well as political, for any renaissance of civility. In recent years, members of Congress have even expressed fear of physical harm. In this light, of course, Wright's resignation still resonates. Looking back, Wright had his own take: calling for Congress's better angels was "the biggest damn mistake of my life."[13]

Wright loved the Congress of old. For many years, committee chairmen ran their own political fiefdoms, sometimes strong enough to counter party orthodoxy. With seniority counting, there remained a degree of independence, pragmatism as much as ideology. With federal spending the coin of the realm—literally—and the backroom the market du jour, it arguably promoted a certain bipartisanship. Leaders accomplished and their constituents saw the proceeds, rewarding them with votes. Wright thrived in this environment. Once when asked why in the age of refrigeration staff still left ice outside offices, Wright replied approvingly that they always had. That was enough; it was tradition.[14] Having cultivated a gregarious, folksy style, Wright became the master of this dealmaking. Cast to the House Committee on Public Works, Wright astutely used his powers of appropriation to advance his own career and the causes he held dear. In the end, history might conclude from all this that Wright was a master of the political craft, the consummate politician who deftly manipulated the system to advance not only his own power but the common good. In a time when public opinion of Congress stands at historic lows, the institution marred in partisan gridlock, history may perceive an admirable productivity in the age of Wright.[15] It may see not an unscrupulous power broker or an example of the devolution in American body politic but a man who knew how the sausage was made and cooked well.

For one, Wright helped bridge a growing chasm within the Democratic Party between its liberal, younger, and more urban and diverse members and its traditional base of Southern conservatism. The Democratic leadership had long represented the "Austin-Boston connection," but a conservative reaction to the 1960s and the civil rights movement tore at the fabric of the party.[16] Wright was critical to stemming this tide, at least temporarily, a fact surely not lost on historians. His moderation helped define a moderate age. This impacted the political landscape for many years, resulting in an impressive array of domestic and foreign policy accomplishments and ultimately winning for Wright the speakership he long coveted. Maintaining unity was never easy. The wave of young, ambitious Democratic congressmen following Watergate—the "Watergate Babies" of 1974—challenged both Wright's personal assent and the congressional culture he held dear. Moreover, bending the old power brokers, such as Dan Rostenkowski, was no small task.[17] History will surely appreciate the tremendous political skill that all of Wright's successful career demanded.

Wright understood early the significance of Ronald Reagan. Today, there is an extensive historiography on the New Right that Reagan cultivated, that political alliance of so-called fiscal conservatives, those who prioritized deregulation and lower taxes, and social conservatives, those like the emerging "Religious Right" who lamented cultural dynamism. The Reagan Revolution today looms large in the literature, with Reagan a political icon for millions. Historians have noted the Reagan Revolution as the consummation of Nixon's Southern Strategy, the 1980 Republican sweep of the South.[18] Wright understood quickly that "Reagan Democrats" promised to shuffle the political status quo even as the Watergate Babies within his own party demanded more. The fact that Wright was able to maintain enough unity to craft an effective resistance to Reagan will not be lost to history. Wright envisioned himself a leader in the tradition of Carl Albert and Sam Rayburn, and, while his tenure as Speaker paled, his political skills were their equal, his impact was significant and long lasting.[19]

As long as Reagan remains a seminal figure both in public memory and in history, Wright's legacy as one of his chief antagonists will grow. Reagan's vast historical shadow will not always shine a favorable light on Wright, but at the same time it assures that Wright will not soon fade from our collective consciousness. Until his dying day, Wright maintained that his success battling Reagan's anti-Communist efforts in Central America underscored the coordinated campaign of slander against him. He had been too effective. This is an argument that may echo in history, if for no other reason than Central America remains controversial today. The battle that eventually produced the Iran-Contra Affair that was so damaging to Reagan's legacy revolved around military support for the Nicaraguan Contras, a right-leaning rebel force, against the left-leaning Sandinista government.[20] Reagan's staunch anti-Communism supported the aid, but Wright and the Democrats believed that diplomacy and economic support to the country promised the best path forward. The battle grew bitter.

Today the argument remains unsettled, if less prominent given the implosion of the Soviet Union. Wright had argued that the Sandinista leader, Daniel Ortega, would moderate in response to American diplomacy and aid. At first it seemed such was the case. In 1990, Ortega lost the election Wright had championed and left office, suggesting a nascent democracy was taking hold. In the new millennium, however, Ortega won reelection and in recent years has strengthened authoritarian controls, suggesting Wright's hopes misplaced.[21] Also unsettled is the question of Wright's diplomacy in the first instance. Had Wright crossed a constitutional boundary in challenging traditional deference to executive authority in matters of diplomacy?

This is no easy question, the answer sure to occupy future historians. The Constitution gave the executive branch the power to conduct diplomacy and wage war but reserved to Congress control of the national purse strings and the power to declare war.

The president was the commander-in-chief, but Congress had oversight. Wright was no private citizen and no powerless bystander; the Logan Act did not apply. While he clearly had a role to play, however, he was arguably negotiating directly with a foreign country contrary to the Reagan administration's position. In this sense, some historians will argue, his efforts represented a second, competing foreign policy that not only complicated international relations but also bent the Constitution. The question of balance of powers is, of course, no small matter today, and other historians will undoubtedly see things differently. With the imperial presidency of lore alive and well today, Wright's assertion of legislative power may resonate still. The future is uncertain.[22]

Wright took pride in his leadership of the One-Hundredth Congress, and with some reason. Mitigating Reaganomics and marshaling into law an impressive array of bills, Wright touched on everything from pollution control to homelessness, from civil rights to trade competitiveness, and from health care to drug abuse. Historians will not record the One-Hundredth Congress in the league of the Seventy-Third Congress, which launched Franklin Roosevelt's "First One Hundred Days," or the Eighty-Eighth Congress, which launched the Great Society of Wright's mentor Lyndon Johnson.[23] Neither, however, will they forget that Wright and his colleagues were able to get all this legislation passed despite the growing dynamism, factions, and contentions they faced in their day. In recent years historians have documented a decline in the volume of congressional legislation and an increase in presidential executive orders, raising broad questions about the health of American democracy. In the Senate the filibuster has replaced regular order, ensuring that virtually all significant bills not covered by the reconciliation process require a supermajority to pass, a high standard seldom achieved. Once again, the present suggests not only a more positive legacy for the One-Hundredth Congress but also Wright's aggrieved defense of traditional political culture.

While Reagan's and Wright's historical legacies intertwine, the final chapters of Wright's career will not totally eclipse all that he had accomplished previously. Wright was in Congress for more than three decades and left his legislative fingerprints on more than just the One-Hundredth Congress, on more than just his battles with Reagan. Aware that history reflects the present, Wright late in life acknowledged mistakes that clouded his legacy and hurt any historical vindication. Wright at first voted against the monumental Civil Rights Act of 1964, in later years conceding that as a Democrat in the South, political calculations dominated. The following year, however, Wright voted for the Voting Rights Act of 1965, whether a change of heart or a simple desire to be on the winning side of history. The reversal was probably wise from a historical perspective. Today in an age of Black Lives Matter and racial redemption, of Trump and critical race theory, issues of race and voting are paramount.

Wright was no racist, but he was arguably slow to embrace the racial reckoning sweeping the country during the postwar years. He did not sign the infamous 1956 Southern Manifesto but did declare that the Supreme Court had "errored in judgment when it said discrimination is inherent in segregation."[24] Wright later came to applaud the *Brown* case and, later still, supported the Martin Luther King Jr. holiday. He also helped override a Reagan veto of the Civil Rights Restoration Act of 1987. For some historians it will all suggest a man with his thumb to the political winds, if not a pragmatic politician operating in a conservative Southern district. To others in an increasingly global and multicultural world it may represent a cardinal sin, not so easily dismissed as a "mistake." There will be little debate about whether Wright ended on the right side of history, but a lot of debate on how.

Wright's support for the Vietnam War will most likely not age well in history, another mistake the elderly Wright acknowledged. Polls today suggest the overwhelming majority of Americans view the war as unnecessary and a tragic error, a conclusion shared by most scholars.[25] The problem for Wright's legacy is that he did more than just voice rhetorical support, he authored and led a 1969 congressional resolution supporting the efforts of the Nixon administration, appearing with Nixon and criticizing the war's opponents. Earlier, during Lyndon Johnson's military buildup, Wright had mocked the antiwar movement. It "ridicules" Johnson, Wright declared in 1968, for "preserving and honoring the very institutions and processes of our constitutional system in which he is sworn to defend."[26] When Nixon signed the 1973 armistice—which extricated American troops but ultimately proved a failure—Nixon thanked Wright for his support.[27] The war was a "stern test notably met," Nixon wrote, a sentiment to which Wright readily assented. The war was not easy for Wright, dividing both his party and his family. Wright was a World War II veteran and an institutionalist who had faith in government. He was not one likely to challenge the Cold War consensus. With the passage of years his perspective evolved, not unlike that of millions of Americans. Indeed, as early as 1973, Wright supported the War Powers Act, which, while asserting congressional prerogative, also implicitly condemned the war.[28] In later years Wright was more explicit, if even then reticent to assign blame.

Wright's position spoke to the institutionalist in him, the faith he had in the system, even as it assured him criticism well into the future. History may view Wright's position on the Watergate scandal from the same perspective. Wright felt that he and President Nixon understood each other and refused to believe in Nixon's complicity until the very end. He cautioned his Democratic colleagues not to go too far, which Nixon appreciated. When reporters asked him with each new revelation if he maintained his faith in Nixon and the system's ability to handle the crisis, Wright replied vaguely that ugly politics was horrible but "most emphatically not commonplace."[29] Today, with Nixon's guilt established beyond doubt and historians regarding him as one of history's most corrupt presidents, Wright's association may not play well.[30] At best, history might see him as naïve. For his part, even later in his life Wright still refused to say whether he would have voted to impeach Nixon. Wright still did not see his position as a mistake as he did with civil rights and Vietnam. While perhaps another example of the bipartisanship Wright valued, it is a position likely best forgotten for Wright's legacy.

There is so much more for history to debate. Wright had a long record of trying to limit the growing influence of money in politics, reflected in many speeches and proposals. At the same time, however, having failed to blunt such growth, Wright fought back in the same vein; he became a prolific fund raiser, a top draw for Democrats across the country. Nor was he shy about using his cash and endorsement, strategically distributing it to his greater end. Whether this was hypocritical or wise will, like beauty, be seen through the eyes of the beholder.

When it came to the national debt, Wright cast himself as a fiscal hawk and warned about the dangers of deficits. The spending he advocated, however, was an investment that paid dividends, and was not the political pork barrel his conservative critics claimed. It stimulated economic growth, he argued, not debt. This, of course, was a question for which there is no simple answer. Economists today debate supply versus demand, monetary policy, and all the complexities of macroeconomics. Wright understood both the public's aversion to taxes and its fondness for what they bought. In the future, one's view of Wright's stewardship of the economy will likely depend on one's own economic assumptions. Was Wright a Keynesian? Did his economic policy evolve? History will offer no simple consensus.

As only one example, Wright argued in favor of lower, not higher, interest rates to battle the persistent stagflation of the 1970s. A tighter monetary policy would hamper economic growth while doing little to battle inflation, he argued. When, however, President Jimmy Carter's Federal Reserve chairman Paul Volcker did in fact raise rates, inflation tumbled and the nation's economy boomed.

There was a cost—just as Wright had predicted, the recession of 1982—but many economic historians have credited Volcker's policies in the macro.[31] America had to take its medicine, but it was worth it. Whether one agrees with this historical conclusion depends on one's larger economic philosophy and, perhaps, one's views of Reagan. Both the recession and the boom played out during his administration and the voluminous literature on Reagan will definitely overlap. History is complex and will hold no complete vindication, as Wright had hoped.

Wright's record on the environment will certainly draw its degree of attention. To the old lion in winter it was "one of the things I am most proud of."[32] Today, when polls indicate growing public concern for climate change and weather extremes almost daily remind us of its threat, history will undoubtedly shine brightly on those who were champions of environmental protection. Wright's long tenure on the Committee on Public Works assured him a prominent role in the environmental battles of his day. It also assures that he is today a subject for historical scrutiny and, inevitably, debate.

Some will note that Wright was no early convert to environmental protection, with his district being strong for agriculture and ranching. They will argue that his advocacy grew more from an interest in utilization and consumption and not from aquatic ecology, a fact Wright readily acknowledged. Wright, for example, supported both the Cross Florida Barge Canal and the Tennessee-Tombigbee Waterway, two large reclamation projects with significant environmental impact. The success of environmentalists in halting the former is celebrated in environmental literature today, and often cited as wise policy.[33] Wright for decades supported development of the Trinity watershed. With the river flowing through Fort Worth and development popular with both civic leaders and the public, Wright was the project's greatest champion. Environmentalists sued, however, and with environmentalism growing nationally, they ultimately blocked the project. "It was a big miscalculation on my part," Wright acknowledged years later.[34] When the famed early environmentalist Rachel Carson testified before Congress about the dangers from pesticides, Wright was skeptical, undoubtedly reflecting agricultural sentiment in his district. He had read Carson's famed book *Silent Spring*, Wright later recalled, but "not as carefully as I should have."[35]

Wright's evolution to environmentalism was part of a broader trend, historian Paul Milazzo has noted. With the matter of pollution still relatively new, jurisdiction fell to the existing committee structure. Congressmen increasingly interpreted pollution as a "water resources problem" that exacerbated already limited supplies and threatened economic growth.[36] In this respect Wright's committee membership exposed him early to the threat of pollution, and the jump from water quantity to quality was a natural step. Wright not only embraced public works, after all, he also proved an early backer of water pollution control legislation and was a committed warrior in Johnson's Great Society endeavors. He did not support every bill, but he came to advocate the need for environmentalism as early as his second book, *The Coming Water Famine*, released in the midst of Johnson's legislative wave.[37] Perhaps most significantly, Wright used his appropriation powers to advance funding for clean water. More than just legislating waste treatment projects—more than the pork barrel many Republicans criticized—the appropriations Wright helped advance proved critical in a time of tremendous growth and aging infrastructure.

Wright worked with the Nixon administration and helped fashion what today stands as the cornerstone of American environmental law, the bipartisan support being arguably another example of Wright's Congress of old. Wright supported air pollution legislation, creation of the Environmental Protection Agency, and passage of the National Environmental Policy Act. When Nixon vetoed the Clean Water Act amendments of 1972, Wright assisted the override effort and fought Nixon's attempt to impound the billions the legislation provided. Fifteen years later, Wright led another successful override of a presidential veto, this time Reagan's rejection of Wright's own Water Quality Act of 1987, the first legislation passed during Wright's One-Hundredth Congress.[38] From this perspective at least, history may conclude, Wright had reason for the pride he held late in life.

Wright's committee work was obviously critical in the growth of the nation's infrastructure, and no more so than in regard to the interstate highway system. Wright worked for bipartisan consensus and as a young legislator won a personal meeting with President Dwight Eisenhower to advocate for the creation of a highway trust fund. In a nod to his aversion of debt, Wright helped convince the president for a pay-as-you-go system. The result was a transportation network that relied on a gas tax as the primary funding mechanism. This, history will undoubtedly conclude, was no small accomplishment. The interstate system transformed America, and the tax remains today an effective way to mitigate deficit spending. While one historian might argue that Wright's promotion of a car culture undercut his claims as an environmental champion, another will point out that in this case at least, Wright lived up to the fiscal conservatism he often professed. Still another historian might claim that it all proved Wright was correct in his economics; here no doubt exists that federal spending paid dividends. All will agree that Wright had a tremendous impact.

Wright took pride in his ability to craft compromise, evident in all such debate. His foreign policy was no different, and his faith in dialogue and reasoned diplomacy was a constant throughout his long career. His position regarding Ortega and the Sandinistas was only one example, even if the verdict of history is today clouded. History tends to favor the peacemakers, and Wright's many other efforts internationally will probably play better. Early in his career Wright worked to unite the United States with its Latin American neighbors, promoting such ventures as the Inter-American Highway and international aid. Wright was ahead of his day in recognizing the importance of Mexico economically and long insisted that close ties benefited both countries. He played a role in facilitating the famous Camp David Accords, leading a bipartisan delegation to Cairo and suggesting to Egyptian leader Muhammad Anwar al-Sadat a personal trip to Israel. When Sadat arrived in Tel Aviv, Wright lobbied Israeli leader Menachem Begin. Wright was not present at the Camp David presidential retreat where the two leaders and President Jimmy Carter hammered out the specifics of the historic peace treaty, but he had helped lay the necessary groundwork for what stands today as one of Carter's greatest accomplishments.[39]

While a strong defender of a robust military, it was Wright who ended up the first American leader ever to speak live and unedited on Soviet television. Part of a spate of détente he helped promote, Wright's nationally broadcast plea for the Cold War rivals to be friends won plaudits on both sides of the globe. The White House approved and no questions of constitutional prerogative existed. Wright told his audience that if they wrote him, he would send a small lapel pin of Soviet and American flags. The response was overwhelming, with thousands of Soviet citizens writing that it was the first time they had ever seen an American live. Although undoubtedly diminished in importance by the subsequent fall of the Soviet Union, Wright's plea to "Ivan" deserves its own mark on history. It arguably proved, as one American put it, "vital to obtaining mutual trust," a small but important ingredient in ending the Cold War.[40]

Wright's impact was not always evident but was frequently profound. When John F. Kennedy visited Dallas on that fateful day in 1963, he was on a campaign trip to North Texas, partially at the behest of Wright, who had pressed his connections to Johnson. Wright had a front row seat for all the horror that unfolded. To top it all off, the killer hailed from Wright's district. Wright lived in momentous times and his long life reflected it in a myriad of ways, great and small. Wright, history will surely note, was an exemplar for what journalist Tom Brokaw termed America's "Greatest Generation."[41]

Growing up during the Great Depression, he was shaped by economic hardship. He volunteered for service in World War II and emerged a decorated combat veteran. Raising a family during the postwar boom years, remaining stalwart throughout the Cold War, Wright perfectly represented the sacrifices and successes of his historic generation. To this degree, like his cohorts, Wright's contributions were profound indeed.

If Wright's legacy stretches wide and deep, the people who knew him best—his own constituents—felt the greatest impact. Early in his career, as mayor of Weatherford, Texas, Wright guided the small town through a period of tremendous growth. With increased tax revenue came expansion of electric and water utilities, more parks, and new street signs, among other improvements. The town's boundaries extended twice and its population exceeded ten thousand. The town purchased a new water reservoir, which is still in use today. Historians might cite Weatherford's success as a by-product of the growth of the Dallas-Fort Worth Metroplex, an example of the suburban sprawl that characterized America's postwar economic boom.[42] Its citizens, however, would attest to Wright's historical importance more directly.

It was not just Weatherford that benefited from Wright's career. Although his district shifted over the years, Wright's base was Fort Worth. Like Weatherford, it too boomed, in no small part because of Wright's aid. Early in his career, Wright's lobbying won for the city's General Dynamics Corporation a large contract with Boeing. Defense contracts followed. This brought thousands of jobs over the years and helped make Fort Worth the player in the aviation industry it is today. Wright promoted the city's north side, which included the city's old Stockyards. Today the Fort Worth Stockyards Historic District is a significant part of the city's allure and a key to the city's tourism industry.[43] Government grants helped with affordable housing and economic development. Grants arrived for utilities and highways, always a priority for growing cities. Wright ensured Fort Worth a place on the nation's growing interstate system and a sufficient highway connection with neighboring Dallas. Grateful Fort Worth citizens even named a portion of the "820 Loop" Jim Wright Freeway. For residents today it is hard to miss Jim Wright's legacy.

History will undoubtedly appreciate perhaps Wright's greatest service to his district, his role in creating the Dallas Fort Worth International Airport, known nationally to any traveler as DFW. The two city's airports—Meacham in Fort Worth and Love in Dallas—competed for their portion of the expanding aviation industry, with Love having the upper hand. Wright helped promote the idea of a large international airport in the middle to benefit both cities. Given the threat of Love, Wright got an amendment through Congress that today bears his name. The well-known Wright Amendment restricted flights to and from the airport, removing competition and facilitating the growth of DFW and the arrival of American Airlines.[44]

Historians today have ample evidence of how farsighted Wright's position was. The airport was perfectly located in the center of the United States, with easy access to Latin America. It combined demand from both cites and had room to grow. Surrounded by relatively cheap land, both cities had space for the suburban sprawl so characteristic of modern America. Aided by low taxation, less regulation, and the tremendous explosion of airline travel, the Metroplex emerged arguably to the benefit of both cities. DFW has grown into one of the nation's busiest airports, an entry point to America for millions. A 2015 study by the Perryman Group estimated DFW's annual economic impact on the region at $37 billion, the airport directly or indirectly supporting almost a quarter million jobs. It represents "the single biggest economic engine," noted Lillie Biggins, the airport's board chair. "If you look at all the companies that have come to this area and talk to them, they will tell you the biggest reason . . . is workforce availability and the connectivity that this airport affords them."[45] The larger metropolitan area of North Texas has remained a driver of economic growth nationally, "poised to dominate America's heartland" in the conclusion of another economic analysis in 2021. History will see this all as a success story of the country's postwar Sunbelt, and it will not forget Wright's key role.[46]

In this light it is no wonder that Fort Worth citizens today still regard Wright highly, a legacy that Wright would have valued. Here scandal receded and few doubted his word. When Wright died in 2015, his service drew national attention, Fort Worth's streets blocked for the procession and a firetruck holding a giant American flag overhead. Dignitaries offered condolences. Republicans as well as Democrats, including President Barack Obama and former president George H. W. Bush, cited Wright as one of the giants of Congress, rhetorical nods to a bygone historical era. Today, Wright's presence is still felt on the campus of Texas Christian University, where Wright donated his papers and taught for many years in retirement. The Mary Couts Burnett Library Special Collection maintains the Wright archives, complete with displays of memorabilia, climate-controlled preservation, a reading room, and a team of professionals ensuring that the next generation of historians does not forget him. Wright's alma mater, Weatherford College, sponsors a Jim Wright Lecture, while the town itself proudly displays a historical marker at Wright's boyhood home.

The people who knew Wright best, who benefited from his efforts, know of his many legacies. The personal costs were real, the accomplishments not without sacrifice. The elderly Wright regretted the stresses his career caused his family, his divorce and the time away from children. It was in a sense a cautionary take for future politicians, if not an example of the challenges public service demanded. At the same time, the successes were many and their ramifications immense. The friendships were real and the mourning at his funeral more than perfunctory. Friends are perhaps a man's greatest legacy, and despite all the complexity of the man and his time, all the controversy of his politics and policy, Wright left a legion of admirers who will ensure that Wright gets his historical due.

In the future, partisans will write their diatribes, looking to history to make their point. Scholars will approach the past from the perspective of their own day. New sources will emerge, and through it all history will grow. Debate will live on. "We cannot escape history," Abraham Lincoln reminded Congress in 1862.[47] Jim Wright, the old lion in winter, knew this. A longtime history buff, he understood the nature and complexity of history and the inevitability of criticism. He foresaw upon his death not only the outpouring of grief and the celebration of his life but also the stain of his resignation. Indeed, when Wright died, the *New York Times* headlines blared, "Jim Wright Dies at 92; House Speaker Resigned Amid Ethics Charges."[48] Today, the controversies and resignation play prominently on Wright's Wikipedia page.[49]

Never resigned to the fate of history, Wright defended until his dying day his reputation. In his later years he wrote a regular newspaper article and several books, including his *Balance of Power: Presidents and Congress from the Era of McCarthy to the Age of Gingrich,* published in 1996, and his *Worth It All: My War for Peace,* published three years earlier as a direct rebuttal to Reagan's policies in Nicaragua.[50] He lectured, taught, and gave interviews. He remained active politically, still pushing the causes he had championed and his case to history.

In many respects he could have rested assured. His legacies were indeed manifold, which history will not forget. From the jungles of Central America to Red Square outside the Kremlin, from the halls of Weatherford College to the halls of Congress, Wright left his mark. From friendships to physical infrastructure—both still obvious today—historians will find much to praise. Wright's life and times offer fertile ground for future research, and there is surely much to come. Hagiography may be rare, but Wright will undoubtedly remain on solid historical footing. The old lion in winter may never win the complete vindication he fought for in his final years, the complete vindication he knew he would never truly win, but he need not worry about his historical fate. James Claude Wright Jr. had nothing to fear from the many verdicts of history.

[1] Jim Wright, interview by J. Brooks Flippen, July 22, 2012. For a detailed discussion of Wright's career, including the actions and positions mentioned in this chapter, see the author's *Speaker Jim Wright: Power, Scandal, and the Birth of Modern Politics* (Austin: University of Texas Press, 2018).

[2] History in the broadest sense, including popular memory and academic study. For a discussion of bias in professional history, see Edward Hallett Carr, *What Is History?* (Cambridge: Cambridge University Press, 1961) and Geoffrey Elton, *The Practice of History* (New York: Thomas Y. Crowell, 1967). An example of the dynamism is the postwar growth of environmental history and women's history.

[3] William Whitehurst, interview by J. Brooks Flippen, December 29, 2012.

[4] Speech by Harry Truman, sound recording, Columbia University, New York City, April 28, 1959, Harry Truman Presidential Library, accessed February 21, 2022, https://www.trumanlibrary.gov/soundrecording-records/sr75-2-harry-s-truman-lecture-columbia-university-constitution.

[5] See T. Harry Williams, *Huey Long* (New York: Random House, 1981); Mike Royko, *Boss: Richard J. Daley of Chicago* (New York: Dutton, 1971); Robert Boettcher and Gordon Freedman, *Gifts of Deceit: Sun Myung, Moon, Tongsun Park, and the Korean Scandal* (New York: Holt, Rinehart and Winston, 1980); Robert W. Greene, *The Sting Man: Inside ABSCAM* (New York: Dutton, 1981); Mills, the powerful Ways and Means Committee chairman, was caught in his car with an Argentine stripper, who leapt into Washington's Tidal Basin; *Washington Post*, October 11, 1974, 1.

[6] See Paul Barrett et al., "How Tech Platforms Fuel Political Polarization and What Government Can Do about It," Strengthening American Democracy Project, Brookings Institution, Washington, DC, accessed February 12, 2022, https://www.brookings.edu/blog/techtank/2021/09/27/how-tech-platforms-fuel-u-s-political-polarization-and-what-government-can-do-about-it/.

[7] For a brief summary of the scandal, see Flippen, *Speaker Jim Wright*, 1–8, 373–86.

[8] See *New York Times*, October 19, 1994, 21; *Los Angeles Times*, July 20, 1993, 1.

[9] Scott J. Basinger, "Scandals and Congressional Elections in the Post-Watergate Era," *Political Science Quarterly* 66, no. 2 (June 2013): 385–98.

10 John Barry, *Ambition and Power: A True Story of Washington* (New York: Penguin, 1990), 448–73; Karl Brandt, *Ronald Reagan and the House Democrat: Gridlock, Partisanship, and the Fiscal Crisis* (Columbia: University of Missouri Press, 2009), 193–94; James Barnes, "Political Focus: Partisanship," *National Journal* (November 7, 1987): 282.

11 Resignation speech of Speaker Jim Wright, video, C-SPAN, May 31, 1989, accessed January 28, 2022, https://www.c-span.org/video/?7822-1/resignation-speech-speaker-wright.

12 Catherine Clark and Jeanne Clark, "Jim Wright's Resignation Speech: De-Legitimization or Redemption," *Southern Communication Journal* 58, no. 1 (1992): 67–75.

13 Rebecca Beitsch, "Lawmakers Coming under Increased Threats: Sometimes from One Another," *The Hill*, accessed January 30, 2022, https://thehill.com/policy/national-security/590058-lawmakers-coming-under-increased-threats-sometimes-from-one-another; Wright, interview, July 22, 2012.

14 Mike Andrews, Texas Democratic congressman, interview by J. Brooks Flippen, July 14, 2014.

15 *Historical Trends in Congressional Approval: Gallup Polling*, accessed February 20, 2022, https://news.gallup.com/poll/1600/congress-public.aspx; *Summary of Polls, Real Clear Politics*, accessed February 20, 2022, https://www.realclearpolitics.com/epolls/other/congressional_job_approval-903.html.

16 See Anthony Champagne et al., *The Austin-Boston Connection: Five Decades of House Democratic Leadership, 1937–1989* (College Station: Texas A&M University Press, 2009).

17 See James Merriner, *Chairman: Power in Dan Rostenkowski's America* (Carbondale: Southern Illinois University Press, 1999).

18 For a quick overview, see Michael Schaller and George Rising, *Republican Ascendancy: American Politics, 1968–2001* (Wheeling, IL: Harlan Davidson, 2012). While polls of historians rank Reagan in the middle, they acknowledge Reagan's impact and share public perceptions that he was a transformative figure. Chester Pach, "How Do Historians Access Ronald Reagan?," History News Network, George Washington University, accessed February 17, 2022, https://historynewsnetwork.org/article/341.

[19] See Carl Albert and Danney Goble, *Little Giant: The Life and Times of Speaker Carl Albert* (Norman: University of Oklahoma Press, 1999) and Alfred Steinberg, *Sam Rayburn: A Biography* (New York: Hawthorn Books, 1975).

[20] See Jane Mayer and Doyle McManus, *Landslide: The Unmasking of the President, 1984–1988* (New York: Houghton Mifflin, 1989).

[21] See "How Daniel Ortega 'Demolished' Democracy," *Public Broadcasting System Newshour*, November 5, 2021, accessed February 18, 2022, https://www.pbs.org/newshour/show/how-daniel-ortega-demolished-democracy-in-nicaragua.

[22] See Mariah Zeisberg, *War Powers: The Politics of Constitutional Authority* (Princeton, NJ: Princeton University Press, 2013).

[23] See Adam Cohen, *Nothing to Fear: FDR's Inner Circle and the Hundred Days That Created Modern America* (New York: Penguin, 2009) and Julian Zelizer, *The Fierce Urgency of Now: Lyndon Johnson, Congress, and the Battle for the Great Society* (New York: Penguin, 2015).

[24] See John Kyle Dale, *The Southern Manifesto: Massive Resistance and the Fight to Preserve Segregation* (Oxford: University Press of Mississippi, 2015); quoted in *Fort Worth Star-Telegram*, March 24, 1956, 2.

[25] See Stanley Karnow, *Vietnam: A History* (New York: Penguin, 1997); William Lunch and Peter Sperlich, "American Public Opinion and the Vietnam War," *Western Political Quarterly* 32, no. 1 (March 1979): 21–44.

[26] Jim Wright, remarks, November 18, 1967, Folder "Speech Files: Democratic Party—Remarks of JW, RCWC, November 18, 1967," Box 1285, Jim Wright Papers, Mary Couts Burnett Library, Texas Christian University, Fort Worth, Texas (hereafter cited as JWP).

[27] Nixon to Wright, January 24, 1973, Folder "Peace in Vietnam," Box 1150, Series 2, JWP.

[28] Zeisberg, *War Powers*, 5–7, 168.

[29] Quoted in *Fort Worth Star-Telegram*, August 14, 1974, 7.

[30] *The Americans' Public Attitudes about Richard Nixon Post-Watergate*, Roper Center for Public Opinion Research, August 9, 2014, accessed January 27, 2022, https://ropercenter.cornell.edu/blog/american-publics-attitudes-about-richard-nixon-post-watergate. In recent years, Nixon has risen in

polls; see Michael Endicott, *After Watergate: The Renaissance of Richard Nixon* (n.p.: Searchlight 37 Press, 2018).

31 See William L. Silber, *Volcker: The Triumph of Persistence* (New York: Bloomsbury Press, 2013).

32 Wright to Henry Black, April 19, 1967, Folder "Legislation – 90th Cong., House Administration, 1967," Box 317, Series 1, JWP.

33 See Jeffrey Stine, *Mixing the Waters: Environment, Politics, and the Building of the Tennessee-Tombigbee Waterway* (Akron, OH: University of Akron Press, 1993) and Richard Andrews, *Managing the Environment, Managing Ourselves: A History of American Environmental Policy* (New Haven, CT: Yale University Press, 1999), 285–88; Victor B. Scheffer, *The Shaping of Environmentalism in America* (Seattle: University of Washington Press, 1991).

34 Wright, interview by J. Brooks Flippen, July 12, 2012.

35 Wright, interview by J. Brooks Flippen, July 8, 2012.

36 Paul Milazzo, *Unlikely Environmentalists: Congress and Clean Water, 1945–1972* (Lawrence: University of Kansas Press, 2006), 5–7, quoted on 7.

37 Jim Wright, *The Coming Water Famine* (New York: Coward McCain, 1966).

38 Edward Walsh, "House Votes to Override Veto of Clean Water Legislation," *Washington Post*, February 3, 1987, 1; see Harvey Lieber, *Federalism and Clean Water: The Water Pollution Control Act Amendments of 1972* (Lexington, MA: Lexington Books, DC Heath, 1975), 80–82.

39 See Lawrence Wright, *Thirteen Days in September: Carter, Begin, and Sadat at Camp David* (New York: Knopf, 2014).

40 Paul Graff to Jim Wright, May 19, 1987, Folder "Russia Trip, 17/60, Soviet Pen Pal Project, of 2," Box 1329, JWP.

41 Tom Brokaw, *The Greatest Generation* (New York: Random House, 2001).

42 See Adam Rome, *The Bulldozer in the Countryside: Suburban Sprawl and the Rise of American Environmentalism* (Cambridge: Cambridge University Press, 2001).

43 See Harold Rich, *Fort Worth: Outpost, Cowtown, Boomtown* (Norman: University of Oklahoma Press, 2021) and "History," Fort Worth Stockyards National Historical District, accessed January 22, 2022, https://www.fortworthstockyards.org/history.

44 See "The End of the Wright Amendment," *Dallas Morning News* series, October 3 and 10, 2014, accessed February 12, 2022, http://res.dallasnews.

com/interactives/ending-wright/.

45 *Catalyst: The Role of the Dallas Fort Worth International Airport in the North Central Texas Regional Economy*, Perryman Group, November 2015, accessed February 14, 2022, https://www.perrymangroup.com/media/uploads/report/perryman-catalyst-11-30-15.pdf; quoted in Bill Hethcock, *Dallas Business Journal*, October 23, 2015, accessed February 14, 2022, https://www.bizjournals.com/dallas/news/2015/10/13/dfw-airport-economic-impact-grows-to-37-billion.html.

46 *How Dallas-Fort Worth Is Poised to Dominate America's Heartland*, Rice Kinder Institute for Policy Research, October 27, 2021, accessed February 7, 2022, https://kinder.rice.edu/urbanedge/2021/10/27/dallas-fort-worth.

47 Abraham Lincoln Second Annual Message to Congress, December 1, 1862, American Presidency Project, University of California, Santa Barbara, accessed February 13, 2022, https://www.presidency.ucsb.edu/documents/second-annual-message-9.

48 Adam Clymer, "Jim Wright Dies at 92; House Speaker Resigned Amid Ethics Charges," archived, *New York Times*, May 6, 2015, accessed February 20 2022, https://www.nytimes.com/2015/05/07/us/politics/jim-wright-house-speaker-who-resigned-amid-ethics-charges-dies-at-92.html.

49 Accessed February 20, 2022, https://en.wikipedia.org/wiki/Jim_Wright.

50 Jim Wright, *Balance of Power: Presidents and Congress from the Era of McCarthy to the Age of Gingrich* (Atlanta: Turner, 1996); Jim Wright, *Worth It All* (Washington, DC: Brassey's, 1993).

INDEX

JW = Jim Wright
Locators in italics refer to images

ABOUT THE EDITORS

JAMES W. RIDDLESPERGER JR. (BA, MA., North Texas State University; PhD, University of Missouri-Columbia) is professor of political science at Texas Christian University. A native of Denton, Texas, he has taught at TCU since 1982. He is co-author of *Texas Politics* (14th edition, Cengage, 2022), *Lone Star Leaders* (TCU Press, 2011), and *The Austin-Boston Connection* (Texas A&M Press, 2009). He co-edited *Reflections on Rayburn* (TCU Press, 2018) and *The Wright Stuff* (TCU Press, 2013). He has been named the winner of the Chancellor's Award for Creative Teaching and Research and Honors Professor of the year at TCU.

ANTHONY CHAMPAGNE is professor emeritus at the University of Texas at Dallas. He is the winner of numerous teaching awards and has written extensively on judicial selection in Texas, Texas politics, and leadership in the House of Representatives. His writing includes books on the relationship between Texas and Boston in the leadership of the House, the home style of Speaker Sam Rayburn, the career of Speaker Nicholas Longworth, along with shorter articles on John Nance Garner and Jim Wright.

Printed in the USA
CPSIA information can be obtained
at www.ICGtesting.com
LVHW021328301124
797960LV00003B/356

* 9 7 8 0 8 7 5 6 5 8 1 7 9 *